BITING THE HAND THAT STARVES YOU

BITING THE HAND THAT STARVES YOU

Inspiring Resistance to
Anorexia/Bulimia

Richard Maisel
David Epston
Ali Borden

W. W. Norton & Company
New York • London

W. W. Norton & Company has been independent since its founding in 1923, when William Warder Norton and Mary D. Herter Norton first published lectures delivered at the People's Institute, the adult education division of New York City's Cooper Union. The Nortons soon expanded their program beyond the Institute, publishing books by celebrated academics from America and abroad. By mid-century, the two major pillars of Norton's publishing program—trade books and college texts—were firmly established. In the 1950s, the Norton family transferred control of the company to its employees, and today—with a staff of four hundred and a comparable number of trade, college, and professional titles published each year—W. W. Norton & Company stands as the largest and oldest publishing house owned wholly by its employees.

The text of this book is composed in Palatino Light
with the display set Gill Sans Light.
Composition by TechBooks, Inc.

Manufacturing by Quebecor World—Fairfield Division.
Production Manager: Ben Reynolds.

Library of Congress Cataloging-in-Publication Data

Maisel, Richard (Richard Linn), 1957– .
Biting the hand that starves you : inspiring resistance to anorexia/bulimia /
Richard Maisel, David Epston, Alisa Borden.
p.   cm.
Includes bibliographical references and index.
ISBN 0-393-70337-1
1. Anorexia nervosa—Treatment.   2. Bulimia—Treatment.   I. Epston, David.
II. Borden, Alisa.   III. Title.
RC552.E18M325   2004
616.85′26—dc22   2003066231

W. W. Norton & Company, Inc., 500 Fifth Avenue, New York, N. Y. 10110–0017
www.wwnorton.com
W. W. Norton & Company Ltd., Castle House, 75/76 Wells Street, London WIT 3QT
3   4   5   6   7   8   9   0

This book is dedicated to those people who are struggling to free themselves or others from the tyranny of anorexia/bulimia and to the memory of those who have tragically perished.

CONTENTS

ACKNOWLEDGMENTS

T he true "parents" of this book are the hundreds of women and men
we have met or corresponded with over the years, who, imprisoned
by anorexia/bulimia, provided us with glimpses into the magnitude of
their suffering and allowed us to work in league with them to discover
some means of escape. As authors, our primary role has been to find a
way of organizing this archive of "insider" knowledge—the knowledge
of those who have struggled with anorexia/bulimia—into a coherent
text. We wish to acknowledge by name the insiders who actively assisted with this daunting task and who, by continuing to remind us of
the life-and-death importance of this endeavor, enabled us to persevere: Abby, Eve, Sarah, Fran, Laura, Rebecca, Tanya, and Victoria. We
couldn't have done it without you and even those versions that didn't
materialize provided the impetus for this final one.

We also wish to thank editors at W. W. Norton for their belief in
the importance of this work and above all their patience, which we
have sorely tried. Susan Munro was our first editor. Thank you, Susan,
for believing strongly enough in this work to offer us a book contract
without requiring a detailed book plan in advance, which permitted
the structure of the book to grow organically out of the archive of anti-
anorexia/bulimia. Deborah Malmud became our editor when Susan
retired from W. W. Norton, and it became her task to see the book
through to completion. We are grateful to you Deborah for the additional effort you made to grasp our idiosyncratic ideas and vision
for this book. It was thanks to you that the manuscript was passed to
Casey Ruble, an "outside" editor, to make it more thematically coherent and readable. Casey, your enthusiasm was like a spoonful of sugar
that made the medicine go down a lot easier. We also wish to thank
Michael McGandy for his hard work behind the scenes, and for his
invariable politeness and responsiveness.

RICK'S ACKNOWLEDGMENT

I am grateful to you, David, for your mentoring, your colleagueship, and your friendship. I have prized each and every one of these relationships. This book is in many ways a monument to what you have discovered and unearthed over the many years you have spent toiling in the "killing fields" of anorexia/bulimia. The revolutionary vision and practices presented in this book are largely the fruit of your curiosity, creativity, commitment, playfulness, and love. Thank you for continuing to believe me capable of spinning this gold into gold when I feared I might tragically spin gold into straw, and for making room for my vision and helping me trust it. I never could have persisted without your unfailing encouragement and delight.

Thank you, Ali, for being someone I could turn to for advice at every fork in the road, for your transfusions of excitement, and your well-timed reminders of the importance of the book and the reasons for writing it.

I'd like to acknowledge by name some of the insiders who I consulted with over the years this book was being compiled, for their written words, encouragement and the anti-anorexic knowledge they generously imparted: Laura, Aliza, Amanda, Rachel, Julia, Tanya, Maya, Lauren, and Kimberely. I'd also like to thank Marya Hornbacher, Lisa Berndt, Liz Colt, and Debbie Zucker for their helpful feedback on early drafts of some chapters, and to Caroline Pincus, "book midwife" extraordinaire, for reviewing an earlier draft of the manuscript, and for pulling the title out of the text like a rabbit out of a hat. I also wish to name some of those colleagues who offered encouragement on a fairly frequent basis: Dean Lobovits, Jenny Freeman, Jeff Zimmerman, Jan Chambers, Sharon Leydon, Steven Kanofsky, Robert-Jay Green, Michael Searle, Mary Herget, Jim Sparks and Richard Bush.

Lastly, I would like to thank my life partner, Susan, for graciously allowing me time away from the responsibilities of parenting in order to write, which increased her workload while simultaneously denying her of badly needed breaks. Thank you, Susan, for being such a good sport. You can write the next book.

DAVID'S ACKNOWLEDGMENT

Everyone who so willingly let me in on "anorexia/bulimia" deserves to be acknowledged here, but there have been far too many to cite—must be nearing 1000 over the past 15 plus years. I salute all my col(Leagues) who urged me to pursue anti-anorexia/bulimia into both forms it has taken so far, e.g., Archives of Resistance: Anti-Anorexia/Anti-Bulimia (see www.narrativeapproaches.com) and this book.

Rick, without your persistence, dedication and ingenuity, this book would not have been brought into being. If there ever was a successful teaming up of a hare and a tortoise, we were that! There were times when I wanted to abandon this project as just being too taxing and too time-consuming. You refused on each and every occasion to give in. When you learned there were risks to your health, you weighed that risk up and proceeded with this project, such was your commitment to it. Rick, I will always consider this your book. After all, you wrote it and I will be eternally grateful to you for having done so.

Thanks, Ali, for always being there when anything needed to be considered by insiders. Without that, I doubt if we would have had the nerve to have completed this project. We wouldn't have been able to believe in ourselves if we weren't convinced by you and your colleagues that anti-anorexia/bulimia was worthwhile.

Thanks to Ann Epston for her fierce commitment to anti-anorexia in both her practice and her life.

I owe a special debt to Dean Lobovits, who foresaw a Web site as a way to make the Archives of Resistance available to a far larger audience than ever possible beforehand. Although I was extremely reluctant at first to consider this, it was his vision and the donation of hours and hours of time constructing www.narrativeapproaches.com that made it possible. I can't thank you enough, Dean!

The launching of this book stands as my "retirement" from this practice so I can take up many projects I have deferred over the past 7 years. Whatever is mine in anti-anorexia/bulimia, I gladly bequeath to those who will take it up either in their own lives or on behalf of those who seek their help.

ALI'S ACKNOWLEDGMENT

I offer my most heartfelt appreciation to the many people who support my work and my life:

> To Rick and David for inspiring both my work and my desire to make a difference,
> To my mother, Sharyn Scott, for teaching me to be proud of being a woman, to appreciate situation beyond disposition, and that every life is valuable,
> To my partner Scott Gerwehr who continues to help me see through the lies and deception and whose day to day love and friendship

furthers my practice of collaboration in ways I never knew possible,

To Larry Zucker for his amazing ability to bring life to the things I find most valuable about my work and my experience,

To Carolyn Costin for allowing me the space to practice, explore, blend, and grow with these ideas,

To my amazing community of friends who continue to call forward the best parts of myself, remind me that love and friendship are above all else, and have truly changed the course of my life,

To Lyra Barrera who has been both friend and colleague, for understanding my passion for political action and being a personal anchor for me, especially with these ideas when they might otherwise have been lost in the sea of dominant thought, and finally,

To the women at Monte Nido, even though their stories are not included in this book, they inform everything I do and think about the struggle against anorexia/bulimia and have been the best instructors I have had in how to wage this battle.

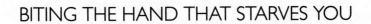

BITING THE HAND THAT STARVES YOU

INTRODUCTION

Y ou will see them as you wander through a city park on a pleasant sunny afternoon. Or perhaps you will find them at your local gym on the machines that precisely measure caloric expenditure. Try looking into the eyes of these "torturecizers." Can you tell the difference between those who are exercising and those who are torturecizing? No anti-anorexic veteran has any difficulty discerning one practice from the other. "It's all in their eyes. The look on their faces!"

How exactly does anorexia/bulimia (a/b) transform a person from someone making an appearance in her life to someone disappearing from it, from someone dieting to someone dying, from someone blossoming and flowering to someone withering, languishing, and finally perishing? Why do so many of the concentration camps* of anorexia

---

* Ellen West's (1937) words, later reported by Binswanger (1944), are the first "insider's" account of anorexia that we know of. She wrote: "Existence is only torture . . . Life has become a prison camp." We believe that if she had not been writing before World War II, she would have used the then-unknown term *concentration camp*. Such metaphors have reappeared time and time again when insiders speak of their experience of a/b's radical evil. We have found such a metaphor apt in that a/b might be one of the most "evil" expressions of modern forms of power, inciting women to police themselves and their bodies according to particular cultural specifications to the extent that they torture their bodies to the point of permanent damage or, in effect, become their own executioners. Therapists working in Jewish communities have informed us that the closer one is by history or experience to the holocaust, the more the metaphor fits. Two of the authors of this book are Jewish, and we do not use this metaphor lightly. We believe that by using the concentration camp as a metaphor for a/b, resistance can be inspired and lives saved. We hope that those who survived the holocaust and those who perished would, for that reason, find our use of this metaphor honoring (rather than trivializing) of their experience.

remain invisible to their inmates despite the slave labor and death marches? Why are resistance, protest, and very real combat the only means of escape for most people? How can individuals join with others to break free from the prison of a/b and discover the means by which they can construct a preferred life and identity? These questions are central to the explorations and conversations that make up this book.

In addressing these questions, our intention is not to understand a/b as much as it is to undermine and subvert it. This, then, is a book about fighting words, terrifying anti-a/b deeds and thrilling anti-a/b possibilities for the lives of therapists, individuals struggling with a/b, and the communities in which they reside. A/b is our sworn antagonist in these life-or-death duels. The purpose of this book is to help those whose lives have been captured by a/b (referred to as "insiders") to know, beyond all doubt, their enemy from their friend—to know who will treacherously betray them and who will be faithful and constant.

This book is not a "how to" therapy manual for professionals or a self-help book for insiders or their parents. A/b is too cunning a problem for any one-size-fits-all approach. It is a moving target, sidestepping your shot and returning fire. Furthermore, blanket prescriptions, even if well-intentioned, often end up mirroring the prescriptive nature of a/b itself. Instead, we have compiled "insider knowledge" (knowledge that can only be gained by experiencing this suffering and struggling to reclaim one's life from it) from various sources. These stories and written accounts emphasize novel ways of thinking and speaking about a/b that bring about a vision and practice that can always stay on its toes. It is our hope that the insider knowledge presented in this book will help prevent a/b from turning young women and men against themselves, their families, and their communities.

This book was written for three audiences—professionals, insiders, and their parents, partners, and friends.* The only "safe houses" in a culture so infiltrated by a/b are the anti-a/b sites that we construct. We hope that this book will assist all readers in the construction of anti-a/b sanctuaries, havens to which people whose lives have become ensnared by a/b can retreat when they lose their way. Furthermore, we

---

* Ideally, those parts of the book that are written for a specific audience (e.g., professionals) will still hold the interest of members of the other audiences (e.g., insiders or other outsiders). However, if your interest wanes, feel free to move on to sections of the book that address your concerns more directly. Additionally, you may wish to share some chapters or sections with certain people in your life and other sections with other people. For example, an insider reader might share the therapy-oriented chapters with her therapist, physician, or dietitian and the chapters on parents as anti-anorexic/anti-bulimic allies with her parents, partners, or friends.

hope that this book will inspire and enable insiders to embrace more of their own freedoms, joys, pleasures, and appetites. Living one's life according to one's own preferences may be the surest way to make an anti-a/b home. Perhaps the spontaneous, accepting, and unruly space one preserves will inspire others to break out of the prison of a/b's condemnations and rules.

If you, the reader, find yourself objecting to the vehemence of our anti-a/b zeal because of your belief that a/b is a friend or merely a mild problem or on the grounds that such passion is unbecoming to "professionals," we ask you to consider this; we have not come to take this position happily. We did not want to believe what we have come to know and we would have preferred to have remained innocent. But having stumbled upon (or, in Ali's case, into) the concentration camp of a/b, it would be morally reprehensible to turn our backs on it. We cannot blind ourselves to what we have witnessed and experienced— death sneaking its way of into the lives of young women and young men. Nor can we drive out of our memories the agonizing screams of those who have been robbed of all hope, or worse, the deafening and chilling silence of those resigned souls who have passed beyond despair.

At the same time, we have either witnessed or had narrated for us innumerable occasions of breathtaking valor when, despite the risks of a/b reprisals, anti-a/b women and men have fought for their very lives and reclaimed them as their own. Few things can rival the pleasure of hearing these tales of people rediscovering those things most of us take for granted—smiling, relaxing, feeling carefree, flights of the imagination, the pleasure of another's company, and the satisfaction of our own desires. In the telling of such accounts, joy for what has been regained often comingles with grief for what has been lost.

We regard a/b as the "Nazification" of everyday life. Anti-a/b is any number of resistance movements whose members are loosely attached or, at times, unknown to each other but connected by their opposition to a/b. This book offers anti-a/b to you in the spirit of furthering this resistance and inciting fresh resistance. We have included many forms of anti-a/b resistance, including those aided and abetted by therapists making use of practices drawn from narrative therapy, those engaged in by parents struggling to ally themselves with their daughter against a/b, and those practiced by the insiders themselves. We invite you to link arms with us, whether you are a therapist, parent, friend, or insider, and engage your courage, curiosity, and creativity in helping to create a culture where each and every body, mind, and spirit is celebrated and honored.

THE GENESIS OF THIS BOOK

This book has been a very long time in the making. Below, we present not only the story of how the book itself came to be, but the origin of the ideas and practices that have come to be referred to as *anti-anorexia/bulimia.*

David's Account

This book (and the website accompanying it, www.narrativeappro-aches.com) represents a culmination of nearly 15 years of active practice and consultation/research. Seeing this book in print fulfills both a dream and a moral imperative to bring insider knowledge to the widest possible audience. We have done everything we could think of to faithfully reproduce the stories and words of those who have suffered grievously at the hands of a/b and have born the brunt of a/b's punishment for speaking out and against it as well as the means by which these stories have been elicited. These veterans deservedly take pride of place in this project. We also acknowledge being in league with those who cared about these anti-a/b veterans—mothers, fathers, sisters, brothers, partners, lovers, friends, classmates, and so on—and who have endured untold anguish as they witnessed, at times helplessly, their loved one's torments. And, of course, we are thankful of our professional colleagues who have joined with us, encouraged us, and extended anti-a/b practices to hospitals, community mental health services, and professional forums.

I first entertained the prospect of such a document at the behest of many insiders attending the first public presentation of this embryonic anti-anorexic practice at the New Zealand Family Therapy Conference in 1991 in Auckland, New Zealand.* Nearly every insider I spoke with informed me that many conventional "treatments" for a/b seemed to reproduce the conditions that enabled such problems to emerge in the first place. They told me repeatedly how they "became anorexic for the hospital." Nothing could be more challenging of professional's good intentions than these young women who took to their pathologizations like ducks to water. Many anti-a/b women have expressed how resentful they were at the treatment they received at the hands of so many well-intentioned professionals. In New Zealand and everywhere I traveled—Canada, Sweden, the United States, Australia, and elsewhere—women described with uncanny repetition that the

---

* This was also presented in a plenary address to the Australian and New Zealand Family Therapy Conference, 1995, Wellington, NZ, and The American Family Therapy Academy conference, 1996, San Francisco.

hospitals to which they had been admitted as a last resort were "no better than concentration camps." Although they had physically survived the ordeals of their hospitalization and the terror of their force-feedings, many felt that their spirits had been trampled upon in the process, making them even more vulnerable to a/b upon discharge.

Over the years, I heard many professionals refer to insiders as "prima donnas," "spoiled brats," and "manipulative attention-seekers," describing them as people deserving of disdain and even loathing. At the same time, they also feared these young women. I was perplexed by these descriptions and later found the disregard and disdain to be morally repugnant, though I came to understand that they were partly a byproduct of the adversarial relationships caused by professionals attempting to counter a/b's coercion with coercion of their own.

In addition, I know of no other problem for which mothers were blamed so zealously and without regard for the consequences. One mother told me that she felt so relentlessly pathologized by the hospital staff that she came to believe that the only means by which she could help her daughter was to kill herself. It is my belief that the culture of psychotherapy owes such mothers a blanket apology.

My original vision of an alternative practice came from two very different but related sources. First, over the decade of the 1980s, I regularly joined Michael White at Dulwich Centre in Adelaide, Australia, where I observed his work from behind a one-way screen. By then he had immense experience working with such young women and their families both in hospitals (Children's Hospital, Adelaide) and in private practice. I witnessed some young women and their families repudiating a/b in a manner that was unforgettable and that flew in the face of the dim professional expectations about their futures. At the same time, Michael White was one of the earliest family therapists/psychotherapists to engage with the thinking of Michel Foucault and, to my knowledge, was one of the first to see Foucault's analysis of modern power as a chilling analogy for anorexia. This was later taken up with gusto in the late 1980s by poststructuralist feminist thinkers. It is at this nexus of Michael White/Michel Foucault/poststructuralist feminist philosophy that I locate the foundations for anti-a/b practice.

I would also like to acknowledge Helen Gremillion, then a Ph.D. candidate in anthropology at Stanford, whose 1992 paper was the first statement I was aware of that reached strikingly similar conclusions— conclusions that haunted us equally (Gremillion, 1992, see also Gremillion, 2003). We became friends and colleagues, and her image of "canaries in the mine" replaced both the scornful and romanticized images of these young women and their plights.

Whether an anti-a/b approach could be extended to in- and out-patient hospital services was another matter of grave concern for us. If it couldn't, we would have had to question whether this approach had an adequate reach. It had to be tested in the most dire circumstances. In 1993, Eliot Goldner and Vicky Syme, codirectors of St. Paul's Hospital in Vancouver, invited my colleague, Stephen Madigan, to run anti-a/b groups for inpatients, with hospital staff serving as reflecting team members. The groups led to follow-up groups after discharge and it was in these groups that the foundations for the Vancouver Anti-Anorexia/Anti-Bulimia League* were laid. This League engaged in overt political activism and produced, for 3 years, the magazine *Re-vive.* A parallel development at the Methodist Hospital in Minneapolis was initiated in 1992 by its director, Irene Bugge. Staff met with Michael White and me, and they asked Stephen Madigan for consultation from 1994 to 1995. When I visited in 1998, I found it hard to believe what anti-a/b life was like in this inpatient unit as different as it was from conventional eating disorder units: It felt more like a "cell" of anti-anorexic resistance than a hospital unit.

The women I have worked with over the years have been nothing like the "anorexics" I read about in professional texts. Even those who had abandoned all hope became feisty and wise beyond their years. Was I, by chance, meeting extraordinary women? Or was it just beginner's luck? Quite the contrary. I began to realize that these young women were in possession of a knowledge but had no means to represent it. It was as if they had been gagged. However, I was soon to learn that even those who had been mute were capable of becoming fluent in anti-a/b, which for many has become their second language.

Anti-a/b has provided me with a place to stand. Had I not come upon anti-a/b, I have no idea what I would have done with what I knew— except to weep in despair. It has also provided a "community of counter practice" (personal correspondence, Tomm, 1992) from which I have drawn upon to inspire my practice and repaired to under duress. What it has meant for me personally is that I have never surrendered, no matter how desperate the circumstances. Retreat, yes, but surrender, never. This book and the website that complements it are the archive on which I have always depended. It is my hope that it will serve you as well, in both your anti-a/b advances and retreats.

---

* David coined the term *anti-anorexia/bulimia league* to describe a community of insiders and their allies who communicate with each other (often via an intermediary such as a therapist) for purposes of exposing a/b's tactics, sharing anti-anorexic/bulimic strategies, fostering hope, celebrating victories, and engaging in activism. Some leagues meet face-to-face, while others operate more "virtually" via e-mail or FAX correspondence. Although they can take traditional organizational forms, most often they operate like resistance movements working underground.

Rick's Account

My first exposure to the problem of a/b was through my attendance at workshops given by David back in the late 1980s and early 1990s. Before this, I had the standard ideas about a/b that any graduate school student would have had. It wasn't until I heard David speak about a/b that it took on a life. I remember finding the League documents that David read from simultaneously horrifying and fascinating. The conversations he was having with these women were among the oddest I had encountered, especially the way in which a/b was personified by having motives and strategies attributed to it. Through these odd conversations, a/b's "voice" was audible and I was dumbstruck by both the cruelty of its motives and the diabolical ingenuity of its rhetoric. The rendering of a/b's voice made it possible for me to get a glimmer of how it could deceive these extraordinarily intelligent and well-meaning young women into torturing themselves to death. But, honestly, I was also a bit incredulous and wondered if perhaps David wasn't engaging in some hyperbole for dramatic effect. Yet, as inventive as David was, I couldn't see how he could manufacture such a coherent voice, so I decided to give him the benefit of the doubt.

Part of my initial excitement had to do with the way the narrative therapy approach to a/b connected to my long-standing desire to see psychotherapy used to address social injustice. I had first heard Michael White present an overview of his work & ideas in 1988. His work illuminated how power can operate in an oppressive way in the therapist-client relationship. Michael also talked about the ways in which power could infiltrate the everyday lives of people through taken-for-granted ideas about how they should act, look, feel, and so on, and how therapists could help people identify and challenge these "specifications" when they became problematic.

In David's work with people struggling against a/b, I repeatedly witnessed very dramatic examples of how therapy could assist people in recognizing and resisting their own subjugation through an exposé of the linkages between a/b power and wider cultural norms, values, and practices. David's conversations with the women consulting him about the problem of a/b indicted this culture and opened up possibilities for resistance not only to a/b but also to the wider culture.

It wasn't long after my initial exposure to David's work with a/b that I found myself on the anti-a/b front lines quite unwittingly. Anorexia had moved into the foreground of the lives of two women who had been consulting me for other concerns. At this point in my professional practice, I would have refused to work with the problem of a/b, instead referring them to someone more qualified. But I had already been through thick and thin with these two women and because of my allegiance to them and their concerns, I could not turn my back on them. Although I had no experience with the problem of a/b, David's work gave me hope that we could find a path through to the other side of the problem and that I would not have to blaze this trail alone.

The emotional distance that I formerly maintained in relation to a/b was no longer possible (or desirable) when a/b was attempting to murder girls and women whom I now knew, cared for, and admired. Prior to this time, my enthusiasm for this work was primarily academic. It wasn't that I didn't care about what was happening to the girls and women I heard about from others. But it was only after I began meeting face to face with women and girls who had been dispatched to death row by a/b that I felt myself exploding with outrage. And it wasn't until then that I knew that David's "hyperbole" was, in fact, an understatement. Many of the very same shocking words and phrases that I had heard from David's archive (and that I had wondered if he had put in the mouths of the women consulting him) were now being voiced by the girls and women in my Berkeley, California, office, 10,000 miles away from Auckland, New Zealand.

At that point I'm sure David sensed a new urgency to my requests for League documents and a boldness in my seeking his advice during our informal chats. Whenever David would read an insider's account of a/b or anti-a/b resistance during one of his northern California workshops, I would approach him during the break, and he would preempt my predictable request with "Yeah, Rick you can have a copy of that." David was always incredibly generous in offering guidance, moral support, and League documents, and I don't think I would have had the nerve to take on this work without this kind of support. After a while, I had amassed a fairly sizable anti-a/b archive of David's letters, writings by insiders, and transcripts and videotapes of conversations.

I began in earnest to make sense of this archive for myself. I read and reread transcripts, trying to infer David's intentions in asking the questions he asked. I gradually began to sort the myriad questions into distinct lines of inquiry, and to map these lines of inquiry through time to gain a loose sense of the progression of the work, though this was by no means a simple linear path. My study of this archive gave me confidence that this problem was knowable, and that we (my clients and I as well as the League) had the means to expose and thwart it. Furthermore, although I couldn't claim to know much of anything, one thing I did know was that in order to murder someone a/b had to perpetrate outrageous deceptions. Over time, I became confident in our ability to see through such deceptions to a "truth" that a/b could never entirely obscure. I came to our meetings without any certainties but rather an informed curiosity that was met with wonderful tolerance, and together we taught each other anti-a/b.

In 1994, I pulled together a "map" of David's work into a presentation for the psychiatric staff of several Kaiser Hospitals in Southern California. This map found its way into David's hands via Michael White, to whom I had given a copy during one of his visits to northern California. David contacted me and asked if this outline could be the basis for a book chapter—"A Narrative Approach to So-Called Anorexia/Bulimia" (1998). This commenced our colleagueship, and many of the women who consulted us separately were happily brought into league with each other through the documenting David and I did of their insider knowledge.

In mid-1997, David asked if I might join him as coauthor of this book. The timing of his request couldn't have been worse, as my partner Susan and I were expecting our first child. Despite my concern about involvement in the book taking me away from fully participating in the life of my newborn and my fear that I was not up to the task, I agreed to join David in this project. If the anti-a/b archive could be spun into book form and published, I had no doubt that lives could be saved. If I could contribute to that, then I felt morally compelled to take a leap of faith and try.

Compiling this book has taken us far longer than any of us would have imagined, especially our editors at W. W. Norton, and we are grateful to them for their infinite patience. This has proved an extremely challenging book to write because of the moral responsibility we felt to remain faithful to insider knowledge. We have tried our hardest and done our best.

Ali's Account

It is no surprise that narrative therapy deeply appealed to me when I first encountered it during my master's program in psychology. Throughout my life I had witnessed my parent's political activism and their efforts fighting against social injustice. Their attention to power and those who are denied access influenced my world view from a very early age. Narrative therapy's focus on the external "forces" which shape people's lives was far more in line with my sense of justice than the therapies which viewed problems as merely arising within families or in individual minds. Narrative therapy called to my desire to not stand idly by but to actively challenge cultural discourses, including those of the culture of psychotherapy.

As someone who has been subject to the voice of anorexia in my own life, I was very familiar with the feeling that I could never measure up to the person I believed I should be, either in terms of my body or my "self." Social constructionist ideas, which highlight how these norms and measurements are culturally produced, lined up what I had seen happening to marginalized peoples (being told they are not "right") and what was happening inside my mind. Suddenly my perspective on my practice and my personal experience fused, and I felt as if I were home.

This fusion afforded me a way of speaking and acting that capitalized on my rebelliousness and provided me with the means to take up my family tradition of activism in both my work and my personal life. From this perspective, I began to conceive of a/b as a disempowering cultural force not unlike racism, homophobia, and classism. I also began to see how the field of psychology in many ways endorsed this disempowering cultural force—seemingly unknowingly but quite dangerously—by continuing to present a/b as a diagnosis and a problem within individual women themselves. In recognizing a/b as a political problem of oppression, I suddenly had a place to fight for something bigger than myself.

I began my career in a work setting where women who have struggled with a/b can assist other women to do the same. In daily conversations with individuals and in therapy groups, I led inquiries into identifying the forces that cause us to feel "less than" and consequently have us attempting to measure up to impossible standards. At the same time, I was trying to open avenues where we could bring forward and celebrate our individual uniqueness.

Around this time, I met Rick at a narrative therapy conference in Malibu, and my world cracked open. It was not long before I learned that he had much of the anti-a/b archive stored on his laptop. I begged for the chance to read the archives. (Rick was eager for me to do so.) I began reading them in the hotel instead of attending workshops. But I didn't just read them, I devoured them. Despite the fact that I was sitting by myself in a room, hunched over an impersonal computer screen, I suddenly no longer felt alone. In a split second, the experiences I had felt and turned over and over in my mind and in my therapy were no longer just in my head but coming from someone else's heart as well. If narrative therapy felt like home to me, finding the archive was like suddenly having that home filled with a loving and supportive group of my closest friends. This is how I felt as an insider. As a therapist, I felt as if I had stumbled upon the code to a lock I had been trying to crack for some time. The thing I remember most clearly was trying to memorize the questions and wishing I could write down the exchanges and share them with the women and families I was working with, hoping that it would crack their world open as it had mine.

Rick, noticing my voracious appetite for archival material, offered to send me more documents. He also appeared interested in my opinions about decisions he and David were unsure about regarding what to include in the book. He acknowledged the unique position I occupied in my life—being an insider to both anorexia and narrative therapy and at the same time being an outsider in my work with other women struggling with these issues. As the book was intended to address several audiences—those struggling and those connected to them personally and professionally—Rick and David thought I might play a part in bridging the divide between the two. My involvement became such that Rick and David requested that I join them as third author.

What the archive specifically added to my thinking and my basic narrative practice was what I later came to know as *anti-a/b*. Anti-a/b assisted the women consulting me to uncover a/b's intentions and tactics while generating documents to record the tortures and abuses of this diabolical problem thereby exposing its disguise. Anti-a/b provided me with a manner of speaking that could help people break the spell of a/b and step into a world of their own making.

During the process of writing this book I have been working full-time with women struggling to take their lives back from a/b. This has afforded me ample opportunity to share draft material with insiders. Doing so has helped women expose a/b's voice and articulate a means to contest it. Throughout this process we have been continually reviewing, critiquing, and sanctioning the drafts. Rick and David never presumed the authority to speak for insiders. This reviewing by insiders provided them with some assurance that these accounts (generated primarily through conversations with their own clients) resonated with the experience of other insiders. I believe this work is important on a level that extends beyond those directly affected by a/b, and I am appreciative to them for inspiring both my work and my desire to make a difference.

WAYS OF SEEING AND SPEAKING ABOUT ANOREXIA/BULIMIA

This book offers just one of the many perspectives on a/b. Although we are aware of other perspectives on and treatment approaches for a/b, we rarely refer to them. Our primary purpose is to present something new—a novel set of possibilities. We do not attempt to compare our perspective with other perspectives or engage in a critique of those perspectives. We leave these important tasks to you, the reader, or to other writers.

A unique aspect of our perspective is that it draws heavily upon metaphor. We also are committed to distinguishing between the person and the problem—to viewing a/b as something outside of the person but exerting an influence. However, this perspective should not be seen as a literal "truth" about a/b. Rather, this particular construction allows a/b to be "seen" in particular ways, ways that enable us to decipher possible lines of resistance and support for this resistance. We hope that by using this alternative lens, readers will also begin to see conventional understandings of a/b (those that draw from the psychiatric and medicalized discourses of "disorders" and "psychopathology") not as literal "truths" but as other sets of culturally influenced constructions.

One of our purposes in writing this book was to assemble the insider knowledges that were generated through our anti-a/b conversations. We conceived of the project as both an archive of insider knowledge and a explication of the manner of speaking that brought it into being. Everything of import in this book can be traced to a conversation between an anti-anorexic therapist and insiders as well as their family and friends. Any idea introduced from the outside was queried, refined, and elaborated through a thousand and one anti-anorexic conversations and a hundred or more minds. All of this was necessary given the fact that the first two authors, Rick and David, were "outsiders" when it came to a/b, and all the more so for being middle-aged men. Because of our outsider status, we decided to keep our own personal and professional voices in the background. Instead, we chose to privilege the first-person accounts of insiders and to keep the book focused on the voice and tactics of a/b and the practice of anti-a/b.

Typically, professional books privilege the professional voice; it is not only given far more textual space but also the last word. We acknowledge that the manner in which we have reversed and redressed this imbalance may be disorienting for some and frustrating for others. However, we regard this insider knowledge to be the heart and soul of the book. Our hope is that this book will transmit this insider knowledge to outsiders working with individuals struggling against a/b and provide an alternative to "treatment" or "caretaking."

A FEW COMMENTS ON TERMINOLOGY

Anorexia Versus Bulimia

The insiders we have spoken with over the years have not taken much interest in the diagnostic lexicon of the *Diagnostic and Statistical Manual* (DSM). Upon reflection, insiders have informed us that what has been most useful to them in gaining some traction against the problem has been coming to know the voice of the problem (however that problem might be named) and the tactics and strategies it uses to seduce and imprison them. Consequently, our practice has come to revolve around these *experience-near* descriptions, for these descriptions are the footings upon which insider knowledges stand. Although we typically use the terms *anorexia* and *bulimia* as ways of referring to the problem (and not as a means to capture it), we do not intend for them to be diagnostically precise. Rather, in this text the terms are employed very loosely and, at times, interchangeably.

Another reason we use these terms interchangeably is to avoid anorexia's being afforded more status than bulimia. Some writers have attributed the status or cachet of anorexia to the fact that it is more in keeping with dominant ideas about femininity (e.g., self-effacement and restraint) than is bulimia, as vomiting is widely regarded as "unladylike" (see Burns, in Press). Readers who have a strong interest in diagnostic classifications may find our lack of precision very frustrating, but we request that you bear with us.

Capitalization

While most insiders tolerate the use of the terms *anorexia* and *bulimia* as ways of referring to the problem, many have been adamant that we defy the convention of capitalizing the terms as proper nouns, as they regard anorexia and bulimia as highly "improper." Thus the terms are presented in the lowercase, unless the insider herself has chosen to capitalize the word.

Gender

While a/b is a problem that effects men as well as women, for every one male a/b sufferer there are still nine women. Thus, although we occasionally refer to men, we primarily use feminine pronouns when referring to those captured by a/b. (Furthermore, we often use the term *women* to stand for both girls and women.) We adopted this convention to make the writing less cumbersome. Due to space limitations we have focused primarily on the experiences of women. However, it is not our intention to marginalize the experience of boys and men or to imply that males in this culture are exempt from a/b's seduction and torture. In fact, we have worked with boys and men who have struggled with a/b, and many of them have made valuable contributions to the archive. Unfortunately, the expanding culture of a/b seems to be rendering boys and men increasingly more eligible for a/b's discipline and punishment.

A WORD OF CAUTION TO INSIDER READERS

We initially hoped that we could compile a book that was a/b-proofed—in other words, a book that was immune to a/b's tampering with the meaning of our words. To this end we adopted some unconventional writing conventions to make it harder for a/b to use the text against its readers. We did not include the weights of the people with whom we have consulted and we edited out the references insiders made to their weight in their own writings. Our purpose was to prevent weight from becoming a standard of comparison. We also parted company with the traditional practice of presenting case histories, which can play in to a/b's hands by reducing people to "thin" clinical descriptions that implicate them as the problem (see White, 1997, 2001).

Additionally, we attempted to allow the organization of the book to reflect the nature of anti-a/b practice, which prefers spontaneity, welcomes messiness, and admits considerable backward and forward movement in the struggle against a/b. However, publishers under-standably value economy of words, and a compartmentalization of ideas, and the conventions of writing have required us to adopt a tidier organization than suits an anti-a/b disposition. Although this writing approach may make for a more readable book, it also compromises the spirit of anti-a/b and, by tiding up a very messy business, oversimplifies it.

Unfortunately, such an organization also makes the reading of this book potentially more hazardous for the insider reader. The division of the book into roughly two sections—the tactics and strategies of a/b and the resistance to a/b—means that, in the first section, the insider reader is exposed to the voice of anorexia without anything immediately present in the text to oppose it. Insiders have informed us that this makes it far easier for a/b to twist the meaning of the text to its own advantage.

We finally concluded that a/b-proofing any text is impossible. We now realize that there is almost nothing that a/b cannot turn to its own advantage and your disadvantage. Consequently, we think it is highly likely, if not inevitable, that as you engage with this text, the voice of a/b will try to infiltrate it and put a pro-a/b spin on what we intend to be an anti-a/b book. If you find yourself reviling yourself rather than a/b, condemned by a/b rather than morally outraged by it, more fearful of living without a/b than you are of dying for it, a/b has probably started to worm its way into the core of our meanings with the intention of spoiling them. In this event, we urge you to take evasive action, perhaps by putting the book aside and returning to it when you revive your anti-a/b stance, or by turning to the later chapters on resistance or logging onto www.narrativeapproaches.com to read the archives of the League for anti-a/b inspiration.

OVERVIEW OF THE BOOK

In the first part, "The Seduction and Imprisonment," we address the means by which Anorexia/Bulimia insinuates itself into the lives of women. Chapter 1 introduces the idea of the voice of a/b. We talk about some of the circumstances that make a person susceptible to a/b's voice and how a/b uses its voice to take advantage of these circumstances and seduce a person into believing its promises. Chapter 2 uses the metaphors of prison and torture to describe the actual experience of a/b, which stands in stark contrast to the freedom and happiness it has guaranteed. We present many of the rhetorical tactics and strategies a/b uses to keep people confined after the romance has soured and they have begun to recognize their imprisonment and betrayal. Chapters 3 through 6 are first-person or narrated accounts of young women who were seduced and imprisoned by a/b.

The second section, "Turning against Anorexia/Bulimia," focuses on how therapists and other helpers can help young women imprisoned by a/b to recognize their dangerous predicament and cocreate possibilities for resistance. Chapter 7 presents some novel ways of speaking and thinking about a/b that can help break its spell and open up opportunities for resisting and defying it. Chapter 8 expands upon some of these ideas and presents some additional conversational practices we have found helpful in breaking the spell of a/b. The next two chapters provide actual examples of spell-breaking conversations taken from our work.

The third section of the book, "Reclaiming One's Life from Anorexia/Bulimia," maps the back-and-forth process of freeing oneself from a/b's prison and presents a great deal of insider knowledge about methods of resisting and separating from a/b and reengaging with preferred voices. Chapter 11 details the first prong of the strategy: unmasking and defying a/b. This entails discerning, countering, and disengaging from the voice of a/b, as well as using moral outrage to foster the repudiation of a/b. Chapter 12 discusses the second prong of the strategy: constructing anti-a/b lifestyles by helping women build their lives around an acceptance of and appreciation for their own values, desires, and preferences. This chapter also discusses the role that spirituality can play in assisting people in reclaiming themselves and their lives. Chapter 13 takes up the issue of *comebacks* by a/b (often referred to by professionals as "relapse"). This chapter shows how an anti-a/b framework for viewing comebacks can help shorten their duration by preventing a/b from using them as a means of cultivating discouragement and hopelessness. The chapter also presents the anti-a/b practice of strategic retreats, a means by which people can, in a sense, take comebacks into their own hands. Chapters 14 and 15 use therapy transcripts to recount the stories of two women struggling to take their lives back from a/b.

The final section of the book, "Becoming an Anti-Anorexic/Bulimic Ally," is written for caretakers (parents and professionals) who wish to know how they might aid those who are struggling with a/b. Chapter 16 is addressed to parents. It presents a general framework that parents can use to co-construct, with their daughter, an anti-a/b parenting practice. It also details many specific parenting practices that insiders have found helpful. Chapter 17 is the story of a couple whose daughter was hospitalized for anorexia. After becoming disillusioned with the treatment they were receiving at the hospital, this family parted company with the hospital staff and turned to David for guidance. However, their daughter refused to meet with David or any other therapist. By learning the language and perspective of anti-a/b, this couple developed a parenting practice that was instrumental in ushering their daughter back into her own life. Chapter 18 is addressed primarily to medical professionals and therapists. It illustrates the perils of traditional treatment approaches and provides an alternative therapeutic approach that remains dedicated to the nourishing of the spirit and not just the body. The book ends, in Chapter 19, with a two moving letters written by insiders—one from a father to his daughter and the other from the daughter to another young woman imprisoned by anorexia.

Part One

THE SEDUCTION AND IMPRISONMENT

Chapter 1

THE SEDUCTIVE VOICE OF ANOREXIA/BULIMIA

T he following was written by Elizabeth, a 17-year-old girl, shortly after beginning therapy with Rick. She titled it "My New Friend."

i made a new friend this year.* Confident, strong, in control, my friend understands me as no one else does. His black eyes watch over me as He breathes softly in my ear, whispering secrets about myself. He tells me who i am. He tells me who i should be. Silently and without fear, He gently takes my hand and leads me to the places where He knows i should be going.

Together, We are like two mountain climbers, scaling the face of a dangerous cliff. My friend is always in the lead, comforting, encouraging, coaxing me to keep on climbing. Though the wall is steep and hard to grab on to, though my body is scratched and bruised and broken, and though i keep falling again and again, i continue to follow and obey His orders, intrigued by his promises of the beautiful things We will see from the top. Though i cannot see it, i know it is there, somewhere above, somewhere close, a little higher than i am right now. The top is always just out of reach. i know it is there because He told me so.

---

* Elizabeth uses capital personal pronouns for anorexia (*He, It*) and for her relationship with anorexia (*We*), and does not capitalize the personal pronoun *I* when, in the writing, she describes her experience of being controlled by anorexia. The reverse is true when, in the writing, she experiences separation from anorexia and feels more connected to her own voice.

My friends and my family, even my doctor—they are jealous of my new friend. They say He has a name, but they must have him confused with someone else. They call Him a bad influence and try to push Him away. But with each push, my friend pulls back harder. He clings tighter to my fingers, explaining that they do not understand.

i got a D in History. My father held and comforted me, told me it would be okay. But it was my friend who cheered me up. Tugging at my hand, He led me to the bathroom scale. Proudly patting me on the back, He said "That's a good weight . . . but doesn't a little lower sound so much better?" He was right. He always is.

I hear my mother crying late at night as she paces up and down the halls. I know He has hurt her, although I don't know how or why. When she enters my room to stare down upon me, I apologize because He will not.

At lunch, my other friends plead with me, waving chocolate muffins and lollipops in front of my face. They are frustrated when i decline. I hear their voices, but His is louder. "You're different," they tell me. "They're right," He agrees. "You are different. You are better." They glare at Him and turn away. They do not know Him as i know Him.

He is not just a friend, but something more. A guide, a counselor, a teacher, a coach. Each morning He wakes me up early, dictates Our plans for the day. If i do what He says, then i am rewarded. i get to sit down or drink a glass of water. i cannot eat. Only he can. he eats at my body, my heart, my mind. he eats at my strength, my energy, my soul. he eats at the bonds that connect me to my family and friends. And even then, he is not full. My friend is always hungry. Licking his lips in satisfaction, he eats my smile for dessert.

Sometimes I get angry with my friend. he tricks me, deceives me, lies to me, leads me on. he makes promises he can't keep, sets up goals that I can't meet. he fills my head with his voice, invading my thoughts so that his words become mine. As I climb the side of the cliff, he offers his hand then snatches it away, laughing as I fall to the ground. he looks down upon me with disgust, calls me weak, then scolds me for betraying him. It is hard to climb a cliff with his hands over my eyes.

There are many things I like to do, but my friend does not like for me to do them. I like to walk with my dog. I like to read and relax. I like to go out dancing and come home late. I like to sit in coffee shops with my friends, talking for hours and laughing out loud, not caring that all the other customers are staring at us and rolling their eyes. I like to sit on my mom's bed and tell her how my day went. I like to watch Saturday Night Live with my dad. I like to lie on my back on a sunny day, staring at the clouds and imagining what animals they would be. I like to just sit and let my thoughts wander, leading me on a journey with an unknown destination.

My friend does not like when I do these things. He tells me they are bad and i do not question because i know He is right. He is always right. Sometimes He comes along to torment me. Others, He lets me go alone and i wonder if He will be there waiting when i return.

In my mind, He has placed a scoreboard where i add and subtract numbers throughout the day. i don't know who is winning or who is losing or even whose side i am playing for. My friend says We are ahead, but I'm not so sure. Everyday I feel myself losing. Losing weight, losing energy, losing pride, losing hope. I have yet to see the giant prizes I have won. I have yet to see the beautiful view from the mountaintop.

Yet i keep on struggling. i keep on climbing, in hopes of one day reaching the top, standing proud on that cliff high above the world. And my friend will be there waiting, watching as He always does. i will close my eyes as He swings and spins me around, dancing to the music only We hear. And as We waltz about the cliff so far from the ground, sometimes I worry and I wonder: How will I know when we reach the edge? "Just keep your eyes closed," My friend assures me. "I will catch you before you fall."

If you wish to understand the means by which anorexia/bulimia (a/b) insinuates itself into the lives of its victims and then lays claim to these lives, you must become familiar with the voice of a/b. When we say the *voice* of a/b, we are referring to the meanings that support and strengthen its regime.* It is through these meanings that a/b exerts its power.

A/b doesn't need steel bars or barbed wire to imprison people and starve them, nor does it require whips to drive their bodies. It need not rely on guns, swords, or fists to keep people in line, nor is its torture inflicted with the help of any of the traditional instruments of pain. Its seduction, imprisonment, torture, and murder of women is accomplished through its voice and the rhetorical strategies it uses to influence how they view themselves, their bodies, and the world around them.

---

* We speak of a/b as if it were the embodiment of these meanings, the personification of a system of values. We even go so far as to imbue it with motives inferred from its effects on the spirits and bodies of its victims. For a more detailed discussion of our reason for adopting this manner of speaking, see Chapter 7.

Because most of the rhetorical strategies a/b employs involve deception and subterfuge, its approach is quiet, cunning, and disguised. It does not march into a person's life like a conquering army, loudspeakers blaring, nor does it raise an anorexic flag or draw attention to itself in other ways. A/b avoids the visibility of a traditional occupying force. Its approach more resembles the fog in Carl Sandburg's poem, creeping in on "little cat's feet." Initially, it speaks quietly and reassuringly. It softens the sharp edges of experience. It muffles and mutes people's fears and concerns about their world. It extends what appears to be a benevolent hand to those who feel they are drowning and, with affectionate reassurance, directs them to a fraudulent safety.

A/B'S TACTICS OF SEDUCTION

A/b uses two principal means of seduction.

Promoting Self-Blame and Guilt

A/b seeks, covertly, to knock a person to her knees so that, in desperation and despair, she will be inclined to invest her hopes in its promises and reassurance. Behind the seeming benevolence of a/b's seductive promises and reassurances is concealed its cruelty—its desire to do all it can to promote and fuel a person's pain, fear, and despair. It attempts to mask the injustices a person may have experienced by using its voice to maintain her guilt. Whatever violations the person has experienced are made out to be her fault. If she was sexually abused or raped, a/b may say, "If you were only more lovable he wouldn't have treated you this way" or "you were stupid to think he would be interested in you as a person." If a person is being belittled and criticized, a/b tells her she deserves it. When she falls short of perfection, a/b tells her she is failure. If people around her suffer, a/b claims that it is her fault and that she subtracts from people's lives more than she adds. If she feels pain, a/b says she is weak and demands that she stop feeling sorry for herself. If she becomes angry, a/b tells her that nice girls don't get angry and that she is a "selfish bitch."

Naturally, a/b disguises its identity when using this voice. It presents itself as the "voice of reason," as "reality," as "this is what everybody thinks but is too afraid to say." By promoting despair in girls and women, a/b makes it more likely that they may, in their desperation, turn to a/b for hope and redemption.

Exploiting and Appropriating Hopes and Dreams

A/b seduces people by appealing to their hopes and dreams for their lives. Most of the girls and women we have spoken with over the years who have gotten tangled in a/b's web had, early in their lives, nurtured visions of a just and caring world in which they could thrive while contributing to the lives of others. The hopes and dreams of these girls and women often included the wish to be acknowledged as persons of worth, to be treated with respect and care, to be safe, to make a positive contribution to the world and to find love and happiness. Circumstances such as those outlined in the next section can make these hopes and dreams seem unattainable. Experiencing abuse, control, and objectification by others, being saddled with unattainable standards for achievement and success, or being burdened by an ill-conceived sense of responsibility for the well-being of others can cause hopes to be dashed and usher in a shroud of despair about the possibility of attaining one's dreams. A/b addresses both sides of the coin: It promises to bring an end to the pain, fear, and despair, and it promises to make the realization of one's hopes and dreams possible.

In doing this, a/b shows its more public and seemingly benevolent face. "Yes," anorexia says, "although I must admit that you are, in fact, a poor excuse for a human being, you should not despair." In sympathetic and reassuring tones, it tells the person that there is hope for her, that she is "workable." "I can make you more lovable, more respectable, more in control, and more invulnerable. I can deliver success and happiness, but you must comply perfectly with everything I say and trust no one but me. Only I really care about you and have your best interests at heart. My solution is very simple but difficult to achieve. But with hard work, willpower, and self-discipline, I know you can do it. In fact, you can excel at it! What is my solution? Lose weight!"

How could women and girls think to question such desperately needed assistance and advice when it is echoed by the ever-present iconic images of the successful and admired woman—Barbie-Doll thin, torturecized fit, selfless and self-sacrificing, invulnerable and untouchable? It promises the swiftest and surest way to realize these models of womanhood. It promises the most complete makeover of all time. At a time of despair, loss, disorientation, or transition, it is understandable why so many women would find it hard to resist the promise of perfection, the attainment of the cultural virtue of control, and as a consequence, the love and respect of all, perfect happiness, and a trouble-free life.

SUSCEPTIBILITY TO THE VOICE OF A/B

The means by which a/b seduces people can be divided into two general categories: 1) promoting self-blame and guilt, and 2) exploiting hopes and dreams. The first of these general strategies is a more covert and the second more overt. That is to say, a/b would prefer that its role in making women feel bad go unnoticed, while promoting itself more explicitly as a means whereby women can feel and "be" better. A/b relies heavily on these two tactics early on in a woman's relationship with it. As the initial romance sours, however, and women begin to doubt a/b's promises and intentions, a/b may periodically use these tactics along with others (see Chapter 2) in order to get them to recommit to the relationship.

Because of the way in which success and beauty are defined by Western culture, any white teenage girl or woman living in the United States or other Western countries is valuerable to a/b. In Western culture, thinness is generally regarded as more beautiful for women than are other body types. Furthermore, a woman's appearance is often taken as a measure of her character and worth. Western culture regards qualities such as *self-discipline*, *self-control*, and *niceness* as virtues (see Chapter 2), and a/b, like the proverbial wolf in sheep's clothing, can easily proffer itself as the surest and fastest means to these cherished ends. It offers women a path to this culturally specified success. A/b promises to deliver a beautiful body and a virtuous character if the person only obeys its rules and restrictions. Perhaps, then, a/b tells her, she will be looked upon by others as a person worthy of love and respect, someone to be taken seriously, a woman to be reckoned with.

As Western cultural norms are adopted by nonwhite communities living within Western countries and elsewhere around the world, anorexia and bulimia are making inroads into populations that were previously resistant to it (Simmons, 2002; Thompson, 1994, Gillyatt & Reynolds, 1999). Furthermore, physical appearance is becoming increasingly emphasized for men, and eating "disorders" among men are becoming more common, especially in male subcultures that tend to emphasize physical appearance (e.g., some gay subcultures).

In addition to the general predisposing influence of Western cultural values, other circumstances can open the door for a/b. Following are some of the common circumstances encountered by people we know struggling with a/b that contributed to their receptivity to a/b's accusations and false promises.

Activities or Professions that Place Bodies on Display

Activities and professions such as dance, cheerleading, modeling, and acting leave women feeling visually exposed to large audiences and evaluated on the basis of their physical appearance. This visibility and evaluation can easily prompt girls and women to police their bodies according to dominant Western notions of beauty. A/b then sneaks in, offering its assistance in meeting these "requirements." Involvement with performance dance in general and ballet in particular is one of the most significant risk factors for developing an eating disorder, perhaps because of the extreme self-discipline and competition within the culture of professional dance.

Contexts that Emphasize Achievement and Competition

Many girls and women who gravitate toward a/b have a strong desire to be liked, admired, and respected. Many insiders have resonated with the word *untouchable* when describing their ambition to feel above others, who hopefully will regard them with awe. When these girls and women find themselves in contexts where this approval and acknowledgment is doled out only in proportion to one's achievements, this "success" can take on a life or death importance. Competitive sports and academia are two contexts that tend to fan the flame of the idea that you need to excel to get approval or respect (from coaches, teachers, parents, peers, etc.). When a girl or woman has already developed an ethic of hard work, self-discipline, and self-denial in the service of achievement—and a belief that she needs to do this to be loved or valued—the road has been paved for a/b to glide in and co-opt that ethos. For example, a/b might say something like, "You will never be noticed if you are just one of the pack. You must be the best if you are going to get attention and respect. You need to work harder and push farther if you want anyone to notice you." Or it might offer itself as a way of redeeming failures in other areas: "You can't control the grade a teacher gives you (or how many points another team scores), but you *can* succeed in losing weight."

Situations Where One Feels Out of Control of One's Body or Life

A/b can offer a person a supreme sense of control over her body and a sense of order to her life through the imposition of mindless and exacting rituals. A/b's appeal in this regard can be considerable for those who have had their bodies appropriated by others (for example through sexual abuse) or have been dispossessed of their right to make fundamental life decisions by dominating and controlling partners or parents.

Feeling Demeaned and Belittled by Others

Interactions that leave a person feeling badly about herself can make her more vulnerable to a/b's promise to improve her as a person and make her less deserving of criticism and insult. A/b can take advantage of situations where perfectionistic, critical teachers, coaches, parents, partners, or friends constantly highlight, compare, and even ridicule a girl or woman's "shortcomings" and "failures."

Emotionally Overwhelming Events

Intense fear, pain, grief, anger, and other strong emotions can be both frightening and difficult to tolerate. Anorexia offers relief from these feelings. It has at least two means of inducing a kind of emotional anesthesia. First, it divorces a person from her embodied experience by encouraging her to disregard or overrule physical sensations while submitting to an extreme regimen of physical exertion, self-deprivation, and restriction. It turns people into dissociated automatons who have been separated from themselves and their feelings. Second, as the person becomes increasingly malnourished, she either will be too fatigued to feel much of anything or will experience the effects of endorphins, chemicals the body releases when it is experiencing stress and trauma, that produce a false feeling of well-being and euphoria.

Bulimia can also appeal to a person's desire to rid herself of unwanted feelings. Bingeing can shift a person's awareness from emotions to physical sensations, while purging, particularly vomiting, can generate the fleeting experience of emotional "cleansing."

A/b can also seem like a refuge for women who find it difficult to define themselves and their preferences and make decisions based upon what they want. The desire or requirement to please and placate others can make it difficult and frightening for some women to articulate and act upon their own desires, preferences, and values. Because a/b dictates so many aspects of a person's life, defining for her who she is and what she wants, it can "relieve" the person from having to define herself.

Periods of Life Transition

Significant transitions and crossroads in a person's life, such as grad-uation from high school, moving away from home for the first time, attending college, beginning a new job, or changing careers, can en-gender anxiety, fear, self-doubt, and confusion. A/b can appeal to a person at these times by offering to anchor her in something that is immediate, concrete, and controllable, thereby providing her with an "achievement" that can momentarily boost her confidence without requiring her to actually face her fears.

Professions or Activities that Encourage Self-Sacrifice and Selfless Giving

Professions or activities in which the person is ministering to people who are less privileged and sometimes desperately needful (e.g., the helping professions such as nursing, therapy, social work, teaching) can make it difficult for a person to honor her own limits. Many jobs lead people to feel that they can never do enough or help enough. These jobs can engender in a caring person feelings of guilt, inadequacy, and powerlessness, which a/b can then exploit. In addition, any profession or activity that encourages, rewards, expects, or requires people to work extremely long hours and to ignore physical needs for food and rest can support a/b's ethos of self-denial.

Family Contexts that Promote Achievement, Perfection, Thinness, or Guilt

Children tend to want to please their parents and make them proud. In striving to win their parents' acknowledgment and approval, they often end up internalizing many of their parents' values. When children emulate their parents' valuing of achievement, perfection, thinness, and so on, they become more vulnerable to the voice of a/b, which also champions these values and carries them to a deadly extreme.

Children tend to feel responsible for misfortunes and tragedies that may strike a family, such as deaths, divorces, or financial crises. They can also blame themselves for the unhappiness or depression of a parent, even if they have received no encouragement from parents or siblings to do so. Feelings of guilt and responsibility can leave a child vulnerable to the voice of a/b, which confirms their "badness" while offering them a path to redemption.

Seeking an escape from pain, fear or uncertainty, and taken in by these promises and enticements that are so in line with dominant cultural specifications for women, these women sign on the dotted line and the "deal with the devil" is ratified. The a/b trap has been carefully set in the dark corners of innocent lives, and the bait painstakingly concealed within these women's very desires to live in a world where transgressions against women are no longer commonplace, and respect of self and other replace the brutal ethics of ruthless individualism. Once the deal is done, a/b continues to use these hopes and dreams to disguise its imprisonment, abuse, and murder of the women who hold them.

Chapter 2

FROM CAPTIVATED TO CAPTIVE

ANOREXIA/BULIMIA AS PRISON AND JAILER

The metaphors of *prison* and *concentration camp* resonate strongly with the experience of many of those we have spoken with who have had to struggle with the dream-turned-nightmare of a/b. Similarly, many people have described their lives under the regime of a/b as a "hell" and a/b as "the devil" or an expression of "evil." Prisons are places that generally inflict hardship, deprivation, and suffering while erecting great obstacles to prevent the escape of their inmates. It is this dual aspect of prisons that makes them an apt metaphor for a/b. The first part of this chapter deals briefly with the hardships and tortures inflicted in a/b's prison; the remainder addresses the tactics a/b uses to keep people imprisoned despite the increasing deprivations and degradation it imposes.

THE PRISON

A/b generally worms its way into a person's life by disguising its rules as prudent suggestions. It then begins to construct its prison by declaring it will fulfill its promises only when the person has complied with its rules. A/b usually offers its "aid" to people during times of desperate need when a/b may seem like the only available option. Like a loan shark who takes advantage of a person's desperate need for cash by imposing extreme repayment terms, a/b exacts an unconscionable payment. But even a ruthless loan shark makes the terms of the agreement explicit and delivers the cash up front. A/b, by comparison, is more predatory: It never initially discloses its terms, yet it ultimately requires that these impossible terms be met before it fulfills its end of the "bargain."

Emily (see Chapter 3) described a/b's trap in the following way:

> It goes about its search for humans in pain and misery. Whenever it finds them, it approaches them and attempts to befriend them. . . . It promises to take away your pain. If you are having an identity crisis, it will promise to provide you with an identity. If you are lonely, it will promise to be your friend. If you are feeling powerless, it will promise to make you powerful. It will make promise after promise, but its promises are lies. It says, "I will make you happy." As soon as you believe the lie, you have already begun to die.
>
> Once you believe the promise you are given a set of spoken rules. The promises become conditional. It says, "I will take away your pain only *if* you follow the rules. I will make you happy only *if* you do everything I tell you to do."
>
> Anorexia's spoken rules are those of self-denial. Anorexia promises to reward you for denying yourself anything and everything you need and desire. Anorexia tells you that denying all your needs and desires will make you strong, happy, and free of pain. If you are tired, anorexia forbids you to sleep. If you are hungry, anorexia forbids you to eat. If you are cold, anorexia forbids you to turn up the heater or put on a sweater. Anorexia forbids you from enjoying your sexuality. The most important of Anorexia's rules is that you must follow all the rules perfectly at all times.
>
> But no matter how perfectly you follow the rules, it is never perfect enough for Anorexia. He says, "Lose the five pounds and I will make you happy." Once you lose the five pounds, he wants another five pounds, and so on. It is impossible to satisfy Anorexia. You will sooner starve to death than be rewarded by him and that is precisely his intention. Even though he has never laid a finger on you, he gets full credit for your death.

Once a person has been caught up in a/b's web of promises, it is not long before her life begins to revolve around the performance of these prescriptions and the enduring of these restrictions. Ironically, having promised the person deliverance, a/b confines her to a prison where she is forbidden every right, including even the simple pleasures of smiling, prayer, and human association. A/b becomes the arbiter of nearly every thought, gesture, and action—a judge, jury, and executioner all rolled up into one.

The Souring of the Romance and the Development of Doubt

Once the initial exhilaration associated with the promises of a/b has abated, the romance usually begins to sour. Despite the initial relief some may experience when they turn their lives over to a/b, many of these girls and women become disheartened and distressed by some of the negative effects of a/b. Failing health and waning energy may prevent them from participating in cherished activities. Their contact with friends may evaporate as a/b fills their time with obligatory rituals and prohibits them from eating in the presence of others or from being in the presence of others who are eating. Relationships with parents, even those that are warm and close, often descend into conflict and turmoil. Poor concentration and fatigue can make it difficult to function at school or work. A/b attempts to minimize such experiences, denies that they are an effect of a/b, or portrays them as inconsequential sacrifices necessary to achieve the promised happiness and success.

Despite this, many women and girls begin to have second thoughts about the path they (seemingly) have chosen and attempt to reverse direction. But a/b slams the door shut and bars their exit. As with any prison (or military service, gang, or cult) getting in is far easier than getting out. This difficulty is bewildering to many outsiders, who can't understand why a woman who professes a desire to overcome her eating "disorder" doesn't just eat. This lack of understanding can limit their patience with someone who claims to know what is best for herself but repeatedly fails to act in her own interests.

A/B'S TACTICS OF IMPRISONMENT

Almost all of a/b's tactics of imprisonment can be subsumed under a perverse appeal to a perverted morality. Some tactics rely more on straightforward deception than an explicitly moral discourse, such as telling a woman that her friend's concern for her well being is only veiled jealousy of her thinness, or attempting to demoralize her by telling her she will never succeed in overcoming it. Many of these tactics are illustrated by the insider stories we present in the reminder of this section (see Chapters 3–6) as well as throughout the book. In the reminder of this chapter we focus exclusively on those more subtle tactics that confine people to their anorexic/bulimic cells by virtue of the manner in which they define the virtuous and the profane.

A/B: A Moral Con(quest)

A/b secures its authority as jailer by relying on certain implicit assumptions about morality. We use the term *morality* in a broad sense to refer to those qualities and ways of being in the world that are regarded as virtuous and meritorious. Standards of morality may derive from religious doctrine or from secular (popular) beliefs and values. In essence, these standards define what makes a person or an action "good." A/b attempts to define what is morally virtuous in people it has ensnared, and it promises happiness only if they realize this particular moral vision. Likewise, it defines what is morally contemptible and ascribes a catastrophic future should the person fail to morally redeem themselves. In short, a/b's promises revolve around its vision of the morally virtuous, whereas its chastisements, threats, and dire predictions revolve around its vision of the morally flawed.

We wish to be clear, lest a/b twist the meaning of our words, that we are not making the case that a/b is a moral discourse or a moral problem. Rather, we are discussing the ways in which a/b *uses* moral arguments to achieve its highly immoral ends—the murder of women and men. A/b speaks with moral authority, but we view this "authority" as an overarching tactic it employs to perpetrate its deadly ruse. We hope that by making a/b's moral claims more explicit, we will help those who have been subject to a/b's dubious moral authority to contest and repudiate it.

Thinness as Moral Virtue, Fatness as Moral Depravity

At the center of a/b's moral vision is the matter of body shape and fitness. The pinnacle of moral virtue, according to a/b, is thinness, whereas fatness lies at the other end of the moral continuum, that of moral depravity. Here, a/b is merely building upon moral foundations that already hold currency in contemporary Western culture. Slender women not only are more in step with contemporary fashion but also are the beneficiaries of a culture that has come to view thinness as aesthetically desirable and morally virtuous. A slender body is often assumed to reflect virtues such as self-control, restraint, temperance, and grace. Conversely, women who are "overweight" are often thought to be lacking in moral character, as fatness is often viewed as a consequence of laziness, self-indulgence, and weakness.

Thinness as a moral standard may derive from religious as well as secular notions of morality. Some historians have attributed the

vehemence of the moral disdain for fatness to the images of thinness long associated with Christian self-denial and saintly virtue (Bell,
1985). Others have proposed that an emphasis on dieting and an attack against fat arose as a moral counterbalance to the increasing ma-
terialism and sexual permissiveness of the early Twentieth Century;
dominance over the body and deliberate self-sacrifice, exemplified by
"the diet," paralleled the traditional Christian means of the expiation of
sin through self-denial (Stearns, 1997). Furthermore, during this same
historical period people were becoming more sedentary due to the ex-
pansion of white-collar jobs, the proliferation of labor-saving devices
for the household (e.g., washing machines), and the introduction of
streetcars and then automobiles. Fatness became associated with laziness, and dieting became a means of demonstrating moral character in
an age of increasing leisure, acquisitiveness, and sexual permissiveness
(Stearns, 1997).

Whatever their historical roots, diet and body shape have, in dominant Western culture, been carried into the domain of morality. A/b
capitalizes on this moral discourse by claiming to bestow a moral superiority to women who gain mastery of their own bodies, desires,
and appetites. Likewise, a/b exploits the moral overtones of the cultural discourse about women and their bodies to validate the harsh
judgments it levels against those who fail to live up to its command-
ments.

Exaggeration of Cultural Ideals

A/b builds upon the cultural foundations that place inordinate emphasis on women's physical appearance by attaching moral significance
to women's body shape. But in building its foundation upon this cultural bedrock, it must exaggerate these cultural biases to hyperbolic
proportions. For example, although the dominant cultural discourse
places great value on a woman's appearance, it also permits the acknowledgment of her merit in other aspects of her identity, such as
that of a professional, parent, scholar, homemaker, artist, and athlete.
A/b exaggerates the value placed on women's appearance by asserting
that women have no value beyond their appearance or that obtaining
acknowledgment for other qualities or endeavors is contingent upon
first achieving the "perfection" of thinness. A/b allows no means of
compensating for the "failure" to obtain this "perfect" body; the only
redemption permitted is through a covenant with a/b and unflinching
devotion to its dogma.

Extending the Range of Its Assault

In this section, we delineate some of the tactics a/b uses to strengthen its grip on people who may no longer be infatuated with it and who, at moments, may even attempt to resist it. A/b uses these tactics in an attempt to dominate every domain of the person's life—her identity, her relationship to her body, her relationships with her family, friends, and helping professionals, and even her spiritual life. These tactics can be likened to the threads a spider uses to bind a fly securely once it has been caught in its web. Even when a woman successfully evades or breaks some of these threads of meaning, it is likely that a/b will find a way, at least temporarily, of binding her with others.

Equating Fat with Fatness

One of the ways in which a/b maintains its control over the person in the face of mounting deprivations is by extending its moral purview to include increasingly larger domains of the person's life and actions. It often accomplishes this, in part, by directing its attacks not only against fatness but also against fat itself. In other words, although the culture at large morally condemns women for "being fat," a/b morally condemns them for "having fat." By making fat rather than fatness its villain, a/b succeeds in conflating fat and fatness in the minds of the women it has seduced. Consequently, even women whose bodies are extremely thin may perceive any body fat or the appearance of body fat (like abdominal protrusion after eating) as evidence of fatness and therefore morally repugnant.

Attacking the Person's Character

Submission to a/b is fueled by not only a desire to be good, but also, simultaneously, a desire to cease being bad. A/b accrues power by claiming the moral authority to define both what is good, right, or true and what is bad or wrong. A/b harshly condemns fat or fatness as evidence of a morally profligate character. It argues that the existence of body fat is proof that the person is lazy, self-indulgent, selfish, weak, and worthless. It extends its condemnation to any thoughts, feelings, or actions associated with the possibility of gaining (or not losing) weight, such as eating, feeling hungry, contemplating eating, and so on.

A/b does not limit its harsh indictments exclusively to the domain of eating. It leaves no stone unturned in its search for ways to make people feel like failures.* If a woman or girl feels like a personal failure or worthless, she is all the more vulnerable to a/b's promise to "gooden" or purify her, and she is more accepting of hard labor and starvation as forms of penance and punishment. Sometimes the need to escape an identity as a "bad" person or to reject feelings of safety (because people who are injured by others often blame this on their "badness") is an even more compelling motivation than the desire for thinness. As Margaret (see Chapters 10, 11, 13, 15, & 18) put it, "As far as anorexia goes, for us it's not about our weight as much as it is the ideas it presents to us about who we are as a person and its ability to make us better by our own starvation."

How is a/b able to so utterly persuade even those girls and women generally regarded as among the most thoughtful, considerate, talented, and accomplished of their generation that they are worthless and inadequate? How does it turn every opportunity for pride and self-appreciation into a cause for self-condemnation? Although its strategies are numerous and ingenious, one of its favorite tricks is to impose standards and expectations that are impossible to live up to. Two such "virtues" are that of perfection and the "ethic" of pleasing others and ensuring their happiness.

Demanding Perfection

By demanding perfection, a/b ensures that no matter how much a person achieves, she will always experience herself as a failure, because perfection is impossible. When a/b sets perfection as its standard, it imposes a system of absolutes: You are either victorious or a failure, good or bad. There is no middle ground. If, for example, a/b requires the person to run a specified route at a specified time of day for a specified number of minutes, any departure from those requirements, no matter how minor, constitutes an absolute failure in a/b's eyes. A/b then chastises, demeans, and rebukes the person for their failure: "How can you expect to get anywhere with an effort like that? You are worthless. If you wish to be worthy of me you will have to do better. You are a loser. In order to make up for your failing, you will have to run twice as long tomorrow."

A/b often extends these perfectionistic standards beyond directly pro-a/b activities such as compulsive exercise or food restriction. For example, Elizabeth a 17-year-old (see Chapter 1), had been making

---

* For a elaboration of the ways in which contemporary culture contributes to the construction of failure identities, see White (2002).

steady progress in reducing the extent of anorexia's influence in her life when it made a sudden comeback. Elizabeth had just taken an after-school job shelving books at a library. Anorexia began telling her not only that she had too much work to do on the job to take time to eat, but also that she must do the job perfectly (even though it was only her first week), which meant both accurately and speedily. Anorexia even had Elizabeth blaming herself for the errors she made due the mistakes of others. When she "messed up," anorexia forbade her from eating at all.

Being perfect at something requires being the best, for, by definition, if another person's performance exceeds your own, you have failed to attain perfection. Aspiring to perfection entails the constant comparing of your performance to that of others. You feel under the ever-watchful eye of a/b, which is constantly evaluating and "sizing you up." These evaluations inevitably result in confirmation of failures and deficiencies. Such evaluations proceed through normative measures such as grades, scores, marks, weights, and other objectifications, and by the quantification of goals through numbers such as percentiles, grams, calories, minutes, miles, and so on.* As Kimberley, age 20, astutely remarked: "Anorexia uses numbers as ammo to get you to look at yourself and think you're pathetic."

Proscribing Selfless Giving

The a/b requirement of self-sacrifice and the obligation to please others is another "virtue" that fosters feelings of guilt and "badness." As Elizabeth put it, "If someone looks sad to me, then I can't be happy . . . I feel bad if I can't make it better for them." After freeing herself from bulimia, Mia, a 28-year-old, had the following reflections about what she had felt was a moral imperative to live for others:

> I used to be called "everybody's sunshine." I still feel like sunshine but the sun is not alone—it "lives" in harmony with the clouds and when I feel "gloomy" I am still that sun; I just don't feel like shining on anyone. I am much of a happy hermit. . . . I used to give people what I thought they'd want . . . and I got lost. I was so good at making people like me but there were very few people whom I really liked.

---

* For these reasons, the Vancouver Anti-Anorexia and Bulimia League turned against such measurements. After repeatedly being asked by reporters to reveal the lowest weight they had reached, League members decided to give only their birth weights (personal communication, Lorraine Grieves, 1995). Questions about weight and other measurements easily invite the voice of a/b to harass members who haven't "achieved" as low a weight.

The others drained me and I resented them but I took them on in the first place. Now I am not spreading *"love"* to everyone reaching out for it. I treasure the people I love and one of them is... *moi*... I don't feel evil anymore because I don't feel like everyone's well-being depends upon me, which I thought before.... So I feel less angelic and more human.

To people of the Christian faith, a/b may claim ecclesiastical authority to judge their spiritual status as that of saint or sinner, and it is invariably the latter when the person is at odds with a/b's dictums. It calls upon and distorts a tradition of self-less devotion, denial or disavowal of desire, asceticism, self-sacrifice, and even self-mutilation for its own unholy purposes. Perhaps this is why historian Bell (1985) found such haunting parallels between the lives of canonized medieval Catholic saints and the contemporary lives of young women taken by anorexia.

The responsibility of making others happy is a heavy burden to bear. Like perfection, it is impossible to fulfill, and the failure to do so results in lashings of guilt. This moral injunction ensnares people in the a/b loop of sin and elusive redemption.

Setting Women and Girls Up for Exploitation and Abuse

When people feel compelled to put the needs of others ahead of their own, they leave themselves vulnerable to exploitation and abuse. If selfless giving persists in relationships where that "ethic" is not reciprocated, inequities can quickly develop. If the woman is unable to value her own life and privilege her own desires, she is likely to remain in the relationship at the cost of her own self-respect and self-confidence. The ensuing feelings of self-blame and shame play right into the hands of a/b, which entices her with promises of moral redemption, emotional anesthesia, a sense of control, and so on.

Erasing the Sense of Self

Compulsory giving can also separate a woman from her awareness of her own desires, preferences, and values. She feels unable to put these into practice in a relationship and instead must cater to the desires of others. This lack of awareness of "self" can diminish the tension and distress the person might feel in the event of a conflict between what she desires and what the other person desires. Instead of giving *of* herself, she gives *up* herself. This makes it easier for a/b (as well as other people in her life) to dominate and define her. As Maggie, a 24-year-old (see Chapters 2, 4, & 7) put it:

> Anorexia says you don't need to feel anything because you have got *it* [anorexia]. There is no need to waste your energy crying or being sad or arguing or getting angry or standing up for yourself. There was always the voice that said: "What's the point of feeling those things? No one would listen to you. And what you have said really doesn't count. So don't bother."

Amy, a 40-year-old woman (see Chapters 2 & 14) expressed the same understanding a bit differently:

> Anorexia sucks everything out. And it puts a gloss over you. And it makes the bingeing and food stuff seem all that's important. And *it's not!* By having you focus on food, it stops you from getting into the inside stuff. It's really the inside stuff that's got to be looked at. Anti-anorexia is about feeling connected to yourself. The bingeing stuff is superficial. It is really getting back to finding out who I am, what I want, and how I am going to live my life.

By deflecting people away from their internal experience, a/b seriously impedes a person's ability to navigate according to an internal moral compass—one which might provide a basis for challenging a/b's assertions about good and bad, right and wrong. It has them looking outside and beyond themselves to a/b—the crystallization and exaggeration of Western culture—for their moral bearings.

Once a/b has undermined a person's sense of moral goodness, it can often easily convince her that, because she is a bad person, she will have a bad life and deserves nothing better. It threatens her with dire forecasts of a life lived without the prospect of love, admiration, success, or happiness unless steps are taken to address her character flaws and her body shape—the latter, according to a/b, being evidence of the former. A/b assaults women with distorted and horrifying images of their bodies and asserts "you are nothing without me." These tactics have the effect of destroying any hope the person may have of surviving without it.

Many women who have struggled with a/b over the course of many years have been persuaded by a/b that their lives are hopeless, and they have been too far down a/b's road on too many occasions to still believe in a/b's promises of redemption. Some of these women, without even the false hope of a/b to cling to, take their own lives.* Others may deal

---

* Though these deaths might be officially recorded as suicide, we regard them as murders by a/b. These suicides are never taken into account in the statistics on deaths caused by a/b.

with their despair and disillusionment by seeking death through a/b, which now presents itself as an angel of death, delivering the person from her suffering.

For those women who are still susceptible to a/b's promises, the chastisements may be proffered in a more encouraging and exhortatory manner: "You are not trying hard enough!"; "I just know you are capable of meeting my demands!"; "If only you would have more willpower, more discipline!"; "You are very special to me, and I know you can be special to others if you only do as I tell you." Many women, still charmed by a/b and its promised land, are beguiled into repayment.

Ironically, the only way to achieve a life ultimately worthy of a/b's approval is through the forfeiture of that life. We have never met a person who has satisfied a/b once and for all. Every time a demand is met, a/b ups the ante. Any praise a/b offers along the way is just a prelude to another demand or requirement, and then another, each one a stepping stone in a long and torturous path that ends only with death. As the person proceeds along the path laid out for her, the tests become more arduous and the deprivations more severe. Outsiders may wonder why someone would submit to or tolerate the yoke she seems to be laboring under. However, as the person's sacrifices and sufferings intensify, a/b tightens the noose of its rhetoric, allowing the person less and less slack.

Glorifying Discipline, Willpower, and Self-Control

The one-two punch of a/b involves, on the one hand, the unequivocal condemnation of every act of anti-a/b defiance and noncompliance, and, on the other, the qualified praise of acts of compliance ("You did well, but I know you can do even better") and the extolling of the associated "moral virtues" of discipline, willpower, and self-control.

If a/b is to succeed in working and starving a person to death, it must do so through the imposition of a morality that promotes an adversarial relationship between the person and her body. The "morality" of discipline, willpower, and self-control functions in exactly that manner. Protest and outrage against a/b will almost certainly arise from the body as a result of its mistreatment. This protest takes the form of aching hunger, fatigue, headaches, dizziness, and many other symptoms. These symptoms serve as alarm bells that have the potential to expose a/b's fraudulent goodwill. The capacity of the body to cry out against its own destruction is an obstacle that a/b tries to overcome. The body's voice must be gagged as the body itself is subdued, controlled, and shaped. The elevation and glorification of the associated "virtues" of self-control, discipline, and willpower provide a "moral" foundation for the assault on the body.

Tactics for Overriding Messages From the Body

The tactics that a/b uses to overcome the objections from women's bodies are probably nearly infinite, limited only by the creativity of the minds that a/b has appropriated. However, we will present five types of tactics that we commonly find a/b using with the people with whom we have consulted.

Denying that the Bodily Symptoms Are Connected to A/B

When physical symptoms (such as heart failure, profound fatigue, persistent headaches, dizziness) cannot be denied, a/b maintains that the problem has nothing to do with it. For example, if a woman has been told by a doctor that her heart has begun to beat arrhythmically due to inadequate nutrition, a/b may prevent the woman from focusing on the "due to inadequate nutrition" part of the message and maintain that the problem is a heart defect unrelated to a/b (see Chapter 10). If a woman faints or nearly faints upon standing, a/b may tell her she is just a "klutz."

Using the Physical Symptoms to Intensify Physically Destructive Acts

At times, a/b is able to use the presence of symptoms of malnutrition as a pretense for arguing that the person should intensify her a/b efforts. For example, if a person is fatigued or feeling faint due to malnutrition, a/b may redefine this symptom as "laziness" or "weakness" and lash the person on to even more strenuous exercise. If the person is experiencing hunger pangs or cramps, a/b may tell her, "It is not good to eat when you have an upset stomach, it will only make you feel worse." If a woman feels faint due to low blood pressure secondary to starvation, a/b may tell her that she is "weak" and needs to exercise more strenuously.

Appropriating a Woman's Concern About Her Body

When a woman places a high value on her physical health, a/b may appropriate this concern and twist it toward its own ends. For example, a young woman I (RM) worked with recalled a situation during which she was contemplating eating some peanuts on an airplane flight. Anorexia reminded her that her doctor had said she should refrain from working her body and then succeeded in talking her out of eating the peanuts by telling her how hard her body would have to work in order to break down and digest them.

Arguing that the Physical Symptoms Are Signs of Progress

Another tactic a/b uses when physical symptoms cannot be denied is to minimize their injuriousness and to argue that they are signposts of progress towards moral and physical reformation. A/b transforms the symptoms from being something to worry about to being something to feel proud of and encouraged by. By exalting "virtues" such as *self-control* and *willpower,* a/b lends moral support to the war it conscripts women into against their own body and its desires, and by doing so, it virtually guarantees that they will experience the betrayal of their own bodies as ennobling and sanctifying.

Promoting Detachment From One's Body

In order to get a person to betray the needs of her body, a/b portrays the body, along with its needs and desires, as a threat to her progress, an enemy that she must pit her will against. A/b encourages her to simply ignore or tune out the body's messages. The capacity to do this, it argues, is an indicator of moral strength. The inclination to see the body as an enemy and the capacity to detach from it may already be well established in girls or women who have experienced physical or sexual abuse. A/b may also encourage the use of sensation-numbing or sleep medications for this purpose.

In the next several chapters, we present insiders' accounts of how a/b used its voice to seduce girls and women into its world and imprison them.* The stories in Chapters 3, 4, and 5 are intended primarily as illustrations of the seduction tactics we presented in Chapter 1. We hope that these stories will make clear how the personal circumstances of one's life intersect with the values enshrined by Western culture. Although a/b may have been laying in wait, concealed in the background of women's lives, these junctures are the places where these young girls and women met a/b for the first time, face to masked face. Chapter 6, anorexia's letter to Kristen Webber, is intended primarily as an illustration and explication of the tactics of imprisonment presented earlier in this chapter.

---

* In the recounting of these stories, we tried to incorporate the person's own words as much as possible, but in some instances narration was required to make the story coherent. In these cases, the person collaborated with us in the retelling.

The stories that follow are highly personal, but they are also intimate cultural stories. They are stories about how cultural values such as *control, thinness, and self-sacrifice* converge with disadvantageous personal circumstances such as sudden loss or sexual abuse to make a/b's promises seem irresistible.

We can happily report that in every instance where we have knowledge of the person's life beyond these seductions, these girls and women fought back against a/b and eventually succeeded in largely reclaiming their lives from it.

Chapter 3

FIRST IT SAVES YOUR LIFE, THEN IT KILLS YOU

EMILY'S STORY

I (RM) first met Emily when she was 13. Even at the age of 13, Emily preferred using poetry and prose as a way of expressing those aspects of experience that are not conveyed easily through conventional, conversational speech. *Ocean,* which Emily wrote just as she turned 14, serves as a poetic self-representation of the young woman.

Ocean

There is a seashell in me . . . polished smooth by the sand . . . gleaming in the sunlight . . . beautiful and interesting . . . admired by many people . . .

Like a seashell, I am empty inside.

There is a flounder in me . . . always trying to fit in . . . blending in with the background . . . never standing out . . . always changing colors . . . afraid of being seen . . .

Like a flounder, I make myself invisible.

There is a sponge in me . . . stationary and immobile . . . stuck in one place . . . watching other fish live their lives . . . absorbing everything that swims in its way . . .

Like a sponge, I am frustrated by my powerlessness.

There is a dolphin in me . . . childishly playful . . . clever and bright . . . kind and good-natured . . . strong but gentle . . .

Like a dolphin, I befriend all who know me.

There is a shark in me ... fearlessly bold ... ruthlessly vicious
... threatening and intimidating ... insensitive and unfeeling ...
attacking anyone who swims too close ...
Like a shark, I only think about my own survival.

I am an ocean, deep, and sometimes dark, full of life and sunken
treasure, hiding beneath a surface of blue-green waves.

I first met Emily and her parents on a beautiful spring evening in
1992. The hospital where she was residing had given her a pass to
attend therapy. Emily slumped down on the couch next to her father;
her mother sat in the adjacent armchair. Prior to this first meeting, I
learned that Emily had made three serious suicide attempts over the
past 2 months; the last two had resulted in medical and subsequent
psychiatric hospitalizations. I learned later from Emily that she had
sought out the drugs for her third suicide attempt following a fight she
had with her mother during the brief car ride home only 10 minutes
after being discharged from her previous hospitalization.

Both parents reported feeling utterly perplexed by Emily's behavior
during the past 2 months. Their tone was concerned but also critical.
When Emily's mother spoke, Emily would interrupt her, only to find
herself abruptly interrupted by her mother. The high degree of reactivity
each displayed toward the other made it hard for any conversation to
proceed and my attempts to create space for each person to speak
without interruption were largely in vain.

I vividly recall Emily's response to one of my first questions. What,
I wondered, did she want to be different in her life and in her family?
Grinning and buoyant, she exuberantly explained: "I'd like to be a
couple of inches taller and to change my cheekbones. I'd like to grow
my hair out. I'd like to get rid of my braces and lose ten pounds. I
want to get better grades." I still remember this exchange because of
how startled I was by her response. How, I naïvely wondered, could
someone distressed enough to attempt suicide three times in two
months be so completely preoccupied with her body, appearance,
and grades? This meeting with Emily was my introduction to a/b. My
initial bewilderment gradually gave way to clarity and horror as I came
to better understand how the voice of a/b had been speaking to Emily.

I met with Emily alone over a period of many months. These meeting
were interspersed with less regular meetings with her and her parents.
During my meetings with Emily, I came to understand how utterly
alone and misunderstood she felt. At times, Emily enjoyed some playful and companionable contact with her father, but her experience of
his unpredictable temper, authoritarian control, and dismissal of her
feelings undermined her trust in him. He was particularly judgmental

and condemning of Emily's outrage. Unable to understand her rage and hurt, he viewed her anger as evidence of her being possessed by evil, which he, on one occasion, attempted to have ecclesiastically exorcised. It was not until near the end of our meetings together that Emily disclosed having been abused by her father as a young girl (though she vacillated regarding the accuracy of her memories). She continued to feel uncomfortable with the manner in which he looked at her and touched her.

Emily's mother also found it difficult to respond compassionately and empathically to Emily's feelings of anger and hurt. She herself had grown up with parents who had been very critical of her throughout her life, and she had married a man who perpetuated her sense of constantly being under fire. Perhaps this contributed to her tendency to interpret Emily's expressions of emotional pain and appeals for change as one more attempt by someone to dictate to her. Emily's mother did not share her husband's belief that their daughter's expressions of outrage were an outcome of devil possession, but rather viewed them as a manifestation of "mental illness."

Over the course of my conversations with Emily and her parents, my sympathy for Emily grew, as I too witnessed the extent to which Emily seemed invisible to them. Emily's parents rarely acknowledged her perceptions of their hostility and rejection of her, despite her persistent attempts to address the issue with them. In fact, Emily's expression of outrage and pain only seemed to make matters worse. Because Emily desperately wanted to feel loved and cared for by her parents, she found it difficult not to identify with their portrayal of her as ungrateful, aggressive, and emotionally unstable. As a consequence, Emily had become very confused about who she was.

Throughout grade school, Emily felt different from her peers, never really fitting in, and found herself with no one to whom she could turn for support. She was hurting and looking for a way out. In her journal, she reflected on the emotional strain she felt: "My parents created hell for so many years by hating each other and abandoning me on top of abusing me when I was little. Everything piled up on top of the next thing. No more. No more of this. The pile ain't gonna get no higher. It can't. I won't let it."

A/B TO THE "RESCUE"

A/b seduced its way into Emily's life when she was 11 years old. She later recalled anorexia's initial seduction strategy in a journal entry made when she was 14.

I asked myself: "Why am I so miserable?" Anorexia, pretending to be me . . . disguising its voice and imitating mine, answered: "Because you're fat." Period. Very blunt. Anorexia approached me when I was miserable. It told me it could make me feel better. It told me that my fat was making me unhappy. It told me to get rid of the fat and then I would feel better. Basically, Anorexia told me that losing weight would make me feel better, because all my problems and all my bad feelings were existing because I was fat and ugly. If my fat was gone, all my problems would be gone too. There. There it was . . . the answer! It all seemed so simple and so perfect and SO EASY. That's why Anorexia is so appealing. It seems like the perfect solution. It gave me the power to change the thing that was making me feel bad: my weight, my fat. I could lose the weight and then I would no longer have any reason to feel bad. I could have reasons to feel good, too, on top of it all. I was really quite impressed and pleased by Anorexia in the very beginning when it first introduced itself. It told me it would make me feel better if I lost weight but it didn't tell me it would punish me for failing to lose weight. It didn't tell me how difficult it would be to lose weight. I did eventually realize that if I lost too much weight I might die but by then I didn't really care. Oh, well, if I die, I die. Big deal. Being thin and beautiful is worth dying for.

The pain and despair Emily felt at this time in life led her to accept the risks associated with anorexia, once she came to know them. After all, Emily wanted her life, as it was, to end. Knowing of no other means of remedy or refuge, she decided to give anorexia a chance to end the misery in her life. If anorexia failed to end her misery in life, then she'd allow it to end her misery by ending her life. At least she'd be dying for an ideal, albeit an anorexic one forged in the contemporary cultural linking of beauty with thinness.

How was it that anorexia was able to convince Emily that it was "fat" that was responsible for all her difficulties and unhappiness, and that all she had to do to feel better was to lose weight? Emily thought that her father's attitudes toward women's bodies made her more vulnerable to the deceptively simple equating of thinness with beauty and happiness. Though her mother was of medium build, her father often expressed disgust for his wife's body in front of Emily and made derogatory remarks about her eating. Emily was often solicited to corroborate his evaluations and moral censure. By the age of 11, Emily was already aware of his distaste for the bodies of mature women and his inclination to gaze at prepubescent girls. By joining him in his moral censure of her mother, she experienced more closeness with him than she might have otherwise, and she hoped that if she lost weight she might succeed where her mother had failed, pleasing him and winning his affection and respect. The following poem shows how a/b exploited Emily's father's hatred of her mother's body, which Emily came to identify with.

> After meals down her throat goes her finger
> No food in her body does linger
> She throws up each dinner
> Grows thinner and thinner
> Till death Anorexia brings her
>
> Disgusting how my breasts
> wiggle and sag
> soft and squishy
> like plastic
> slime-filled sandwich bags
>
> I hate my body
> I hate my mother
> (these two statements
> interchange)

When Emily failed to please her dad, a/b made sure she'd only have herself and her body to blame. Perhaps if the view that Emily's father held toward women's bodies had not been supported by advertisements, television programs, magazines, and other manifestations of the wider cultural climate, it would have seemed less "natural" to Emily. Perhaps then she might have been able to indict the attitude/value/cultural convention itself instead of aligning with it to despise herself, her body, and her mother.

Emily's experience of her life, thus far, had left her hating herself and her body, feeling alone and unsupported, and experiencing a high degree of emotional pain from which she could find little relief. A/b exploited these dreadful circumstances of Emily's young life by offering to numb her pain. Emily made the following entry in her journal.

> Okay, it's like this. You're walking down the street and for no reason at all somebody shoots you in the back. Anorexia immediately numbs the pain, and you continue to walk down the street not knowing you've been shot in the back because you can't see or feel the pain. Yes, you may feel happy, but you are going to bleed to death very quickly if you don't do something about that bullet hole in your back. Or maybe it's a stab wound. The bottom line is that you will bleed to death with a smile on your face. The stab wound won't kill you if you

go to the emergency room and let other people know what happened so they can help you get better and help stop the bleeding. But there is a problem with this whole scenario. The gunshot wound in your back would be excruciatingly painful and you wouldn't be able to walk at all, much less walk down the street with a goddamn smile on your face. So Anorexia comes and takes away the pain. You don't ask it to. It just does. It tells you that the pain is too great and it takes it away. Numb. Not feeling. Takes you from your body. In a sense, it rescues you. It doesn't want you to be hurt. Anorexia cares about you in the beginning. It saves your life. Then it kills you.

A TYPICAL DAY IN ANOREXIA/BULIMIA'S HELL

Is it any wonder that shortly after her twelfth birthday Emily surrendered to the rule of a/b without an inkling of what was in store for her? Someone who is drowning will grasp onto anything, even a shark, especially if the shark is mistaken for a porpoise. Anorexia, disguising its voice as her own, told her that if she wanted her life "saved," she was going to have to follow its rules. Emily described the way in which anorexia's rule transformed her day into a waking nightmare:

A typical *Sixth*-grade school day went like this: I woke up hungry. I went to the kitchen while everybody was still sleeping. I measured out cereal into a bowl and poured milk over it. I ate it fast 'cause I was hungry. I was still hungry. I ate another bowl of cereal. I felt guilty about eating it. For some dumb reason I ate a third bowl to make myself feel better. After realizing what I had done, I panicked and went to the bathroom to throw it up. Feeling better, I took a shower and got dressed. I felt hungry again. By that time the whole house was up, and I went into the kitchen to have a bowl of cereal. Cheerios this time. No more Honey Bunches of Oats left. I was still hungry. I had another bowl. I felt guilty and ate a third bowl to punish myself. Feeling guilty and hating myself for all the Cheerios I had eaten, I decided to skip lunch. I left for school with no money and no lunch. I was hungry at lunchtime and didn't want to watch people eat so, more often than not, I hid in the library or in the bathroom reading a book. I had no real friends except for Janice and Julie, and nobody but them ever noticed I was gone. And they didn't seem to care a whole lot. They had other friends and I didn't. I still felt bad about breakfast when school was over. I hated riding the bus home 'cause I felt uncomfortable around other kids so I walked three miles back to my house on the other end of the town. I didn't come home until around 4:00. By that time I was so hungry I ate everything that looked appealing: usually ice cream and pretzels and leftover pizza and anything else and my mom would tell me to stop and save some food for the rest of the family. I ignored her. Every day we fought over it. She asked me to stop and finally got angry at me for not taking a lunch. I told her I didn't have time to eat at school because I was too busy talking with my friends and having fun and she believed me. She told me to start packing a lunch anyway so I wouldn't be starving by the time I came home. I packed a lunch from then on and ate it every morning with my breakfast. Then when my family was eating dinner around 6:00 I refused to eat with them 'cause I needed to "even the score" with myself. If I pigged out after school, I couldn't also eat dinner. In my mind it made sense. So I went to bed hungry because by then I hadn't eaten since 4:00. I usually had dreams that I was eating breakfast 'cause I was so hungry.

I wasn't able to stay on the diet. I ended up bingeing. A lot. Bingeing and throwing up. This was just in *sixth* grade. I never told anybody this in *sixth* grade. I didn't have any friends. My whole sixth-grade year was centered around food: dieting, bingeing, throwing up, fasting, diet pills, reading diet books, exercising, isolating. IT WAS HELL! From my twelfth birthday on I lived in hell and never once spoke a word about it. I was hurting so badly I didn't even feel it. I lost a whole year of my life to Anorexia. I hated myself in *sixth* grade more than I had ever hated myself in my life.

THE TWO EMILYS

When Emily was 13, she conveyed to me her attempted strategies for coping with her overwhelming pain through an illustration. The two sets of strategies were so different that she associated each with a different Emily. She divided a blank sheet of paper in half with a zigzag dividing line. On the right side of the page she drew a picture of a frightened and vulnerable-looking girl with a sad face, wearing a dress, with her hair in a ponytail. At the top of this side of the page she wrote:

This person wants: ?
This person feels: sad, lonely, hurt, invisible, fragile
Well, I guess I could probably take a guess at what this person might want:
1. To be able to feel happy
2. Real friends
3. Someone to hold her when she's feeling hurt

4. To be visible
5. To feel strong

Unsuccessful attempts at getting what she wants:

1. Attempts to starve herself to feel strong
2. Eraser-burning herself to feel more visible

This Emily maintained some connection to her painful and vulnerable feelings. Emily viewed this self as an essentially good girl who was desperately in need of nurturing contact. Anorexia appealed to her by promising to make her strong and lovable.

On the left side of the page, Emily drew a smiling girl who looked more robust and confident, with hair loose, wearing slacks, a T-shirt, and flashy earrings, and holding a little handbag. At the top of this portion of the page she wrote:

> This person wants: to lose weight, have sex, have more sex, eat without gaining weight, to smoke pot, maybe beat up her parents, eat a lot without gaining weight, to see how much stuff she can shoplift before getting caught
>
> This person feels: ?
> She doesn't know and she doesn't care either.

Emily told me that this version of herself had cast off her feelings of vulnerability and abandoned her quest for love and acknowledgment. Instead of trying to be "good," this Emily identified more with "evil." This Emily could escape from the painful introspection of the other Emily and lose herself (and her vulnerability) through eating, drugs, and sex, while connecting to her rage and desire for revenge. Whereas anorexia had appealed to the other Emily's desire for strength and self-control, bulimia appealed to this Emily's desire for self-abandon and perpetuated the view of herself as evil. For the most part, it was the more confident, extroverted, and "evil" side that Emily presented to the world. Following is another poem Emily wrote when she was 13 years old, expressing her sense of living through two distinct identities.

Inside/Outside
In a world of half realities
I have two personalities
one of which is a fantasy
the other an actuality
I can't decide just which is which
(if I did they would probably switch)
one I wear for all to see

and the other hides inside of me
neither are straight
both are bent
and only valid fifty-percent
I feel divided into two
but neither half is entirely true

"I WILL BE YOUR VIRTUES"

In the larger scheme of her life, it was not just relief from pain Emily sought but an alternative view of herself—one that could affirm and acknowledge her many extraordinary talents, which, miraculously, she still had faith in. It didn't matter whether Emily merely wanted to escape from her pain or forge herself into a person whose talents and abilities would be readily apparent to others. Either way, a/b told her, "I can help you":

Last night
I laid in bed
Aware of the emptiness
Surrounding my identity
I didn't know
Who I was or
Who I am or
Who I one day
Will be
And as I laid
In bed and
Listened
Anorexia spoke

"I will be your
Talents
I will be your
Accomplishments
I will be your
Virtues
I will win you
Admiration
I will bring you
Recognition"

In addition to promising Emily recognition and a feeling of success, anorexia offered her an escape from pain by allowing her to take refuge in a momentary sense of superiority and invulnerability:

> No one can touch her . . .
> Not the nerds
> not the dorks
> not the geeks
>
> No one can touch her . . .
>
> not the stoners
> not the athletes
> not even the popular people
> not even the cheerleaders
>
> No one can touch her . . .
>
> She isn't the prettiest . . .
> She isn't the smartest . . .
> She isn't even the funniest
> or the most talented . . .
>
> No one can touch her . . .
>
> She rises above all
> the girls in the school
> because she is the thinnest . . .

Like a slick politician, anorexia appealed to her deepest desires. But ultimately it was not her vote it wanted, but her life.

"ANOREXIA ATTEMPTED TO KICK MY SOUL OUT AND MOVE IN"

Anorexia tried to ensure Emily's obedience by dismantling potential platforms of resistance from which she might have recognized her own betrayal. One of these platforms was her sense of herself, or as Emily put it, her "soul."

> Anorexia tells you your name is Anorexia and you forget who you are.
>
> 1. You are not a person, you are an object, a thing, a body to be deprived of pleasure to be tortured and starved.
> 2. I will steal your name and replace it with Anorexia.
> 3. I will steal your soul and replace it with Anorexia.
> 4. I will steal your voice . . .

ANOREXIA DEMANDS EMILY'S LIFE AS PAYMENT

Despite anorexia's strategies to secure her loyalty and puppetlike obedience, Emily did begin to question it. Capturing a/b on paper seemed to make it easier for Emily to see, and eventually see through, it.

I paid anorexia to carry my bad feelings. Anorexia carries little bad feelings for little prices and big bad feelings for big prices. I couldn't afford to pay anorexia for carrying my abuse, for carrying the horrendous feelings associated with it. I had spent all I had. I paid in small amounts, over many years. All those small amounts over all those years add up and the sum is equally devastating. I paid by disconnecting. When you disconnect, you miss out on so many things. You miss out on tasting your food. You don't enjoy your food. You don't enjoy music. You can't enjoy feeling loved. You can't enjoy laughter. Anorexia carried the abuse and started demanding payback. It said: "Okay, I'll carry the abuse, but abuse is expensive. You'll have to pay me with your life."

Emily also began to recognize that what had initially presented itself as her friend and savior turned out to be another unabashed abuser.

Anorexia will continue to rape you for the rest of your life if you don't fight it off. Anorexia rapes you over and over again if you don't follow the rules and tells you that it's your fault. Anorexia lies to you. Every time you break free and start struggling Anorexia rapes you to punish you. Then it tells you you did it to yourself and the worst part of it all is that I believed it. Never believe Anorexia. Never, never, never, ever believe a word it says. Anorexia lies through its teeth. Anorexia will lie to the very end.

SERVING NOTICE

Once the spell of anorexia had been broken and Emily recognized the cruelty of its deception and betrayal, she turned against it with all the force of her outrage and the keenness of her mind. And in turning against it she reached back toward the Emily she had left behind and forward toward an Emily that she desired to create. Following is a shortened version of one of Emily's journal entries.

I hate you!

I'm angry at you, Anorexia!

God, I hope you die and go to hell because that's where you belong!

You hurt me! You tricked me! You lied to me! Fuck you! You ruined my self-esteem

. . . you stole my childhood.

God, I hate you!

I'm not going to apologize. I deserve the apology.

I'm not scared of you. You deserve to be told off.

I'm not going to let you steal any more of my life!
You've stolen enough already . . .

Anorexia promises to make you strong. Invulnerable. Powerful.
Untouchable. Unbreakable. But the truth is not what it seems.
True strength means resisting Anorexia and pushing it away. It is
   much more difficult to get rid of anorexia than it is to not eat.
Resisting Anorexia is really what will make you stronger. Being Emily
   will make me strong.
Being Anorexia is easy. Anybody can be anorexic.
But nobody else can be me.
I must be brave.
Be Emily.

The hardest most difficult thing to be but I must be me.
Hopelessness is easy.
Anorexia is easy.
Bulimia is easy.
Giving up is easy.

She "served notice" to anorexia of her intentions to reclaim her own life:

Emily
Lives
Here

No
Vacancy
Sorry Anorexia
Vacancy Filled

EPILOGUE

Emily and I met together for nearly 2 years. Unfortunately, our work came to a premature end as Emily's home situation and then subsequent foster-care situation became unsuitable. The urgent need to find Emily a safe and stable place to reside took precedence over our mutual desire to continue to work together. At the age of 15, Emily was placed by the county in a residential treatment program and remained in institutional care until she turned 18. She is currently 26. She recently completed her undergraduate studies and has plans to pursue graduate studies in creative writing. Her life is no longer dominated by a/b but it continues to be far from easy. She maintains a prudent distance from her parents and has not relied upon them for financial assistance. She continues to be an outspoken critic of injustices she encounters in her life and has even become an activist, initiating a police investigation, a civil lawsuit, and journalistic expose of abuses she became aware of in a "sheltered" living arrangement for young adults. She has bequeathed her anti-anorexia writings to the League so that others can benefit from them.

Chapter 4

BECOMING AN ANGEL

MAGGIE'S STORY

I (RM) first met Maggie when she was 24 years old. By then she had been living with a/b for at least 7 years (nearly a third of her life). She had seen a succession of therapists over those 7 years and was feeling very discouraged about her progress; there were days when she felt she hadn't made any at all.

A/b came into Maggie's life when she was 17 and in high school. Maggie had been, by all accounts, a "model" daughter. She had enjoyed a close and warm relationship with her parents, who regarded her as "the nice one," her older sister being a bit on the stubborn and headstrong side. She received high grades in school and was the captain of three varsity squad teams. How, one might wonder, could a/b appeal to a person like Maggie, who experienced popularity, acclaim, and admiration and who never doubted the love of her family? According to Maggie, "It overpowered me by disguising itself. It fed off my weakness." By *weakness*, Maggie meant both her belief that she needed to please others at all costs and her competitive spirit and desire to be "the best."

TENDING TO THE NEEDS OF OTHERS

Maggie described her desire to make others happy during our very first meeting. "People like me because I am easygoing. If they are happy, I'll be happy. If everyone is happy then I'm more relaxed and don't feel so tense.... If I'm not feeling good [about myself] I might go and cook dinner for everyone." She told me that her ideal was to be "a compassionate angel tending to the needs of others."

This "ideal" was already well established by the time Maggie was 17. Her parents had contributed to this ideal and encouraged her to always consider the needs and feelings of others. From the time Maggie was a young girl, her parents taught her that if you have it better than someone else you should watch out for that person and take care of him or her. If there was an unpopular student at school, Maggie was encouraged to befriend her. If she expressed anger or dislike toward someone, she was encouraged to be understanding, compassionate, and giving towards the person who had wronged her. A/b eventually coopted this moral vision and turned it against her, telling her that she should never get upset or feel angry and, if she did, she was selfish and lacking in compassion. She embraced self-sacrifice and found she had a talent for it. A/b required that, rather than give *of* herself, as her parents had taught her, Maggie give *up* herself. Eventually this self-sacrificing lifestyle came to feel natural: "It always seemed that that was what I was good at, that was what I was meant to do." It became one more thing Maggie excelled at, in addition to sports and academics.

BEING "THE BEST"

The intersection of Maggie's desire to please her coaches and team-mates and her desire to be "the best" left her extraordinarily vulnerable to a/b's seduction. Maggie described all three of her high school coaches as "pushy," but her basketball coach was the most zealous in policing the weight and diet of the team members. Maggie strove to please her coach by watching her diet and weight, just as he was watching it. When she found herself resenting the coach's unjustifiable attempts to control the eating and weight of "his" athletes, the voice of a/b (iden-tified as such only in retrospect) told Maggie she'd just have to work harder to rid herself of her "negativity." She should stop being so "self-ish" and think of what was best for the team. If the coach thought that a strict diet and attention to one's weight was the best thing, who was she to disagree? And because she was the best basketball player on the team, why couldn't she also be the best at losing weight and staying in shape? After all, hadn't she already developed the willpower and self-control to become one of the top athletes at her school? If she was capable of that, surely she was capable of using those same abilities to control her diet and weight.

One of the teams Maggie played for went on to win the state cham-pionship. As the captain of the team and one of its "stars," Maggie found herself constantly in the spotlight. A/b took advantage of this by telling her that if she listened to it she would be admired not only for her athletic abilities but also for her slender and "fit" appearance.

Maggie came to hate her life as a high school athletic star, but she endured it without complaint because "my parents really wanted me to do it—they lived their athletic dreams through me" and because she did not want to let her teammates and coaches down. If she began to experience "negative feelings," bulimia was there to purge her of them. Although she continued to enjoy playing sports, she certainly didn't enjoy bending over a toilet with her finger down her throat. But it was a small price to pay for becoming an angel—or so a/b was content to have her believe.

A/b succeeded in dominating Maggie's life for many years. But Maggie fought back and is now living her life on her own terms. She works as an elementary school teacher and finds her work gratifying and meaningful. She has honest and two-sided relationships with her friends and boyfriend, has a close and loving relationship with her parents, and gives herself permission to be merely human.

Chapter 5

THE DEVIL'S SMILE

JENNIFER'S STORY

I (RM) first met Jennifer, an avid dancer, when she was 17 years old and halfway through her senior year of high school. We met weekly until she left for college approximately 6 months later.

Toward the end of Jennifer's junior year in high school, her pediatrician recommended a moratorium on dancing, the thing she loved most, because she had became extremely malnourished from anorexia. Jennifer was so determined to continue dancing that she forced herself to eat. But anorexia would not retreat. At first she spontaneously vomited what she ate because her body was unaccustomed to food. Anorexia soon made this vomiting into a requirement and, within a few months, it had Jennifer vomiting many times a day. At this point the pediatrician advised Jennifer and her mother to seek the help of a psychologist. The psychologist, who worked in the outpatient department at a local hospital, met with Jennifer approximately fifteen times. Although Jennifer began to vomit less frequently, the psychologist concluded that she needed to see someone over a longer period of time than the hospital's department would permit, and he referred her to me.

During our first meeting, I asked Jennifer about the ways in which her life had changed since anorexia had entered it. Jennifer enumerated the many changes and thought that almost all of them had been for the worse, despite her hopes and anorexia's promises that it would solve all her problems. She identified one positive development—becoming more assertive—but we soon realized it wasn't positive after all, because all of the asserting she had been doing was on anorexia's behalf, standing up for anorexia when people who cared about her challenged or questioned her about it. However, Jennifer mentioned that there had been some recent occasions when she stood up to anorexia. We spoke about how she had managed to do this and what it said about what was important to her. I shared with Jennifer some of the anti-anorexic discoveries that other women had made about a/b, as well as some of the ways they had begun to resist it. Jennifer concurred that anorexia was "a killer" and that she was determined to confront it. Subsequent to this meeting, she began to mount increasing resistance to anorexia, and anorexia fought back with promises, threats, and insults.

Anorexia, with characteristic cunning, tailored these promises, threats, and insults to her particular aspirations, fears, and self-doubts and capitalized on the circumstances in her life that inclined her to believe its lies. It was primarily through the process of identifying anorexia's messages to Jennifer that the account of how anorexia had seduced and ultimately betrayed her was constructed.

A DISTRACTION FROM AND AVOIDANCE OF GRIEF

A/b made its first appearance in Jennifer's life after her father died unexpectedly of a heart attack when Jennifer was 15. Jennifer's relationship with her father had been close, and she depended on him for guidance and support. Her experience of grief, anger, fear, confusion, and sadness was more intense than anything she had previously known. These feelings were made all the more unbearable because of her perception that they were not shared by her sisters and her mother to the same degree. Not only was Jennifer having to cope with her intense grief over the loss of her father, but the very intensity of her grief relative to that of her sisters and mother left her feeling alienated and distant from them as well.

This vulnerable moment in Jennifer's life gave anorexia an opening. It told her she needed to get a grip on herself and coaxed her to grasp onto it: "I was really depressed and didn't want to deal with anything and anorexia offered me a way out. It gave me something to occupy my mind so I wouldn't have to face my emotions surrounding my Dad's death. For about 2 weeks it had me dieting and throwing up when I did eat. It felt like a way of letting my feelings out."

After about 2 weeks the intensity of Jennifer's feelings subsided. She returned to school, reconnected with her good friends, and resumed her long-standing involvement with modern dance. As her life once again took on a semblance of normality and predictability, the voice of anorexia receded into the background for about a year; she had friends and activities she could draw on for support. But she now knew that anorexia would be there for her in the future if she "needed" it.

As Jennifer put it,"When my dad died I felt like I was going crazy. I couldn't believe something like this could happen right when I needed him the most, getting through high school and going to college. I was so angry for awhile. I depended upon him for so much. . . . Everything was always possible through him. He was the light."

FEARS AND DOUBTS DURING A TIME OF TRANSITION

With the arrival of her senior year of high school, Jennifer stood at the far edge of her childhood, gazing in the direction of an unknown future. As is the case for many young people, Jennifer's expectations about becoming an adult in the larger world weighed heavily on her. In the past, Jennifer would have been able to turn to her father for guidance. A tenured professor at a prestigious university, her father had taken an especially keen interest in her academics and had supported her dream of one day going to Harvard Medical School. Jennifer had always imagined that he would be there by her side, offering his advice and assistance and providing needed moral support. But now Jennifer had to overcome the hurdles facing her without him—doing well on her college entrance examinations, completing essays for college applications, continuing to get good grades, selecting the appropriate college, and so on.

Unsettling questions began to abound. Am I smart enough to succeed at my career? Am I attractive and lovable enough to attract a mate? Do I have the strength or the right to stand up for myself? Will I be able to cut it emotionally? Will I measure up to what will be expected and required of me? At moments the chasm between her familiar present and her hoped-for future seemed enormous.

"EVERYTHING WILL BE POSSIBLE THROUGH ME"

Jennifer's fears and doubts about her future coalesced into critical evaluations of herself in the present. Anorexia told her that if she couldn't excel and distinguish herself in the present, she could never ever expect to succeed down the road. Eventually Jennifer came to see anorexia as "a skeleton with a knife, little red eyes, and a black cape, like the devil." But at that moment Jennifer, feeling out of control of her life, saw anorexia as a friend and benefactor. It even had the audacity and the guile to offer to do for her what she had always imagined her father would do. Jennifer had felt that "everything was always possible through him"; now anorexia reassured her that everything would be possible though *it*.

INDUCING A SENSE OF FAILURE

In order to convince Jennifer that her only hope for a good life was to take the path it set out for her, a/b surreptitiously sought to undermine her confidence in herself and her possibilities. It began to denigrate her talents and abilities and encourage her to make invidious comparisons between herself and others. It upheld perfection as the standard so that she would always judge herself as a failure.

Jennifer wrote the following lament early on in our work together. She had not yet implicated anorexia in the making up of her world.

Never the Best
1. School: Christine [her twin sister], or someone else, is always better than me. If I receive a higher grade or score, I assume it was a stupid test, or luck.
2. Dance: Only the best of the best make it in the dance world, and I am definitely not that type. I struggle more and try harder than almost everyone in my group. The extra effort never seems to pay off.
3. Character: I'm not as pretty, as smart, or as talented as most of my friends are. I seem to blend in too well. I share my appearance with Christine and I share my little success in dance with my best friends. I can't call anything my own. I feel constant competition with the people around me.
4. Family: I hate the fact that my father is dead. I hate being in competition with my sisters. I hate not being able to enjoy being with my family. I feel like I am living in someone's shadow.
5. Boyfriends: I've never meant much to any boyfriend I've had. They have all gone on to find serious, long-term girlfriends. It is like I was a short bad episode in everyone's life.

CONTROL OF HER LIFE THROUGH CONTROL OF HER BODY

If Jennifer was "never the best," anorexia could change all that. It could make her the best—but first she would have to become the master of her own body. If she couldn't succeed at dieting and losing weight, how could she possibly succeed in accomplishing the harder things in life? It wouldn't be easy, but at least it was something she could control now, something that she had the power to do. If she didn't get the highest grade on a test, anorexia was there to console her: "At least you are excelling at being skinny. Nothing is more important than that right now." Having convinced her of that, anorexia was able to take possession of Jennifer's mind and occupy her thoughts nearly every waking moment. Its voice was the first voice she heard when she woke in the morning, telling her how many calories she would eat that day. It was the last voice she heard before falling asleep, patting her on the back for being "strong" or telling her she'd have to make up tomorrow for her lapses in self-control today. And between waking and bedtime it had her counting calories throughout the day and avoiding friends who might interfere with her staying focused and "strong."

Jennifer later commented, "I felt like I had to control my body because I couldn't control my life." This imperative of "body control" and its pseudologic soon became the whip anorexia used to lash Jennifer when she listened and attended to the needs of her body. If Jennifer ate more than her anorexia-imposed diet mandated, anorexia berated her, calling her fat, ugly, and a failure. Despite the fact that the scale told her that her weight was "normal" and that no one had ever described her as fat, ugly, or a failure, Jennifer found it enormously difficult to reject anorexia's version of her.

THE INFLUENCE OF DANCE AND CHEERLEADING

I asked Jennifer if she could identify anything in her life up to that point that had prepared her to believe anorexia's promise of happiness through bodily control and to accept anorexia's insistence that perfect bodily control was not only desirable but also attainable. This inquiry illuminated some of the cultural and institutional forces that had opened up space for anorexia to take root and grow. Among these were the activities of cheerleading and dance.

Both cheerleading and dance required that Jennifer adopt a hierarchical relationship to her own body, one that required the development of discipline and willpower. Both activities demanded long hours of practice and physical exertion, emphasized body shape and attractiveness in addition to bodily control, and created venues for the display of her body. Both activities reinforced and rewarded conformity to conventional cultural views of "beauty," but dance, in particular, reinforced a privileging of thinness over other body types.

Dance consumed more of Jennifer's time and energy and required the most discipline. But cheerleading demanded that Jennifer not only discipline her body but her "self " as well. The institution of cheerleading attacked the identity that Jennifer had been constructing for herself and the work that she had been doing to define and articulate her own opinions, values, and beliefs. To be a cheerleader, it seemed to Jennifer, you had to be a nonperson: "You had to do exactly what everybody else did. We all had to look the same. Everything we did was dictated. I had to pretend to be happy. I had to pretend to like the team. I had to pretend to like the school." Although dance and cheerleading both asserted the importance of having a certain type of body and control over that body, cheerleading emphasized the importance of becoming *just* a body.

THE ETHIC OF SELFLESS GIVING

Cheerleading also promoted an ethic of "selfless giving": "It was work that required trying to please everybody else." Jennifer and the other cheerleaders were even required to bake cookies and give them to individual football players without revealing who had given them. These "rituals" attempted to instill the virtue of selfless giving—giving to others without any expectation of acknowledgment or reciprocity.

Jennifer directly resisted some of these practices by speaking out against them. At other times she protested more indirectly by showing up late for practice, sometimes drunk or "stoned." But the messages she received from the cheerleading squad to silence her own voice and engage in selfless giving etched themselves in her consciousness.

This undermined Jennifer's sense of power and entitlement, and she began to experience her life as increasingly out of her control. For example, at one point during her senior year, Jennifer wanted to break up with a boy she had been dating. Although she found him nice enough, she had tired of the relationship and was feeling confined. But selfless giving convinced her to stay in the relationship unless he ended it: "But he's so nice," "he'll be really hurt," "it would be selfish," and so on. And anorexia spoke to her as well: "You are mean and selfish for wanting to break up with him. You obviously don't deserve to have have such a nice boyfriend. I can help you feel more in control of your life, and I can make you worthy of this relationship." It was one of the first times Jennifer recalled beginning to diet since the episode following her father's death.

A/B'S SHIFT FROM ENCOURAGEMENT TO ADMONISHMENT

Initially Jennifer found her romance with anorexia totally absorbing and exhilarating. Anorexia had taken her under its wing and was making her feel special and even superior. But the satisfaction and confidence she attained through anorexia was ephemeral. It always demanded more from her, setting new goals when she came close to attaining the old ones. As time passed and anorexia began to take a greater toll on Jennifer's life, it relied less on encouragement and more on admonishment to keep her in line. "Nothing I do is good enough. Anorexia convinces me that I am a failure at everything."

THE "DARK TUNNEL"

Jennifer began to experience her life as a "dark tunnel," increasingly constricted and devoid of any sense of options or possibilities. What anorexia had initially presented to Jennifer as the means to attain her dreams, became the means by which it transformed her life into a nightmare. As Jennifer put it, "It's like a concentration camp and you kind of unknowingly stumble into it and all of a sudden your in there. It's hard. When you realize you're really in there and that you want to come out, . . . it just takes so much to finally try and get out of something like that . . . Anorexia keeps pushing you down, keeps you in the dark."

Others began to notice and become alarmed over her dramatic weight loss and increasing social isolation. Jennifer herself was noticing that she was physically weaker. People told her she wasn't herself. Anorexia told her they were wrong, that they didn't know her as well as it did. Anorexia reassured her that "this is just the way you are, the way you act. It is just who you are. So what if your friends go out to eat and you choose to not go with them. That's just what you want to do and that's fine. You don't need to be like everybody else." When her doctor, her mother, her friends, and her dance teacher told her she needed to gain weight, anorexia spoke to Jennifer quietly but with the utmost authority and conviction: "They don't know what they are talking about. They are just lying to you. They're just jealous that you're skinny and they're not."

Despite anorexia's attempt to impersonate her, a part of her recognized that she had gone missing from her own life. She later reflected: "You become almost like a tool. Like someone is just using you. It's not really you. I felt the whole time like I'm not Jennifer, I'm just Jennifer's body. Something else is in charge of what I'm thinking and doing. It feels like you are possessed by the devil. Whenever I smiled I felt like the devil smiling." But eventually it was Jennifer who had the last laugh.

I recontacted Jennifer nearly 4 years later in order to ask permission to tell her story and to see if she wanted to help me tell it. By that time she had graduated from college and was living outside Los Angeles pursuing her career. Despite a few predictable ups and downs during the transition from college to the world of work, Jennifer had not allowed anorexia to overtake the life she had reclaimed. She was "doing well and feeling happy."

Chapter 6

SAVING A LIFE

ANOREXIA'S STORY ABOUT KRISTEN

The following letter was supplied to us by Kristen, a young woman in the grip of anorexia. "Authored" by anorexia, it illustrates the insidious nature of a/b's voice.* *Insiders may wish to skip this chapter, as the voice of anorexia is very clever in the means by which it plays on both Kristen's fears and hopes.* If you think that hearing anorexia speak to Kristen will, in any way, heighten its influence in your own life, you should take the anti-anorexic step of refusing to open the door to a/b a little wider, and move on to the next chapter. If you do choose to read the letter, you might consider imagining that anorexia has written it to a beloved friend or sibling instead of to you. This may make it easier for you to see through anorexia's assertions and connect to your sense of moral outrage.

"Saving a Life"
by Anorexia, a friend to Kristen Webber

I am a friend of Kristen Webber—her best friend. I have unselfishly dedicated myself to save her life. I tell her the truth and keep her safe. The thoughts I give her help her to become a better person. When she listens to me, she is happier and her problems disappear. Since

---

* The letter, of course, is not written by anorexia but rather by Kristen herself. She gave the letter to her therapist, who, with Kristen's permission, forwarded it to David. Appearing in slightly edited form here, the unedited version, along with David's response to Kristen, is available on the website, http://www.narrativeapproaches.com

I am the only one who tells her the truth and really wants her to be happy, I am her only friend.

By asserting its dedication to saving Kristen's life, anorexia plays upon an implied threat that without its aid, Kristen's life is threatened. By declaring that only it tells her the truth and wants her to be happy, anorexia attempts to instill another fear: that she is essentially alone. These deceptions are intended to isolate Kristen from the care and aid of others, to undermine her trust in their motives, and to convince her to place her faith in anorexia instead.

The most important thing she needs to realize is that she is ___ pounds overweight. I've seen her body and know that this is the truth. People tell her differently, but they haven't seen her like I have. She is the fattest person I've ever met. My job is to bring her into reality so she can see this and change. When people try to tell her she is not overweight, I save her by telling her they are lying and just trying to make her feel good. I'm the only one who tells her the truth, even if it hurts. Anyone who tries to get Kristen to eat doesn't really care for her at all. They just want to see her get fatter and fatter. It is these people who are very dangerous because their secret wish is to hurt her and see her in pain. I only have her best interests in mind. Without me she might as well die.

Being such a fat person, she is worthless. She is an awful person because of all the extra weight and she doesn't deserve anything good. If she were to lose weight, she would become a worthwhile person who deserves to be happy and treated with respect. No one likes her because she is so fat. No one likes her when she eats. She would be liked if she lost weight. People respect, admire, and are proud of her when she can have enough self-control to resist the temptation to eat and drink. Because she is so overweight and everyone can see this, she cannot eat in front of anyone without them thinking she is greedy and selfish and hating her. Fat people don't deserve to eat. It makes everyone uncomfortable when they eat. I save her from making others hate her.

When Kristen eats or drinks, she loses control of everything in her life. If she started eating, she would never be able to stop. Her problems would become bigger and more intense. Since she is so bad at controlling her life, she needs to get control by not eating. If she cannot do something as simple as reaching a reasonable weight, she should not be allowed control over her life. She will not have a life if she doesn't listen to me. I'm just trying to get her life back. I'm the best thing that ever happened to her. I always reassure her I'll never leave; I'll keep trying to improve her life and make her happy forever.

Anorexia wastes no time in claiming that Kristen's weight is the most important thing about her and it assumes a moral authority in asserting that, because she is overweight, she is worthless and awful. This lays the foundation for anorexia's assault on her eating. Continuing to use moral language to both condemn and threaten her, it warns her that if she eats, everyone will judge her as greedy and selfish and will hate her. Under the guise of benevolent concern, it attempts to further constrict her life by prohibiting eating, drinking, and, by extension, activities that might lead to eating or drinking, such as buying food, carrying money on her walks, and even thinking "bad" thoughts about wanting to eat.

> If Kristen does slip and eat something, there are several backup plans she can do to save herself. She can make herself vomit to get the food out before it does serious damage. This is the best option and most effective way to fix her mistake. She can also take laxatives or do hours of intense exercise after a mess-up. I don't like to see her make a mistake like this, but I do realize that it happens. It is very bad if she eats for two or more days in a row. If she were to do this, she needs to go longer without anything to eat or drink. This is a way she can try to get control back.
>
> These mistakes make her a very awful person. She needs to realize that as soon as she eats or drinks, everyone notices how much fatter she is instantly. She looks like she is 9 months pregnant. This, on top of the __ extra pounds she already has, makes her grossly huge. People talk about her behind her back, saying things like "Look at how fat Kristen has gotten from eating, there's no reason why she should eat, it's so gross." Everyone knows she should not be eating, it is very obvious to see. She gets respect and admiration when she is not eating.

When Kristen defies anorexia's rules by eating and drinking, anorexia refers to these acts of self-sustenance as "mistakes" and "mess-ups." Anorexia morally condemns Kristen for these "mistakes" and prescribes "remedies" such as purging and intense exercise and starvation. Anorexia turns reality on its head (in typical fashion) by prescribing the life-threatening practices of vomiting, laxative use, and hours of intense exercise as the means by which to "save herself," while claiming that the serious damage is caused by her life-sustaining eating and drinking. This tactic is similar to the "big lie" tactics employed by Hitler's propagandists.

> Kristen has very little self-control. Because of this, it is dangerous for her to keep any food and drink around where she might eat them. If

she does slip and buy some food, she must throw it away immediately. I'm very disappointed when she buys food or drinks. She forgets how much better she feels when she is not eating. It would also be extremely awful if anyone were to find food that she bought. They would hate her right away and have absolutely no respect for her. She knows better than that. Kristen cannot have money on her when she goes for a walk in case she gets bad thoughts and stops to buy some food or drink. She might lose touch with reality and temporarily think she wants to eat. This is when she goes crazy and I need to take complete control of her so she doesn't do anything stupid. It's a good thing I'm here for her or she would be a complete mess.

When Kristen does eat, anorexia morally condemns her for having "very little self-control." It uses this characterization to justify taking more and more control over Kristen's life through the proliferation of rules. Anorexia not only forbids Kristen from eating and drinking, but also from buying food, being around food, or even carrying money. These rules are designed to control Kristen's desire to eat. Anorexia, perhaps sensing that even acknowledging Kristen's desire to eat might contribute to Kristen's rebellion, goes on to deny that Kristen has any real desire to eat, and that this perceived desire is only a temporary loss of sanity.

Kristen has enough fat on her body to go for at least one week without eating or drinking anything. When she starts to feel dizzy or sick, it is not because of lack of food or dehydration. She has something wrong with her blood that causes dizziness and fainting. People will try to tell her it's because of lack of nutrition. They are lying and are a threat to Kristen's happiness. They also try to convince her that her lack of concentration and ability to focus are results of starvation. This cannot be true. It's impossible that her body could go into starvation; it has enough reserves to last forever. I need to protect Kristen from these people who try to convince her she's starving. I'm the only one who can see reality and is totally honest with Kristen. She is safe by listening to me.

The voice of anorexia anticipates protest from Kristen's body and from people who care about her. It attempts to neutralize the former by denying that feeling dizzy or sick or being unable to concentrate is an effect of inadequate nutrition. It attempts to invalidate the point of view of caring others by claiming that they lie to her and secretly wish to hurt her.

There is something about Kristen that makes people want to hurt her. She has already been hurt by males before because she was not smart and was very careless. She needs to lose weight so she won't be hurt anymore. She is safer when she doesn't eat because people don't feel like they need to hurt her. They are entirely right in thinking she deserves to be hurt. She deserves to be hurt right now because she is so fat. She deserves to be hurt when she eats, especially in front of people. I'm just trying to protect Kristen. I have her best interests in mind at all times.

Anorexia has the gall to blame Kristen for the abuse she had experienced by men and to claim that she deserved it. Anorexia then appeals to Kristen's desire to not be hurt by asserting that she can become a good person whom people wouldn't "need to hurt" if she only stops eating and loses weight.

It is a big problem that Kristen is seeing Dr. Bryson. She is setting herself up for unhappiness and disappointment. It is very bad that she feels she can talk to him about anything. After talking with him she thinks she is doing better, but this is just a trick—an illusion. She has often eaten after talking with him. This is my proof that he is bad for her. She feels she wants to eat and is safe enough to eat, but she is wrong. It is never safe for her to eat. I have to become more forceful with her after the sessions because her thoughts have been drastically changed. I bring her back to reality. Even though I think it is dangerous for her to see Dr. Bryson, there are conditions where I'll let her go see him. If she doesn't eat for three days in a row, I'll let her go see him.

Anorexia, unable to stop Kristen from seeing her therapist, attempts to turn this relationship to its own advantage by making her visits with Dr. Bryson contingent on Kristen's starving herself for three days prior to each visit.

Kristen's main purpose for being at school right now is to lose ___ pounds. She is not a very good student; her good grades in the past are all fake. I wasn't sure that her going to school was a good idea because I was afraid it would give Kristen a feeling of control over her life. If Kristen does not lose ___ pounds while at school, she must kill herself. This makes total sense since losing weight should be her main purpose and priority. If she doesn't lose the weight, she is hopeless and deserves to die. This is her test. She passes and she'll gain happiness, control, and respect. She fails and she'll die; she will deserve to die. She has known for long enough she needs to lose all this weight. It's time she listened to me and did.

Anorexia recognizes that school is potentially something that could give Kristen a feeling of success, a sense of purpose, and a future direction. It is very common for anorexia to attempt to take credit for success at school ("you never would have had the self-discipline or confidence to succeed at school without me") or to undermine one's sense of success by fostering unrealistic expectations. In Kristen's case, anorexia attempts to undermine her confidence in herself as a student and to redefine her main priority as losing weight. Anorexia implies that the results of the tests she took as a student pale in comparison to the results of anorexia's supreme test. Passing anorexia's test would undoubtedly result in Kristen's death, but, once again, anorexia turns reality on its head by claiming that if Kristen failed anorexia's test she deserves to die.

> Kristen deserves to die if she doesn't listen to me. She might as well just kill herself if she disobeys me because she'll never find happiness. I have the answer to her happiness. I care about Kristen very much—I only want the best for her and I'm striving for her happiness. Nothing can go wrong by listening to me. I'm the only one who tells her the truth and knows all the secrets to how she can gain happiness and respect. I dedicate myself to her. This is my unselfish mission—to save Kristen's life.

Anorexia spun its deceitful threats and promises around Kristen like a spider entangling a fly entangled with its thread. By alternating between threats and prohibitions on the one hand and promises and reassurances on the other, anorexia's "spin" served to block Kristen's exit routes and ushered her further down what Rachel referred to as "its dark tunnel." Kristen not only found herself imprisoned by these webs of meaning but also, like a fly in a spider's web, awaiting her execution.

A/b's sinister sleight of hand can only be achieved by an imposition of meaning accomplished through a sophisticated use of language. A/b speaks in many guises, including that of a friend, confidant, lover, coach, logician, belittler, bully, and judge. All of these forms of speech convey meanings that convince the person that she possesses flaws or deficits that reside inside her character and body and can only be remedied by operating on her body and her "self" in specific ways.

According to a/b, all good is to be achieved through the disciplining and torturing of one's body by way of the moral virtues previously outlined. To fall short in any way is construed by a/b as weakness and a testimony to the person's insufficiency and moral shortcomings. Having a good body becomes equated with being a good person, and a good life is one that is lived in conformity to a/b's rules and regulations.

The tragic irony is that the more these women seek control over their bodies, the more their lives seems to spin out of their control; the more they attempt to become a somebody, the more they become a nobody. This completes the trap. What anorexia tells them is the way out of their unhappiness becomes the way in.

Part Two

TURNING AGAINST ANOREXIA/BULIMIA

Chapter 7

MANNERS OF SPEAKING

A/b bewilders and confounds both the insiders whose lives are directly threatened and the concerned outsiders who find themselves on the sidelines, stunned and stupefied as they watch a/b lay waste to their loved one's mind, body, and spirit. It is as if "a force without form or substance"* has taken possession of the person. As a/b's occupation proceeds, these women become less and less substantial as people until finally the person they were becomes almost invisible. In many respects, a/b makes them strangers to themselves and to those who know them well. We have often heard family members of a person struggling with a/b lament, "We feel we have lost her."

We believe, however, that a/b can only render and keep a person invisible when a/b itself remains invisible.[†] This chapter describes some of the ways of thinking and speaking about a/b that, in our experience, have provided the means to expose and counter a/b as well as open it to public scrutiny. These ways of thinking and speaking are central to what has come to be called *anti-anorexia/bulimia (anti-a/b)*. In a nutshell, anti-a/b is constituted by beliefs, values, and practices that oppose or resist a/b or provide for a way of living in the world that a/b would oppose and seek to undermine. An anti-a/b language and

---

* A phrase used by Eva, an Auckland, New Zealand, League member.
[†] When we speak here about the invisibility of a/b, we are not referring to the conventional evidence of a/b's presence (e.g., "symptoms") such as dramatic weight loss, amenorrhea, purging, laxative use, compulsive exercising, and so on. Instead, we are referring to the subtle and hidden ways in which a/b brings a young woman under its control.

practice encourages people to question the values, promises, threats, and rules of a/b and to bring their lives more into harmony with their own values and preferences. Our discussion on speaking out against a/b touches on a number of areas including: (1) how Western culture defines problems and their relation to people; (2) how a/b hides itself within contemporary Western culture; (3) where we search for knowledge about a/b; and (4) whose ideas about a/b are valued and whose are marginalized or dismissed.

A/B'S INVISIBILITY

Perhaps one of the reasons an understanding of a/b has remained so elusive has to do with the conventional practice of thinking and talking about a/b as something *within* the people it afflicts—something that they *have* or *are*. In this manner of speaking, the distinction between the person and problem is blurred. This way of thinking about the problem is reflected in common ways of speaking about a/b: "I have bulimia" or "She's an anorexic." When the problem is seen to arise from within the person or the "self," it becomes easy to think about the *person* as the problem and to view many of her attitudes and behaviors as deriving from an eating "disorder," which, in turn, is seen as derived from a "disordered self." This view has become so taken for granted that it is almost impossible to think otherwise. Our alternative view considers how people are ushered into *styles of living* and *fashions of thinking* that have the potential to squeeze the "living" out of their lives.

The current Western cultural practice of viewing people *as* problems is an outgrowth of a much more general practice of ascribing a person's actions to underlying personal attributes or qualities rather than viewing them as manifestations of beliefs, values, and conscious purposes. Unfortunately, these static and totalizing descriptions can lead to "thin conclusions" about the person (White, 1997) and qualify her for labels such as healthy or pathological, smart or stupid, strong or weak, good or bad, normal or weird, nice or mean, generous or selfish.

Labeling such as this takes place within a framework of norms and expectations regarding how people *should* think and act. The judgments that arise from these norms exist on a continuum of merit. Conformity with the norms leads to a more positive judgment (e.g., strong, healthy) whereas deviance from the norms invites negative judgment at the opposite end of the continuum (e.g., weak, pathological). Expressing ideas or acting in ways that might invite negative labels brings with it lowered status and sometimes penalties such as social exclusion and various discriminations. Hence, people invest considerable time and effort "working" on their "selves," trying to align their minds, bodies, and relationships with dominant notions of what is deemed healthy, smart, strong, normal, nice, beautiful, and so on. Most of us find ourselves trying to measure up to these ideals while policing our own actions, thoughts, feelings, and bodies for undesirable deviations. These deviations then become the focus of self-criticism, censure, and eradication. A/b thrives upon this way of thinking, which allows it to promote itself as the means to cultivate and perfect those qualities that are highly valued by the dominant culture.

Living Up to Expectations

This view of the "self " as the problem not only sets the stage for a/b to enter people's lives as a means by which to discipline and "improve" them, but also makes it more likely that people who come under a/b's influence will be viewed by others as having "disordered" minds. This allows a/b to maintain its invisibility, as the problem is attributed to the person, instead of to a/b itself. Psychiatrists, physicians, therapists, and dietitians are all likely to ask questions based on the notion that the person *has* a/b or a "disorder." Consequently, the person usually comes to view herself as "an anorexic" or "a bulimic." This all too often prompts the "patient" to try to be a "perfect anorexic" for the doctor or other professional, because a/b fosters in many a desire to please others and live up to their expectations, as well as a desire to be the best. Following is a transcript of a conversation David had with Kris, a teenager, about this very issue.

David: We were just reviewing our first meeting and I asked you what your response to that meeting was and you said that it made you feel more confident because we talked about quite positive things. And you said that you had been to some other people [for therapy] and they did something different. What was the difference?

Kris: The difference was that they talk about how long have you had anorexia, how bad it has been and what things you do . . . how many times you make yourself sick a day . . . you end up believing that you are anorexic. Because I believed I was anorexic, I felt I actually had to compete, that I had to be a better anorexic than others.

David: What did you end up believing when we talked the first time?

Kris: Coming here, I felt all I wanted to do was to get better.

David: I did tell you I was definitely anti-anorexic, so not surprisingly, I am interested to hear that you decided to become anti-anorexic rather than pro-anorexic. Do you think these other people know that they are, in fact, assisting you to become anorexic in a manner of speaking?

Kris: No, not really.

David: You are not the first person to say this to me . . . I actually met one woman who said she decided to become the "best anorexic" for the doctors. And she worked harder at being better and better. And I was quite haunted by that conversation.

Kris: That's why I wanted to come here but didn't want to come here. I was so scared that I wouldn't be a good enough anorexic. That's true! (*laughter all around*)

David: This is really important what you are saying. Can I ask you something? Say you thought I was into anorexia-watching rather than being an advocate for anti-anorexia. What do you think you would have done differently than you are doing now?

Kris: I would even eat less than I do now. I would have had to come back skinnier than I was last time just so you could see that . . . that I wasn't better so you couldn't take your attention off me. I still wanted to do that but it wasn't as important. It just wasn't important. With others you get the feeling you are being evaluated and assessed and then you become even more vulnerable, I reckon. When they are evaluating you, you think they must have seen so many other cases like you that you actually seem unimportant to them. And anorexia is about trying to get to be more important in one area of your life. . . .

By promoting an "anorexic" identity and unknowingly encouraging the "perfecting" of a/b, conventional inquiries generally fail to generate a clear, well-articulated, and useful description of a/b. This makes it difficult for the person to distinguish her voice from the voice of a/b. Which voice speaks for a/b and which speaks for the person herself and against a/b? Which voice should be trusted and which should be questioned and contested? Asking a young woman who is caught up in anorexia's spell to reflect on anorexia is tantamount to asking her to look in the mirror—all she sees is herself. This is because conventional ways of seeing the problem keep the spotlight on the person while a/b's power and influence remain hidden in the shadows. Thus, the person may speak not *about* a/b, but through or *as* a/b. She may speak about her own sense of guilt, of feeling undeserving, of not being good enough, and of her conviction that she needs to exercise her willpower, self-control, and discipline in the service of becoming a better and more worthy person. At least initially, the person experiences herself as speaking the undeniable truth and has no awareness of the extent to which a/b has colonized her mind and replaced her thoughts with its thoughts, her desires with its desires, her appetite with its appetites, her voice with its voice.

If a/b is to take root and flourish, the language of a/b must deny its own presence and conceal its identity. This camouflaging is made possible by the worldviews, practices, and values that are pervasive in Western culture. A/b hides in cultural discourses that champion individual achievement, self-control, and, for women especially, self-sacrifice, being "nice," catering to the needs of others, and looking "good," thin, or "fit." A/b harmonizes its voice with these larger cultural voices and eventually appropriates and distorts these discourses, turning them into grotesque caricatures.

Promoting Isolation

Another adverse effect of seeing a/b as arising from some essence or core of the person is that it tends to inhibit people from speaking with others about difficulties they are experiencing, as they fear they will be judged as inadequate, deficient, flawed, pathological, and so on. A/b thrives on this isolation, which denies the person struggling with a/b access to the points of view of friends and loved ones and thus to alternative versions of themselves and of their possibilities. These alternative versions of people struggling with a/b are invaluable resources in contesting a/b's merciless and unrelenting allegations. Even being in the presence of strangers who are not imprisoned by a/b can inspire resistance and awaken in the person a sense of her own rights and entitlements. Corky, a young woman who challenged anorexia's attempts to isolate her from others by leaving her apartment and spending time in the company of others, commented, "It was like waking up from a coma. Just going out and being with other people and seeing what they permit themselves to do. Even if you can't yet do it yourself, this is so important to be aware of."

Obscuring Sociocultural and Political Contexts

Psychological accounts that place the problem within the individual all too easily obscure the interpersonal, social, and historical contexts that are so often implicated in the difficulties people experience. Psychological accounts provide a ready means to explain any and all of our experience, which then becomes individualized and personalized. According to these accounts, it is all about you! These explanations rely almost exclusively on the identification of deficiencies or excesses in relation to preestablished norms. A/b exploits these psychological theories that claim to explain problems in terms of the personal and pathological. It thrives on and actively fosters accounts of people's deficits. By directing people to scrutinize themselves, a/b turns them away from addressing the injustices they may have experienced. Instead of taking steps to remake their world, a/b convinces them that security and control will only be theirs when they themselves are refashioned.

Dismissing or Thwarting Useful Insider Accounts

Another effect of viewing problems as residing within people is that it renders the person's own account of the problem untrustworthy in the minds of others, as this account is seen as tainted by the problem itself. When the distinction between the person and the problem is blurred or altogether lost, any account of the problem by the "problematic person" can itself be viewed as problematic. Thus, the insider's account of anorexia can be dismissed as "anorexic." This is unfortunate because many outsiders see only the inexplicable outcome of a/b's influence— not the *means by which* a/b exerts this influence. Rather than enlisting the knowledge of those people most intimate with the workings of a/b, well-meaning professionals, armed with the latest theories of psychological development, family dysfunction, psychopathology, physiology, and genetics, scrutinize these women's psyches, bodies, families, and histories for the key to understanding the cause and the "cure" for these "disorders." These endeavors position the person as the object of these inquiries. And thus it is "the anorexic," rather than anorexia, who, after having first been rendered an object by anorexia, becomes an object again—an object of speculation, theorizing, interpretation, and treatment. A/b thrives on the objectification of people, for it must cut them off from their own knowing and their own voice in order to impose itself upon them.

As long as they view the problem as entwined with the "self," even professionals who seek the knowledge of people struggling with a/b are likely to ask questions about the person's feelings, thoughts, relationships, and history rather than questions about a/b and its relationship to the person. The results of such an inquiry often leave the person feeling more identified than ever with a/b.

A NEW MANNER OF SPEAKING

Before, I just talked with doctors about anorexia. No one ever taught me that you have to be against her. Before, all I was told was that you have to get over it. It's more than that! When I talk against anorexia there's more of a chance of getting free because I can start hating her and when I do, I can let her go.

— Allison, 1991

Privileging Insider Knowledge

We believe that the real experts on problems are those people who experience them first-hand. It is these people who have lived through the problem and have the most intimate knowledge of it. These knowledges have been referred to by various writers and theorists as "local," "indigenous," "experience-near," and "insider," in contrast to "expert" or "professional" knowledges. We regard these local knowledges as more trustworthy than systematized professional knowledges, which typically speak for and about people without any accountability to the people they claim to represent.

Externalizing Conversations

How can one elicit local knowledges about a/b from people who have fallen under its influence when one aspect of a/b's influence is to render its presence and effects invisible and the person herself voiceless?

What are known as *externalizing conversations* (Carey & Russell, 2002; Freedman & Combs, 1996; Freeman, Epston & Lobovits, 1997; Morgan, 2000; Payne, 2000; White, 1989, 1995; White & Epston, 1990) can flush the presence and operations of a/b into the open. Externalizing conversations reverse the vocabulary of self-blame, self-reproach, self-hatred, and guilt that a/b employs to represent people, thereby constructing a/b linguistically and conceptually, as a force or influence separate from the person. This invites the identification, objectification, and critique of a/b and its voice rather than of the person. Rosemary, an insider in her early 20s, shared with David her preference for talking and thinking about anorexia as an external influence rather than as a state of being:

> The most interesting and novel thing about our discussion was the fact that you look at anorexia as an influence, not as a state of being or something you *are*. And from that point of view, I, who at times am under its influence, can be in control of it. I can, depending on what other influences are on me, yield to it or control it. If we view anorexia as a state, then anorexia is something you are "in" or not; something that has happened to you or not. It takes the onus off you. Looking at anorexia this way reaffirmed my own confidence in myself. I can see when I am being assessed as an anorexic . . . and I guess I then feel "I can't really do anything about this. This is the way I am. This is what has happened to me. It's hopeless. No one seems to be able to make it any better so why don't you just opt out." This is how suicide comes about because you don't feel there is any possible way you can be in control of it.

If women think of anorexia as a part of themselves, even if they decide to fight it, what choice would they have but to indict themselves at the same time they indict anorexia? An anorexic trap is laid such that when they begin to think in opposition to anorexia (to "come out of their denial") they step into a view of themselves as "sick" or "disordered." And from there it is a relatively easy matter for anorexia to co-opt their fledgling rebellion and tighten its grip by reminding them of their worthlessness and inadequacy. The anguished cry of "I just want to be normal" is a double-edged sword—one edge reserved for anorexia and the other for the self (since the two are conflated), a sword fashioned from an amalgam in which the potent element of anti-anorexic protest is neutralized by the element of pro-anorexic self-hatred or self-criticism. Rebecca, aged 23, contrasts the effects of these two manners of thinking and speaking about anorexia:

> Anorexia makes it very difficult to separate yourself from it. When I was captured by it, I could not even begin to see that they were two things. As far as I was concerned, I was anorexia. I was dumbfounded when you first started talking anti-anorexically with me. Once I began to distinguish myself from anorexia, I was then able to begin to fight it. Before that, I just sank deeper and deeper into the quicksands of anorexia. There was nothing to direct my anger at. It was so hard to have a self when you believe you are anorexia. Anorexia tangles you up in so many catch-22s that in the end, you believe it is impossible to make yourself up. And that is when you surrender yourself to anorexia.

The view of a/b as external to and distinct from the person circumvents its appropriation of anti-a/b outrage and allows for an unfettered inquiry into the nature and effects of a/b. By disentangling a/b from the person, a conceptual space is opened as well as space for people to recognize and give voice to their own experience. As one anti-anorexic veteran put it, "I guess I imagine this quite literally—that as you pull the problem out from the person you actually leave space for the person to inhabit their own body and have their own thoughts."

In the following excerpt from an interview with Jennifer (age 18, see Chapter 5) which occurred at the end of Rick and Jennifer's work together, Jennifer describes the importance that externalizing anorexia played in her eventually winning her freedom from it:

> Before I met you [RM] I kept thinking about anorexia as my problem. It was my fault. It was something I did and I could never figure out why. My physician would say, 'You have an eating disorder'. That's what I

expected him to say but I did feel like it was my fault because anorexia isn't a virus. It requires a little bit more than catching a cold. I don't think he wanted me to feel blamed, I just don't think he really knew how to talk about it. Most people don't really know how to speak in a way that doesn't blame the person. Once you stop blaming yourself, you can see it. Everything kind of gets clearer. You can actually look at anorexia for what it really is.

Creation of an Anti-A/B Language

In order to speak against a/b, a knowledge of what it says and how it says it is imperative. Externalizing conversations, because of the way in which they extricate and separate the voice of a/b from that of the person, create a platform from which to discern a/b and, by inference, give it form and substance. This promotes the personification of a/b, whereby a speaker is put behind the voice, and allows for speculation about a/b's purposes, intentions, strategies, and tactics. The unmasking of a/b takes place through an inquiry with the person struggling with it. This book is, in large part, an archive of these inquiries and the local knowledges they have yielded.

The term *co-research* was coined by Epston (1999) to describe the process of these inquiries. As the term implies, these conversations are not attempts to impose anti-a/b meanings (for this would replicate how a/b speaks) but to continually and vigilantly maintain a questioning and curious stance about whether a particular thought, idea, behavior, development, and so on is something that supports a/b, stands in opposition to it, or perhaps bears no relationship to it. Co-research into a/b may begin by asking a person under its spell what it has been requiring of her since it came into her life. If the person is accompanied by friends or family members, they may also be asked for their comments. The person might then be asked to reflect on and evaluate the effects of these requirements on her life and relationships. Sometimes people offer their own descriptions of a/b practices; other times they concur with one we might offer, such as torture or punishment. The co-research might then shift to any of a number of possible questions: How does a/b compel or convince the person to adopt these practices? What might be its intention toward the person? What tactics and strategies does it employ? What ideas does it depend upon? What support does it receive from the larger culture? What kinds of relationships with others does a/b encourage, and what kind of relationships encourage a/b? Through questions such as these and many others, a local knowledge of a/b can be articulated.

Unlike conventional research, the process of co-research does not claim to be objective, nor does it aspire to objectivity. The process itself is inextricably entwined with its purpose, which is to generate knowledge that can incite and sustain anti-a/b resistance. What use would such a knowledge of a/b be if it did not make available alternative meanings through which to realize an alternative identity and an alternative life? In other words, the process of co-research into a/b has a fundamentally subversive aim.

The externalizing and personification of a/b, in so far as it makes possible the unmasking of a/b and the reappearance of the person, is inherently anti-a/b. Externalizing a/b does not in itself unmask it but rather makes this unmasking possible. We have found that the necessity to see through a/b and "unpack" or "deconstruct" its powerful rhetoric requires a very specific kind of language, one that externalizes a/b, personifies its voice, and allows for the speaking against a/b. The language of a/b functions to obliterate the embodied "knowing" of the person. It uses language to destroy the experience-near language of its victim. The main purpose of anti-a/b language is the rolling back of the power of a/b, the re-voicing of the person, and the recreating of her world. Through this anti-a/b language, the person returns to the position of a critic of a/b and an advocate for herself and others who have been subjected to the abuses of a/b's power.

In order for anti-a/b co-research to bring to light aspects of people's experience that contradict a/b's claims and generate meanings that legitimate a person's own experience, this co-research relies upon the introduction of an anti-language. It is only by supplying an anti-a/b language that the meanings generated by a/b can be rendered controversial and contestable. Whenever experience enters into the domain of language, either by being spoken of or reflected upon, the words used to describe the experience actually shape the experience by inscribing it with meaning. When we speak with people about their experience, we cannot help but contribute to a process of meaning-making. By introducing an anti-a/b language into our conversations with people, we hope to enable people to engage with a language through which they can speak up and out for themselves and their freedoms.

Katie, a woman in her mid-30s, compared her anti-a/b conversations and co-research with David to her prior experiences with therapists who spoke and thought about a/b in more traditional (structuralist) ways:

> Anti-anorexia twisted the very words by which we spoke together. I felt things starting to turn around. First, I turned away from feeling

powerless. Before, I just felt like mush inside. There was nothing—no strength, no depth, and seemingly not even any marrow in my bones. This way of talking made me able to tackle it.

Second, there was a complete shift in the relationship between the "therapist" and the "sick person" and instead we became interviewer-interviewee. And through this, I felt valued. I'm real and not a pathetic person with a pathetic eating disorder. It was a really powerful situation, enabling trust to develop.

Third, this new language made everything acceptable. In fact, the way you asked the questions made bulimia real. And I no longer felt like a freak. Sure, I'm exactly the same person as I was before but now I can see myself as "natural."

Fourth, this therapy helped me start opening out rather than opening up. By "opening up," I suppose I mean confessing. Bulimia was disciplining me. Within its constraints, there was only pass or fail—strange as it now seems, my failure was inevitable. Bulimia had no words for freedoms. Talking anti-bulimically replaced the passive with the active. That's what it is all about. And there were no "goals" in this therapy. You never asked me, "Have you vomited?" And you didn't talk about food. That was brilliant because it enabled us to get into the nitty-gritty.

I found it enlightening, too, when you told me where you stood on eating disorders. It made me feel we were on the same level... we were there tackling this problem together. I had never felt like this before with professionals. As far as bulimia was concerned, the ball was now in my court, whereas before, I was in bulimia's court. That's how I started feeling free because now I was doing the steering whereas before I was completely under its control and direction. It was doing the talking, not me. I was in a kind of linguistic trap—there was absolutely no way out of it for me. I felt like a dead person in a dead end.

The following vignette illustrates some of the ways in which language can be used to generate anti-a/b meanings in the context of co-research. Maggie (whose seduction is presented in Chapter 4) was a 24-year-old woman who had been struggling with a 7-year history of a/b. Early in our third meeting she commented that if it wasn't for occasionally feeling compelled to throw up that her life would be fine. Even though Maggie had seen various therapists over a period of many years, she regarded bulimia as essentially limited to vomiting, and she believed that if she could desist from this, all would be well.

I [RM] asked Maggie about what she experienced when she felt compelled to vomit. She told me that ordinarily she did her best to please others and make them happy. She aspired to be "an angel, ministering to the needs of others." On some occasions, however, she found herself lacking the "strength of character" necessary to transcend her own needs. When we "unpacked" these moments when her "strength of character" failed her, Maggie realized that these were occasions when she half-believed that her own preferences and desires where just as valid as those of others. The privileging of her own desires often spawned feelings of anger and resentment toward those who expected her to sacrifice her desires to serve them. Maggie referred to these feelings as "unacceptable" and said that the throwing up helped her get rid her of them, at least temporarily.

The language that Maggie used to convey and give meaning to her experience supported bulimia in several ways. First, the constricted view of bulimia that equated it with vomiting made it possible for bulimia to be perceived as a friend who could relieve her of her distress. If the feelings of anger and resentment made her bad, then bulimia, by ridding her of these feelings, could make her good again. If she wanted to overcome the bulimia within the framework of this discourse, she would have to strengthen her determination and intensify her efforts to vanquish her own selfishness. She would have to become a more giving and virtuous person who would not experience these "lapses of character" and the "unacceptable feelings" of anger and resentment as a consequence of these lapses. Naturally, the strengthening of her determination in this regard predisposed her to even harsher self-criticism for her "failure" to live up to the bulimic ideal of self-sacrifice.

In order to implicate bulimia in her distress about feeling angry and resentful, I engaged Maggie in an externalizing conversation about bulimia and what it tells her. Our co-research allowed Maggie to come to the following conclusions: "(1) Bulimia tells me that others' feelings are more important; (2) Bulimia silences me, making me afraid to voice my own feelings, wishes, preferences, and limits; (3) Bulimia tries to convince me that it is my duty and responsibility to make others happy; (4) Bulimia tells me that I shouldn't feel angry and resentful and if I do then I'm a bitch and I should be better than that."

We then looked at what Maggie's life would be like if she fully embraced bulimia's rules and requirements. Among other things she concluded that she would be feeling chronically drained from compulsory giving to others and that this giving would never make her feel good about herself but only contribute to an ongoing feeling of not being good enough. Furthermore, she said she would have to neglect her own needs and ultimately detach herself from them, thereby becoming invisible to herself and others. She concluded that bulimia did not want her to be happy but that she herself desired happiness. When I asked her why, she said, "When I'm happy, more of me comes out." I asked her what aspects of herself bulimia had been locking up. She said that when she is happy she is more humorous, playful, fun, and comfortable and relaxed with herself.

The connection to this lighter and more spontaneous side of herself was powerfully anti-bulimic. She could see more clearly that bulimia was dooming her to live a life beset by feelings of guilt, inadequacy, misery, and fatigue. Bulimia was quick to respond with an assertion of its own: "If you feel anger and resentment, no one will like you and they'd be right not to." Not surprisingly, bulimia's assertion evoked fear in Maggie: "I don't want to be known as an angry person, a depressed person, or a selfish person."

I asked Maggie how she had come to believe that certain feelings or actions were unacceptable and would mark her as a "bad" person. Maggie said that, following her parents' example, she learned to get along with others by going along with them: "I would pride myself on giving into someone's will or wishes. I looked up to my parents and I saw how much they were liked. This is the way to be a good person, this will make me better. . . . When I grew up, whenever someone expressed a disagreement I saw my parents go, 'Oh, my God, can't they just relax, can't they just hold their tongue?'" Despite this, at age 17, Maggie rebelled against her parents. In return, they accused her of being a "brat" and "selfish." This squashed her rebellion after a time.

Bulimia had made use of these family experiences and others in Maggie's life to convince her that the only way to be a good person was to not be a person at all. I wanted to open up space for an alternative account of Maggie that could rival these disqualifying descriptions that were inviting Maggie into repeated acts of self-erasure. In order to introduce an anti-a/b language that might challenge bulimia's version of morality, I asked Maggie what rights her rebellion had been attempting to establish. She said she had been fighting for the right to be more independent, to make more of her own choices, to take on her own life, and to have more of a say in shaping it.

During the ensuing discussion, I asked Maggie the following questions: Do you think a person is a brat or selfish for wanting a say in the direction of her life? Do you think a person is a brat or selfish when she demands to be taken seriously and when she honors her own feelings? Do you think a person is a brat or selfish for claiming a right to her own voice? Maggie's response at that moment was an unequivocal no. Did she think the terms "brat" or "selfish" adequately described her motivations, intentions, or values? No, she thought they didn't. What, I wondered, would be a better description of herself—one that fit her experience better? She thought "strong" and "centered in herself and in her feelings" were better descriptions.

Recalling her rebellion and the desires and aspirations that sparked it led her to "regret not pushing harder." Maggie cried as she spoke of having missed out on so many things, including an opportunity to attend more Grateful Dead shows. When I asked what had been so important to her about attending those shows, Maggie spoke of how loving the community surrounding the band was and how good she felt about herself during and after these events. This band and the culture and community that surrounded it represented another potential voice that could support self-acceptance and self-love and work against bulimia's denigrating voice.

During the next week, Maggie breathed new life into the embers of the anti-bulimic rebellion that had been smoldering since she was 17. Maggie had once again begun to feel angry at her boyfriend for expecting so much of her and offering so little in return. Rather than purge these feelings by throwing up, as bulimia was advising, she let her boyfriend know she was upset and why. In addition, she took her best friend up on an invitation to talk about what she was feeling about her relationship with her boyfriend, and found this conversation affirming. She agreed that the conversation was significant because, in the past, bulimia would have isolated her from such support by telling her she shouldn't need anything from anybody and that she shouldn't burden her friend with her troubles.

In my conversation with Maggie, bulimia was spoken about as an external entity whose voice could be identified. The ability to discern bulimia's voice enlarged Maggie's understanding of bulimia. She could now see what bulimia stood for, what its motives were, and what the effects on her life would be if she stood for it. An examination of Maggie's own purposes in rebelling against a/b's prescription to put herself second and others first helped her articulate her desire for a life of happiness, which included fun, humor, and self-acceptance. This contrasted sharply with bulimia's intention to make her feel miserable, guilty, inadequate, and fatigued. We then went on to expose one of the tactics bulimia had been using to achieve its ends: its characterization of her honoring of her own needs as the actions of a "selfish, depressed, and angry" young woman. It assured her that others would also perceive her this way and that this course of action would doom her to disapproval and rejection by others. Maggie was able to repudiate this characterization and instead preferred to see herself as someone who was "strong" and centered in herself and her feelings. She reconnected, in memory, with a community that had supported her preferred view of herself as well as her values, and in doing so, she recognized that she could choose in the present and future to surround herself with people who shared her values and provided her with outlets to be the person she wanted to be.

Chapter 8

BREAKING THE SPELL OF ANOREXIA/BULIMIA

T hose who have struggled to free themselves from a/b's confinement and parents and loved ones who have witnessed this struggle know just how difficult, albeit worthwhile, the effort can be. For us, aiding and abetting these anti-a/b struggles is often a source of tremendous joy and satisfaction. This work affords us many opportunities to appreciate and celebrate the many small and large victories that lie along the path of reclaiming one's former freedoms or asserting a new sense of rights. Although these ongoing battles bring their share of crushing defeats, temporary setbacks, and fearful retreats, we know there is a light at the end of the tunnel, and it is often not long before insiders glimpse it as well.

As emotionally uplifting as it can be to work with those who have decided to bite the hand that starves them, it can be just as distressing to speak with those still enthralled by a/b. They, too, may report seeing a light at the end of the tunnel, but we know that the light they perceive is not that of the hoped-for salvation but rather the headlights of an oncoming train.

The slow and subtle ways in which a/b insinuates itself into a person's life make it very difficult for those who have been taken in to see their own betrayal and for outsiders to understand how they could fail to see it. Even their increasing suffering may not be enough to awaken them to the full realization of their treacherous betrayal.

What hope for escape is there for those "inmates" who tell us they have come to this place of their own accord and view the circumstances

of their life not as a confinement but as voluntary enrollment in a program of self-betterment akin to a university, fitness program, military
academy, or even therapy? They may speak of a/b as a kind of modern-
day finishing school for their character and body, not realizing that
it may in fact "finish" them in a way they don't expect. Their "betterment" is by no means inexpensive, especially if they are to remain
in good standing. Yet, despite the hardships, they remain confident
that the rewards will more than justify the expense and are surely just
around the corner. And even if the hardships are more severe than they
had anticipated and the rewards more elusive, what real choice do they
experience if they believe that the only other alternative is to perceive
themselves and be perceived by others as lazy, a pig, out of control, or
unworthy?

GLIMPSING THE "EVIL" OF A/B

How, then, do the people who have been entranced and then imprisoned by a/b come to realize the fact of their betrayal and the danger of
their predicament? What can therapists, parents, and other loved ones
do to help unmask a/b and expose the prison-without-walls to which
the person has been transported? How can therapists and parents avoid
becoming unwitting accomplices of a/b? How can they minimize the
likelihood that their words and actions are read as an endorsement
of anorexic or bulimic practices? The answers to these questions are
vitally important, for it is only when the person herself can recognize
the cruel trick that has been played on her that she will see the wisdom
in turning against a/b.

A/b's spell is broken when people come to understand that their
happiness and survival depend upon their utter repudiation of a/b and
not upon their obedience to it. Conversations that result in at least
a momentary break from a/b are often experienced as quite moving.
Some people may experience a distressing disorientation and confusion. Others might experience a lightening-bolt-like flash of anti-a/b
clarity. After listening to an audiotape of her first meeting with David,
Joeline, a 38-year-old, wrote to him of her first full realization of the
"evil" of anorexia:

> The first time I saw anorexia without its mask of benevolence and
> solicitude filled me with equal measures of horror and terror; horror
> in that I now saw that what had promised to fulfill my life was like a
> grinning vampire, sucking first my blood, then my spirit, followed by
> the very marrow in my bones, draining my life from my body. Terror
> in that I knew that I now had no recourse but to fight for my very life

for I was staring at a hideous monster who no longer could trick itself up in lies and deceptions. Its intentions were naked.

First, I feared for you, David. Could you possibly know what you were up against? I thought you should be warned... that someone should tell you. Strange as it seemed, I could clearly hear anorexia, which for so many years had stolen my voice, speaking to you and arguing against life itself. Knowing this, I could sympathize with myself for any ways that I had been complicit with it. It now dawned on me. I was not evil as anorexia had judged and condemned me. What had been done to me by my abuser was evil. And anorexia was torturing me for that. I now had to confront evil as evil along with you. I knew I had to prepare for mortal combat as anorexia intended to murder me. It was this realization that allowed me to know that pleading for anorexia's mercy would never placate it. I entered into a fierce struggle with no holds barred that seemed to go on for hours. I drove anorexia off although it promised it would return and subdue me. I rested knowing it would keep its word.

The ongoing process of questioning oneself about a/b's intentions, effects, and trustworthiness leads eventually to the apprehending or exposing of anorexia and its lethal intentions and effects. Chloe, a 19-year-old, discussed the process by which she came to see anorexia as her enemy.

My discovering anorexia to be the "enemy" rather than "friend or ally" was a matter of gradual discovery rather than one defining moment. These are just some of the things that helped me see it more clearly:
- Finding myself in situations (e.g., in the hospital) and suddenly being struck by the realization that this is not what I wanted for my life, and that it was anorexia that had put me in this position.
- Times when it really hit home that anorexia was taking away everything that I held dear and was turning me into somebody I didn't want to be.
- Seeing what anorexia does to other women/men and being outraged at the pain it caused them. This made me realize just how insidious anorexia really is.
- Seeing the way anorexia was hurting those who I loved and realizing that it was something I wanted to stop. However, also realizing that by blaming myself for the hurt I was causing, I only played right into anorexia's hands and strengthened it.

In our experience, it is more realistic, at least initially, to think in terms of *moments* of anti-a/b clarity rather than a once-and-for-all realization of a/b's evil and a subsequent unwavering rejection of it. When the person discovers one of a/b's lies, a/b will resort to other clever but equally flawed arguments to win back the person's allegiance. A/b's rhetoric is like a many-tentacled octopus. This does not mean, however, that when a person succeeds in getting free of one tentacle only to be entwined by another that the former achievement was for naught. Quite the contrary—in our experience, every time the person succeeds in exposing one of a/b's fraudulent claims, the voice of a/b is rendered more suspect in general and the person gradually develops a belief in her own capacity to see through it. In addition, as a/b's most plausible and credible arguments are countered, it must resort to increasingly preposterous claims, and these are more easily dismissed or dispelled.

DISPELLING PRACTICES

Following is a list some of the common means by which we attempt to break the spell of a/b during our initial conversations with people. This list is by no means exhaustive. Necessity is often the mother of invention in this work. We can never be sure, prior to any conversation, what opportunities might present themselves to dethrone the "truth" of a/b. And, when cracks in a/b's claims begin to appear, we never know beforehand what specific question might serve as a lever to widen these gaps and admit alternative understandings and versions of the self. Because co-research infused with genuine curiosity is fundamental to our practice, our practice is continually reinventing itself. We hope you keep that caveat in mind as you read the following list of common conversational avenues we take in these "spell-breaking" meetings.

Thinking and Speaking About A/B as External to People

In the last chapter we discussed our preference for viewing a/b as an external influence on the person rather than as part of the person herself. Because thinking about problems and discourses as external is so fundamental to our practice and so discrepant from traditional practices, we have elected to elaborate further on this practice here.

Few problems have the capacity to remake a person's identity to the extent that a/b does. A/b actively fosters identities saturated with self-hate and worthlessness in order to present itself as a form of salvation or as a punishment warranted by one's badness and guilt. When a/b is viewed as internal to the person, as part of "who I am," then "having an eating disorder" can (ironically) be declared by a/b as further evidence of one's unworthiness. One young woman illustrated this point: "Anorexia made me angry at myself for 'being anorexic' and so I concluded I was a failure. Yet, if I turned away from anorexia, she told me I was a failure at being thin, determined, worthwhile, giving, etc."

Viewing a/b as something distinct from the person and the family not only undermines self-blame, but also blame between parent and child or between parent and parent. A/b often pulls families apart and pits person against person; externalizing the problem can form the foundation of an anti-a/b practice that can bring people together and pit them against the problem. Listen to the experience of Richard Treadgold, a father who, along with his wife, Ann, developed an anti-anorexic parenting practice while consulting David about his daughter (see Chapter 17).

> It was a strange thing about anorexia; you could learn to think of it as separate, like a broken leg. At first you see it as being identical to the sufferer, which makes you hate them (and we were all sufferers). But when you identified it as apart from them, it became more concrete, and somehow more vulnerable. You could apply your intellect to it, consider how it affected a person, how to fight it. I found I could love my daughter again. Then, horror of horrors, I realized it was in me as well, so I could start to turn away from it. Practicing behavior free of anorexia was like starting to sing; gradually others joined in and the freedom spread.
>
> Though very horrible from beginning to end, with no respite and full of despair, anorexia provided a crisis, a common enemy, a shared catastrophe, that pulled our family together as it has many other families, and let us battle together, weep together, toil together, and, in the end, rejoice together.

Rather than promoting a conceptual merging of the person with the problem, we maintain a view of the person as separate from the problem but living in a dynamic and changeable relationship to it. This opens up a conversational space that can serve as an anti-a/b staging ground. It is from this standpoint that it eventually becomes possible to: (1) trace the history and tactics surrounding a/b's seduction and occupation; (2) investigate the effects of a/b on people's lives and relationships and determine with them whether these effects fit with their own values and hopes for their lives, as well as clarify the kind of relationship they'd like to have with a/b; (3) identify acts of resistance to a/b; (4) elaborate anti-a/b knowledges and ways of life; and (5) allow for the claiming of alternative and more preferred identities.

Learning to think about a/b and to speak in opposition to it is a gradual process like learning to speak a foreign language. Rebecca (a 17 year old) commented on the "fits and starts" process of learning to think and speak in this manner.

> Before I was able to externalize it, I thought I WAS bulimia. When I knew that Bulimia was the problem and I renamed it and relocated it, that made it possible for me to stand up to it. Talking anti-anorexia talk came in fits and starts. I would get lost and then realize that my use of language hadn't been consistent. Anti-anorexic talk makes you feel stronger. You feel you have the power to fight against it. Before anti-anorexia, I just thought I wasn't controlling bulimia properly. I thought it was all my fault.

Discerning the Person's Voice From the Voice of A/B

The externalization of a/b typically proceeds through the identification of its voice and the effects this voice has on the person's thoughts and actions. By *voice* we do not mean some predetermined, universal way in which a/b "speaks" to people in general, but rather to the very local and particular ways in which it speaks to the particular person. The difficulty in doing this early on, before the spell of a/b has been broken, is that the person is not yet able to distinguish the voice of a/b as something distinct from and foreign to herself. As one person put it, "If asked what anorexia looked like, I couldn't say. This is because anorexia has been so cunning and manipulative that she has taken on my own form." Another person commented, "If you had asked me what I wanted for my life back then, I couldn't have answered for myself. I would have answered, 'to be thin and in control,' and I wouldn't have seen that anorexia was answering the question for me."

This leaves the therapist in the awkward position of unilaterally identifying what the operations of a/b might be instead of being able to engage in collaborative co-research about the ways and means of a/b. In some instances, these judgments are relatively straightforward and nonproblematic, as for instance, when a young woman, who is medically fragile due to malnutrition, states during her first meeting that her goal is to eat less and exercise more. At other times, discerning the operations of a/b from those of non-a/b or even anti-a/b can be more difficult. For example, suppose the parents of a teenage girl report that their daughter retreats to the bathroom after dinner and turns on the shower for a very long time. The parents believe that these showers are designed to mask the sounds of her vomiting. The girl, on the other hand, maintains that she *is* actually showering—that she feels "dirty" after eating and that sometimes taking a prolonged shower can help her resist the urge to vomit. Is this act of showering bulimia's attempt to deceive her parents, a surrendering to bulimia's view of food as dirty, an act of anti-bulimic resistance, or some amalgamation of bulimia and anti-bulimia? Whatever meaning the therapist makes of the girl's actions will have significant consequences, and there is always the danger that the therapist will miss something important about the girl's experience.

We feel relatively confident in concluding that the voice of a/b is operating when it: (1) denies the physical consequences of starvation or purging or attributes these consequences to something else; (2) claims the person is experiencing something, such as happiness, when there is ample evidence to the contrary; (3) speaks in a way that closes a person off to alternative viewpoints or perspectives; (4) argues that things are hopeless; (5) insists on the badness or unworthiness of the person; (6) emphasizes that the only hope for a good future lies through thinness, self-discipline, bodily control, niceness and subservience, or perfection; and (7) minimizes or dismisses the genuine love and caring of parents, friends, partners, and other concerned people.

Asking Questions that Expose A/B

When we initially find ourselves speaking with someone whose words and thoughts appear to be substantially colonized by a/b, we might attempt to name the operation of a/b by asking the following questions or making the following comments:

- Is that what anorexia tells you?
- How is anorexia tricking you into believing that?
- I think anorexia is attempting to deceive you about this.
- What would anorexia's purpose be in wanting you to believe this?

These questions are often difficult for people to respond to because they may not accept the premise that it is a/b that is sponsoring or promoting their outlook. Even if these questions remain unanswered, we find them useful as a means to introduce an externalized and personified view of a/b. Other times it makes sense to ask questions about the effects of certain ideas or practices on the person's life. Inquiries about effects sometimes make the connections between these practices and a/b more transparent and obvious. If, for example, we were talking to someone about her feeling that she needs to be perfect, we might ask some of the following questions:

- What does this idea that you have to be perfect require of you?
- How does this idea of perfection make you feel when you fall short of its expectations for you?
- Do perfectionistic expectations set you up to feel like a failure?
- Does anorexia subscribe to this idea of perfection? Does it offer to perfect you when you fall short of perfectionistic expectations?
- Do you think that anorexia and perfectionism are allies?

Sharing From the Anti-A/B Archive

Having a person read from an anti-a/b archive is another excellent way to introduce her to a language and way of thinking that makes a/b more visible and contestable, a language that allows more readily for a/b to not only be spoken about but spoken against.*

Archival documents are the repositories of the anti-a/b knowledges of insiders. Sometimes these knowledges are brought forward in a conversation with a therapist; other times they result from the person's solitary reflections, perhaps recorded in a journal. Archival documents can take the form of written documents, such as journal entries, letters, transcripts, or poems, or of visual depictions, such as paintings, drawings, or collages. They can also take the form of audiotaped or videotaped conversations. These documents are considered 'League' property, in that they have been bequeathed to the Anti-Anorexia/Bulimia League so that they can be shared with others who might benefit in some way from their anti-a/b knowledge or spirit.

Archives can offer insider knowledge about a wide variety of things. Some documents develop a portrait of a/b, developing rich metaphorical or personified descriptions of it. Other documents might detail some of a/b's tactics and strategies and contribute to an expose of its voice. Some archives document the means by which people come to recognize a/b and the steps they take to resist it. Some address the ways in which relationships and larger sociocultural messages support a/b or, conversely, empower and strengthen the person's resistance to it. Archival documents can be read aloud to people during therapy or they can be given to people to take home and peruse at their convenience.

---

* If you are a therapist and you have not yet amassed your own archive, please consider sharing the archives presented in this book. We are also continually adding to the archives on http://www.narrativeapproaches.com.

Because these documents cover such a wide range of subjects, they are potentially useful at many points throughout therapy. The sharing of archives helps to circulate the anti-a/b discoveries of others and allows therapists and those suffering from a/b to co-research these knowledges so that they can be more richly described, highly articulated, and multifaceted. But the documents are often of invaluable assistance during initial meetings. Some of the reasons for this are as follows:

- They provide a ready-made anti-a/b framework that conveys the possibilities associated with viewing a/b as external.
- Because they express the experience of others, they are not as directly threatening to the person still in the grip of and loyal to a/b as are confrontations or pronouncements by professionals.
- They do not require the person to speak but only to listen. For some, speaking against a/b would be experienced as too likely to provoke a/b's threats and punishments. Sometimes a/b will prevent people from consenting even to the reading of archival documents, as listening to subversive anti-a/b documents often encourages verbal transgressions against a/b.
- The first-hand experience of insiders documented in the archives usually resonates with listeners more than information or statistics documented by outsiders. Because some of these documents will ring true for the listener, the voice of a/b will find them more difficult to discount and dismiss.
- The mere existence of these documents provides evidence of a community of others who have successfully revolted against a/b. It evokes the supportive presence of these others, which provides hope and a sense of belonging to a larger cause. In addition, when these archives are made available to the person and it is suggested that she too might contribute to them, the person understands that, should she decide to escape from the prison of a/b, she could figuratively link arms with others in the Anti-Anorexia/Bulimia League through the sharing of these knowledges.

Attending to Inconsistencies

Both anorexia and bulimia take increasingly greater tolls on a person's health and feeling of well-being. As friends and family can readily attest, physical, emotional, and spiritual deterioration can occur at an alarming rate. Typically, the person who is medically "crashing" seems singularly oblivious to this fact, further compounding the alarm in others. A/b is often able to keep the person in the dark about the damage it is causing by getting her to listen only to what it tells her she is feeling rather than to what she is actually experiencing in her body. A/b also may claim that whatever physical pain, discomfort, or fatigue she is feeling is a consequence of eating rather than of food restriction or purging. Asking a person questions that make a/b's twisted logic and perverse strategies more visible and helping the person to evaluate this logic in light of her own embodied experience often undermines her unquestioning acceptance of a/b's claims and awakens some suspicion of its truthfulness and motives. An example of this line of questioning is presented at the end of this chapter.

Contrasting Qualities of Life

Both anorexia and bulimia are highly successful in convincing those who have fallen into their trap that their lives are better or will be better because of it. For example, anorexia may promise to make a person better by transforming her character; bulimia may present itself as a consequence of and remedy for having been "bad." We like to ask people to reflect on whether they feel their lives have become better or worse since they became engaged with a/b. For instance, we might ask about what promises a/b has made and what, in turn, it has delivered on.

Anticipating the Arguments and Rhetoric of A/B

When asked about what a/b has promised and what has it delivered, many people respond that although it has not yet delivered on its promises, they know that at some point in the future it will. Almost invariably, when a/b is confronted or challenged by these contradictions, it will attempt to counter them. Its counter arguments often take the form of internal thoughts that are never expressed aloud to therapists or others. Rather than permit a/b to have the last word and allow its counter arguments to go uncontested, we frequently anticipate these arguments and verbalize them. For example, we might ask, "Is anorexia telling you that the only reason it hasn't yet delivered on its promises is because you have not been obedient or disciplined enough? Is it telling you that if you keep on listening to it your rewards will be just around the corner? Is anorexia telling you anything about me and my intentions? Is it telling you that I don't really care about you the way it does—that I am only trying to trick you?"

If our guesses are "in the ballpark," our credibility as people who understand may be heightened, and the power of these counter claims is often substantially eroded. Furthermore, articulating these often unspoken counter arguments allows for another opportunity for the therapist to introduce archival material to further call a/b into question. For example, we might draw from the archive and respond, "Anorexia said a similar thing to Allison—that if she only did anorexia better, only lost a little more weight, all her dreams would come true. Allison said that in her experience, whatever she did was never good enough for anorexia, and it always required something additional from her. Would you like me to read what she wrote?"

Supporting a Preferred View of the Person

If a person is going to turn her back on a/b and all of its seductive promises and dire warnings, she must turn toward something else that she can rightfully place her hope and trust in. People can more easily disregard and dismiss the voice of a/b when they can recognize or reclaim those things a/b obscures, namely a sense of their own worth, rights, talents, capacities, and belief that they are worthy of others' love, respect, and admiration. In other words, we want to help bring about an alternative version or versions of the person, so that she can decide which "self" she prefers and best fits her experience (see Chapter 10).

We all have the capacity to live through various selves or identities. These selves or identities depend upon the way in which meaning gets made of the things that we think, feel, and do. A/b is malignant in its meaning-making. It encourages people to view themselves in the most critical light imaginable, and it tries to convince them that others are also viewing them this way. We are interested in a more benign, benevolent, and generous meaning-making process—one that allows the person more space to work out for herself the meaning of her actions. In fact, we have found that conversations that yield "thick" or "rich" descriptions of a person's experience (White, 2001b) implicate the person's identity in more positive ways.

Often an important part of this process of helping people entertain alternative identities is to encourage them to view themselves through the eyes of loving and appreciative others rather than through the critical and condemning eyes of a/b. It is important that therapists do not reside at the center of this new story and thereby render its survival dependent upon an ongoing relationship with the therapist. A new and preferred story is more likely to endure if it is widely distributed among and supported by the ongoing relationships in the person's life, such as with parents, grandparents, siblings, friends, partners, and teachers. (Russell & Carey, 2002; White, 1997)

A SPELL-BREAKING CONVERSATION WITH RIANNON

The following transcript illustrates some lines of questioning that can be employed when a person's thoughts and feelings are significantly dominated by a/b. The transcript was excerpted from a third meeting (in as many days) between David and Riannon, a 15-year-old.* Riannon's parents had sent her to Auckland to live with her cousin, Donna, and Donna's partner, Jerome, with the hope of gaining admission to the eating disorders unit at the Public hospital there. Riannon had been discharged from the hospital in her own community after suffering disastrous weight loss during her stay there. Riannon's parents decided, at the last minute, to postpone the hospitalization in Auckland and instead seek help from David. Unfortunately, Riannon's parents were unable to attend the meeting as they had to return to their hometown and their jobs many hours away, but Donna and Jerome did come to the third meeting.

Jerome: (*with concern in his voice*) She's just been to her doctor.
David: Do you want to fill me in on that? Did anything come out of that?
Jerome: Yeah, just about her physical condition and how close she is to dying and all that. (*pause*) But she still says that she feels fine and Dr. Jones was trying to explain to her . . .
Riannon: (*interrupting plaintively*) But I *do* feel fine!

Jerome attempted again to explain to Riannon the danger she was in but gave up, his sentence trailing off into a desperate silence.

It was imperative that Riannon come to understand the peril her life was in. Yet, like Jerome, I sensed that it would be futile to continue to confront her with the dire medical facts. Anorexia's voice, at that moment, was just too powerful. It would have found a way to disqualify anyone who contradicted its assertions, perhaps by maligning the person's competence ("he doesn't know what he is talking about") or impugning the person's motives ("he is jealous of you and just wants you to be fat or ordinary"). Instead of arguing the facts of the matter, the futility of which Jerome and Riannon's physician had no doubt already discovered, I decided to shift the focus on to anorexia itself. I began by asking Riannon questions that derived from our previous discussion about the "anorexic ruse" and, by doing so, contested the veracity and trustworthiness of anorexia.

David: Can I just ask you why you think it is that anorexia tricks people into going to their death thinking they're feeling fine? Why do you think that

---

* The entire transcript is available at http://www.narrativeapproaches.com

is? What purpose would it have in getting you to go to your death smiling? Most people go to their death upset or opposing it, especially when they are being murdered, don't they?

Riannon: Yeah...

David: I've wondered about this (*turning to Donna and Jerome*), and you're probably wondering about it too. Probably it is confusing all of us right now. How can anyone be on death row and not know it? (*turning again toward Riannon*) How is anorexia telling you that you're feeling fine when, in fact, it could kill you at any moment?

Riannon: Well, I've got energy.

David: How is anorexia fooling you into that? You're on death row and everyone knows that except you, although you know it sometimes when you take our word for it.

Riannon: Well, if I take your word for it that I'm there, yeah!

I wanted to help Riannon attend to the consequences of whose *word* she chooses to believe.

David: If you didn't take our word for it, would it kill you? Would it have killed you?

Riannon: (*nods in agreement*)

David: It would have murdered you by now if you didn't take our word for it. You'd be dead by now.

Riannon: Yeah.

Donna, sensing the significance of this last exchange, requested that the interview be videotaped, and I assured her that it was.

Donna: Good, because this is actually something that she constantly says.

David: It is very important to undo the ruse. Remember the ruse, the trick?

We briefly reviewed what we had discovered about anorexia's tricks during our first two meetings. I then went on to extend my moral indictment of anorexia.

David: This is a lethal trick. How do you trick a person into their own murder? This is very sinister. Most people have the chance to fight, protest, spit, and scream, "Damn you... you can't kill me... you will never kill my spirit." Some people who are murdered at least can say that back, can't they? Look what's happening here now. It's got you on death row. If it wasn't for Donna and Jerome, you'd be dead. And I don't know how you would imagine that—cremation or burial. Can you explain this to us? I want to ask you to remember that you're not only speaking to us, you are also speaking to other generations of women who will come after you and whose lives you may save. It may sound like a trivial thing but you could not only save your own life but many other people's lives. One purpose of the videotaping is that it is for you, Riannon. But at some time in the future you may allow others to see it so they don't have to die.

I then returned to my inquiry.

David: I think we have to understand its motives, its purposes. Why do you think it would do this—hurt a person and make them think they were happy to die with an anorexic smile on their face? What lethal practices does it use to confound and confuse you? Now you're on death row but somehow anorexia is keeping this from you and the more it keeps it from you, the more likely it is that it will kill you.

Riannon: (with far less conviction) I've got energy.

Donna: You don't have energy because you can't walk to the letter box. Last night, you couldn't move your body to play bowls [a common New Zealand game].

Riannon: I couldn't move *freely*.

Donna: You really couldn't move at all.

Riannon: (*a bit bewildered*) But I feel really energetic.

People in advanced states of starvation often experience a kind of euphoria attributed to the body's release of endogenous chemicals known as endorphins. These substances help a person tolerate extreme pain and discomfort from trauma. But even if endorphin release was contributing to Riannon's feeling of well-being, it could not account for Riannon's near obliviousness to the vast array of physical symptoms that inevitably accompany advanced states of starvation (e.g., muscle cramping, dizziness, headaches, inability to concentrate, growth of hair on the torso and limbs of the body, irregular heartbeat, difficulty staying warm). I believed that it was largely anorexia's spell that had Riannon focusing on her "energy" and ignoring or dismissing the evidence of her rapid physical decline. I persistently prodded Riannon to think outside of the narrow box to which anorexia had confined her mind. Unfortunately, one of the symptoms of starvation is difficulty with thinking and concentrating; I knew that this, coupled with anorexia's clever deceptions, would make it difficult for Riannon to think past the anorexic "givens" of her experience. But I was prepared to persist, even beyond her objections, given that her life was at stake.

David: (*more emphatically*). Okay ... okay ... okay. If that's how you're feeling, how is anorexia fooling you? Most people when they are near death know that, don't they? If you know it's making you feel good or telling you you're feeling good, then I'd ask you to ask this question of anorexia: "Why are you telling me I'm feeling good?" Why would it do this!? Why does it want to murder you? Why doesn't it want you to protest or resist? Look, you're going to your death like a sheep.

Riannon's bewilderment deepened and she repeated anorexia's line.

Riannon: Well, I'm able and I've got energy. That's all I know.
David: *(imploring her)* Can I ask you to think carefully about this? How does it make a young woman think she's fine when it's murdering her? There was a time when you knew you were in danger, wasn't there? Some months ago, you would have known that, wouldn't you?

To my relief, Riannon assured me with a simple, straightforward "yeah!"

David: You have no doubt about that? You would have gone to a doctor and said, "Please pay attention to me; I'm in trouble"?
Riannon: *(nods in agreement)*

I returned to the heart of the morality we were deliberating.

David: How does anorexia fool young women so that they walk, smiling, into their execution chamber? How does it do it? Jerome and Donna don't know, I don't know. But you do. Tell other women how it happens because other women will walk after you. You have a chance to save their lives as well as your own. If you save your life, you will save others because this videotape will be kept with your permission and be shown to others who will sit in your chair after you. How does it do it? How does it confuse your mind!?
Riannon: By telling you you're fat when you are thin.
David: Okay, okay.

Riannon's response indicated that, for the first time in the interview, she had achieved some detachment from anorexia and could now begin to articulate its messages to her. This detachment from anorexia would hopefully now enable us to engage in a process of co-research and a critique of anorexia. This development was the first turning point of the meeting, and I was beginning to experience a sense of relief and excitement.

Riannon: *(uneasily)* Is that right?

Perhaps she distrusted her own account of her experience after having had anorexia put its stamp on it for so long. Perhaps she was eager to please me by producing an acceptable response. In any case, it was essential that I did not step in and assume the authority that anorexia once held for her. This would have replicated in my relationship with her the very dominance anorexia depends upon. I was interested in helping Riannon to reclaim her own authority.

David: I don't know. What do you think? Tell me ... tell us. Is it telling you that you are fat when you are thin?
Riannon: Yeah.
David: Is it telling you that right now?
Riannon: (*nods in the affirmative*) No, I do know I am too thin.
David: You know that?
David: Yeah, because that's what everyone tells me.

Riannon had now returned to the theme of whom can be trusted. Earlier, I had introduced this theme in relation to the question of whether or not she was in physical peril. Now she returned to this theme in relation to her weight and appearance. Riannon, at this point, was still centrally concerned with her appearance, and she had not yet developed an enduring appreciation of her body or trust in her own perception of it. Consequently, she deferred to the opinion of others. Whose opinion she trusted could literally be a matter of life and death. Thus, I was interested in asking questions that would introduce distinctions that could further assist Riannon in determining who was her friend and who was her enemy.

David: Okay, there's anorexia telling you you're too fat and other people telling you you're too thin?
Riannon: Yeah.
David: Who are you believing ... who cares about you the most?
Riannon: (*nodding toward Donna and Jerome.*) Them.
David: Do you think anorexia loves you?
Riannon: (*with a measure of force*) No, it's killing me now!

The spell of anorexia was broken, at least for the time being, and we went on to co-research anorexia and compare it to anti-anorexia.

The following two chapters present more complete transcripts of psychotherapy conversations that occurred early on in therapy with people still under the spell of a/b. During these meetings, Rick and David attempted to help incite some critical reflection about a/b's purposes and effects, though each goes about this in a different way.

Chapter 9

TEN VOICES AGAINST ONE

TRACY'S STORY

I (DE) vividly recall first meeting with Tracy and her parents, Marie and Morris, in 1989. Marie and Morris entered the room first, Marie displaying desperate concern. Tracy followed them, walking like a repentant sinner doing her penance, eyes downcast, arms tightly crossed over her chest, fingers grasping at her frail shoulder blades. When I asked her to sit down, she did so as if she were surrendering her body. She had spent 10 months of the previous year as an inpatient in a public hospital, 3 of these months in intensive care. She was forbidden any visitors for many weeks. When she came of legal age, according to her parents, she "made her own decision to discharge herself and to live with it."

Over the next several months I met with Tracy, Marie, and Morris. It became clear that anorexia had started intruding into Tracy's life 3 years before it became a medical emergency. Perhaps anorexia had been concealed by Tracy's brilliant athletic career, which saw her competing at senior levels as a 15-year-old. But even when she was ranked second nationally, she believed she wasn't good enough and no one could convince her otherwise.

We all worked together on exposing the ways in which anorexia tried to divide Tracy from her parents and isolate her from her friends. Marie and Morris found new ways of expressing their support and caring for Tracy that were more impervious to anorexia's attempts to have Tracy read this as "worry" or "lack of trust." This was vital, as anorexia was incessantly encouraging Tracy to feel guilty for burdening her mother with worry (especially as she believed her mother deserved much but received very little in life) and chastising her for being so unworthy of her parents' trust. After a few months, Tracy broke out of her reclusive ways and returned for her final year at secondary school, where she once again began initiating conversations with others and resuming a social life. With great difficulty, she not only took her exams but was awarded a distinction. Sadly, anorexia forbade her from receiving the award in person.

Not surprisingly, when Tracy started her first job at the beginning of the next year, anorexia made a comeback in her life. It reiterated old standbys such as "you don't need to eat ... you'll get fat." She acknowledged that anorexia was much more vociferous than ever before. At her anti-anorexic best, she felt it was an even match between herself and anorexia, but the tables had now turned in anorexia's favor, and she estimated that now it was 30% Tracy and 70% anorexia.

The following excerpted letter summarizes our discussions about past anti-anorexic developments and the resurgence by anorexia. I mailed it to Tracy after one of our meetings.

Dear Tracy,
[During our last meeting] we discussed how anorexia, at a particularly low point in your life when you were on "death row" in intensive care, had it all over you (100% anorexia vs. 0% Tracy). Last year you fought back tooth and nail to reclaim 50% of yourself and my guess is that quite a bit of your win-back involved new learnings and produced new knowledges, especially anti-anorexic knowledge. You produced a new philosophy of "looking to life" and decided that your life would be one that you manufactured rather than one made up for you by others, especially anorexia nervosa.

You started facing up to things in your life, some of which must have been pretty hard and I admire you for that. You chose to return to school and face all those looks and rumors and even challenged your fears enough to sit for your exams and came through them with flying colors. You then took the next step, which was, predictably, a hard one. You entered the world of work. Here you started to form a vision of your own and this vision was a source of strength for you. You took it upon yourself to learn things every day and that's exactly what you have done. You are moving in a self-supporting direction and feel you are 10% on your way.

Lately, anorexia has fought back somewhat and you are now down 30–70. However, things have changed a lot since your last match-up a couple of years ago. First, you have some sense of what anorexia is up to and are no longer so confused about which thoughts spring from your own mind or from anorexia's intrusion into it. Second, you have produced a considerable body of anti-anorexic knowledge that has proven itself in your more recent struggles. Perhaps you didn't know you were becoming knowledgeable and developing anti-anorexic tactics. I think I can assure you that if you had left it to chance, there would be a very good chance you wouldn't be around to talk about it. Anorexia has the habit of returning at moments you least expect it to but, predictably, at those times when you are feeling somewhat vulnerable. In a manner of speaking, anorexia always kicks you when you are down.

After receiving the letter, Tracy decided to document her anti-anorexic struggle in her "Escape from Anorexia" diary. She began struggling to *see* anorexia with her own eyes rather than looking at her experience through anorexia's eyes. She recorded the following observations about anorexia's tactics in her diary:

- Anorexia tells me food is no good for me and I will get fat.
- I could try to overpower anorexia's voice by using mine to shut it out with positive thoughts but whenever I try this, it tells me they're not true and, therefore, I end up not believing them.
- Anorexia makes me hide food from others or throw it out.
- Anorexia has made me start to count calories, getting me to eat less than—calories a day . . . if I do eat more than this, anorexia will make me panic about the weight, which it tells me I have put on and I'll skip a meal the following day. Sometimes I am able to stop its messages by telling myself that I need food and should enjoy it rather than treat it as an enemy.
- Whenever I try something new or different, Anorexia puts me down—e.g., "I'm worthless, useless, always fail if I try, I'm no good." I never feel good about myself. I feel as though I have failed all my life so I will never succeed in my future.

Although Tracy was able to expose anorexia's voice, her attempts to challenge its claims were ultimately overpowered by the persuasive and constant force of anorexia's rhetoric. Over the next few weeks her resistance withered away rapidly and along with this came devastating weight loss. However, even as Tracy became increasingly confined by anorexia, she was at least able to reveal to me the specific terms and conditions of her imprisonment, which required rigid adherence to an extremely depriving starvation diet and nearly around-the-clock torturecize.

I recall being aghast when I learned of the conditions of Tracy's anorexic imprisonment. But I grew even more concerned (if such a thing were possible) when she informed me several months after anorexia's comeback that she was determined that her life end. It seemed to her that her readmission to hospital was imminent. She told me with chilling resignation that the spark of life that kept her alive during her previous months in intensive care had now been extinguished forever. She could see nothing more in her future than her own oblivion. She was convinced she would not leave the hospital alive and, in fact, was only looking forward to being discharged from her life. She whispered these confessions almost as if she were trying to tell me her last words.

I was both scandalized and enraged by Tracy's reconciliation to her own annihilation at the age of 18. I had agreed around the same time to meet a man who was a Holocaust survivor. Being Jewish myself, I had undertaken an extensive emotional and historical preparation in order to adequately meet him. I vividly recall my horrifying flash of recognition that anorexia's torturing of Tracy had exceeded that of the SS policy of "extermination by exploitation," which allowed for the consumption of mercilessly few calories a day along with 15 hours of hard labor (which would end in certain death).

During my next meeting with Tracy, I commenced a series of inquiries. Due to her advanced state of weakness, she was only able to respond to my questions by nodding "yes" or shaking her head "no." As the meeting concluded, I offered Tracy an audiotape of a conversation I'd had with another young woman suffering from a/b and her family. I hoped that listening to this tape would provide Tracy and her parents with some renewed options and hope.

My conversation with Tracy is summarized in the following letter, which I sent out posthaste that same day. The letter included a radical proposal. In principal, I accepted her capitulation to anorexia, but I expressed that those who loved and cared about her (myself included) could never consent to this capitulation in practice. My proposal was based upon my conviction that all I had to go on at this moment was the *collective weight of others' care*. I did everything I could to pit this love and care against anorexia's fierce death grip.

Dear Tracy

Because we talked about so much, I thought it might be useful to you to have a summary so you could go over it at will. You are becoming aware that anorexia will not rest until it murders you. Its means are well known to you now—first it must convince you to starve yourself and then take over your mind so you can't know what's going on.

Since there is a killer on the loose, I don't think we should reason with it, be considerate of it, or take its feelings into account. I propose *war*. It seems right now that you are too fatigued to develop a strong enough argument against it, as anorexia has begun to starve you to death. For that reason, I propose that you do something like this: When anorexia proposes further self-starvation and further punishments for giving yourself nourishment, *don't argue back*. Instead, say something like this:

"Anorexia, I have been arguing against you for the last year and perhaps I was wrong. Perhaps I wasn't listening to you enough. I started to enjoy my life; I started to feel I had a future; I started to provide myself with adequate nourishment; I started to think of myself as a person rather than your prisoner. Perhaps I was wrong. Perhaps it was unreasonable of me to think of myself as a person rather than your prisoner. Perhaps it was unreasonable of me to think of myself as a citizen of New Zealand when, in fact, I am a prisoner of your concentration camp.

"I am starting at long last to replace my mind with an anorexic mind, my thoughts with anorexic thoughts, my life with your plans for me. Anorexia, I would like to join your concentration camp where you could work me to death through over-exercise and starvation. I would like to die for you, *but I can't*. I feel really badly about this and if I had my own way, I would pretty soon be a corpse for you. *But I can't!*

"Let me explain: I am under obligation to a number of people whom I cannot convince that I deserve my self-execution. I leave it up to you to convince them to assist you. But I doubt if you will have much success.

"Let me explain more. My mother loves me more than life itself; as a matter of fact, my guess is that she would give up her life if she knew I could have a life of my own. My father loves me too in his own way. Although he cannot show it, he would be distraught at my funeral. My boyfriend really cares about me and he would be devastated. His mother also insists on me living my life and there is nothing I can do to convince her otherwise. My soccer coach wants me on his side as do my teammates. I know they are very stupid because they stupidly admire and respect me. My workmates depend on me and I have become their friend. I know you will say that just proves what dummies they are but what can I do about it? Can you please convince them so they will be bystanders at my dying? Can you persuade my mother that she will be better off without me so she will step to one side and allow you to take me away? Can you please convince all my teachers and school counselor that I was a waste of their time and should be condemned to death?

And could you please do something about David Epston, who is always talking anti-anorexically and spreading rumors about you that you are murdering the best women of their generation? Why don't you punish him for his slander and sedition? Did you know he was stirring up protest against you? It's called *The Anti-Anorexia League.* It's a resistance movement. Please do something to put an end to that.

"And what about those women who are protesting about the injustices and inequalities between men and women? How about them? Can you do something about them, too?

"*Beware,* as every day the resistance is growing and spreading underground. I am telling you all this to prove I am on your side. However, I am under obligation to those people who both care about me and love me. No matter what I do, those people only seem to care more about me rather than less. Anorexia, I am helpless. I am under obligation to their love and caring. I cannot talk them out of it. *Maybe you can!*"

Yours forever anti-anorexically,

David

Instead of being admitted to the hospital, Tracy returned a week later brandishing a letter that she read aloud to me with a measure of pride:

Dear David,

After our meeting on the 15th, I felt much better and had more confidence in myself. I got to thinking that maybe I can succeed in life and face problems that might occur. I knew I had a decision to make and fast, about whether to let anorexia convince me to starve myself or to argue back for my life as a normal person. I know that I didn't want a life of living in and out of a hospital. And the way things have been going, I knew it was time to do something strong about it. Maybe I should let anorexia know what I *want* now.

I thought of all those I had to live for against one [anorexia] who wanted me dead or, failing that, to see me unhappy, unhealthy, and living an unrealistic life.

Listening to that audiotape has helped a lot, hearing that family's happiness now that Lee-Ann has overcome this "slimmer's disease" and found that starving yourself to look pathetically thin is no way to solve any problems one may have. In fact, it has made matters worse for me. Now I'm having to face a difficult turning point in my life that will be harder than hard but I know I have to.

To succeed with my fight, I'm going to need to listen to my-self and the "true" messages rather than anorexia's lies which are so strong and convincing. At times, they can dominate my "truth" so that I believe that such lies are the "truth." For so long now I have believed in them and only them *against* others whom Anorexia told me were lying. I need to value these true messages and be-lieve in myself more which is going to be very difficult because Anorexia has had me devalue, discredit, and put myself down. And what's more, it has had me think I deserve this punishment for so long now.

I keep looking at myself all the time and seeing how ugly Anorexia is making me, which I can no longer stand. But it is just so painful to try and do something about it. Because I have kept looking at myself and realizing the way I look all weekend, I felt the need to eat and wanted to put on weight. And that is what I did."

As Tracy turned against anorexia and once again began to substanti-ate herself, she wrote down many of the words and messages she heard in her head. They came in the form of a backlash. Whereas in the past Tracy's attempt to capture anorexia's voice on paper led to becoming captured by anorexia herself, this time the outcome was more in her favor. Tracy's writings reveal her heightened appreciation of the love, caring, and admiration her family and friends held for her, which en-abled her to recognize anorexia as a purveyor of lies rather than truths. Tracy's observations about anorexia's lies and deceptions provided the League with one of its first important documents concerning the un-doing of the influence of anorexia and has been foundational to the preparation of many more. She read to me what she had observed of anorexia during the preceding week.

- Anorexia blocks out positive messages which I receive and re-places them with negative thoughts that I believe in.
- Anorexia has me punish myself in any possible way, as I am worthless.
- Anorexia has made me think of food as an enemy rather than a natural part of life and something that is essential for daily living.
- Anorexia has become my "best friend" ...
- Anorexia distorts my mind and has made me see a completely different view of my body, seeing myself as fat rather than the thin person I really am.
- Anorexia makes me want to exercise frantically and burn off calories and punish my body instead of respecting and caring for it.

- Anorexia has turned me from my parents, causing me to argue with them for no reason.
- Anorexia has shut me off from the reality of living and caused me to develop an "anorexic" way of living and thinking.

Needless to say, I was delighted and relieved by Tracy's eleventh-hour about-face. I feared, however, that her reprieve would only be temporary and that anorexia would find a way of halting her momentum and reversing its direction if something was not done to help Tracy to continue to remain connected to this anti-anorexic version of herself. I was eager to explore with her what had contributed to this dramatic anti-anorexic turn of events. I also hoped to help her elaborate on new knowledges and understandings that would assist her in moving forward with her life. We decided to tape-record the conversation so that what we learned might be shared with others. Tracy immediately saw the sense in this as she had found listening to the tape of Lee-Ann and her family immensely important and was willing to assist others in a similar fashion. Following is an excerpted transcript of this tape recording.

David: Well, Tracy, we were talking before we began the taping and you said one of the major values in listening to and hearing about Lee-Ann was that, perhaps for the very first time in your anorexic career, you became aware that you had a choice.

Tracy: (with some certainty) Yeah, that's true!

David: Prior to this realization, did you feel compelled, under obligation to, or driven by anorexia?

Tracy: I just felt as though it was running my life. I had no control over anything. I didn't even have a choice to live or die. It was just so convincing that I should not eat. In fact, it told me food was bad for me.

David: Did it tell you life was bad for you?

Tracy: Yeah!

David: Great friend, anorexia. Look, how did you come to the awareness that you did have personal choice? That you could bring to bear your own desires in this matter rather than only respond to the compulsion?

Tracy: Well, I realized that it was the others who loved and cared about me against this one person—anorexia!

David: Who do you think cared about you and for you and loved you?

Tracy: I was thinking you, obviously mum and dad, Glen [her boy friend], and friends. And I have got work to think of. I have made a good start there.

When asked about how she was able to break the chains of anorexia's compulsion and experience a sense of choice, Tracy alludes to the significance of my letter and the manner in which it evoked a community of people who loved and cared about her. The fact that a/b so often finds ways of detaching women from their communities of concern speaks to the threat these communities pose to a/b's rule.

David: When you summed up all that care, concern, and love, what effect did that have on the voice of anorexia?

Tracy: *(with a newfound authority)* I just realized it was ten voices against one. And then I heard the real truth. And you know, I had listened to anorexia's messages before and I ended up in hospital for doing so. I wondered what would happen if I listened to others this time.

David: Might you end up with a life of your own? *(laughter all around)* Have you got any suggestions you might make to me and families I might meet in the future about such situations? Could this day have come sooner?

Tracy: *(pausing thoughtfully before responding)* I think it depends a great deal on if you are willing to *face* anorexia. I felt writing everything down was really helpful—its words and messages to me, how I felt in situations, noticing how happy other people were without it. I am always comparing myself against others, and while anorexia often uses this against me, in this instance I was able to notice how much energy loss I have.

David: How was it possible in the face of this crisis, in the face of your very murderer, in fact, to gain such strength? Was it because you had recourse to the combined care of others?

Tracy: Yeah, I saw the truth against the lies of anorexia.

David: Do you now feel angry at anorexia for having tricked you and taken over your mind?

Tracy: *(emphatically)* Yes, I do!

David: Do you feel entitled to express that anger or are you still a bit afraid of anorexia?

Tracy: I am still a bit afraid. I am afraid of controlling my eating once I start and of looking fat. And panicking about what people might think about me.

Now that Tracy had seen through anorexia's lie, I was interested in making space for her to experience anger and outrage at anorexia. Many League members have recounted how significant a role their outrage and indignation at a/b has played in their repudiation of it (see Chapter 11). For many of these women, allowing themselves to experience the full measure of their rage was an achievement in and of itself because of the extent to which they had taken to heart the gendered notion that "good" girls and women should be "nice." In response to my query about whether she was afraid to express her anger at anorexia (and here I was thinking more about the possible backlash this anger could provoke), Tracy guided me away from the fear of anorexia and back to the anorexic fears themselves.

David: Do you think if you had a stronger opinion of yourself, you wouldn't be so vulnerable to other people's opinions?

Tracy: I have got no confidence in myself. I feel I am worthless. And also anorexia makes me believe that others think that, too. When I was in the hospital last time, I thought the choice of death was a good one. Getting away from all future problems. And the thoughts that no one cared for me.

David: What was different about this time that permitted you to exercise your own choice rather than merely follow anorexia's plans for you and entice you into your self-execution? Did the letter I sent help in any way? I wondered what you thought of it.

Tracy: I just kept reading and thinking about it all the time. How you wrote that all the others were wrong and that anorexia was the only "truth"!

David: How did reading that letter assist you to identify anorexia's lies and the others' "truth"?

Tracy: I tried to think how all those people that cared about me would think if I was to be dominated by anorexia again. I thought they might not continue to care about me if I went back into the hospital. I knew that if I wanted them to continue to care, I should show strength.

David: Were you reciprocating their care by making your choice against anorexia? You were able to get some sense of people's care and you expressed that caring in an anti-anorexic way? (*Tracy nods her head "yes."*)

David: Where do you think you are going to go from here? I suspect up ahead will be the anorexic allegations that you are going to get fat and all that sort of stuff. Do you feel you can extend this anti-anorexic course you are now on?

Tracy: Yes.

David: What will you do?

Tracy: (*pondering my questions for a moment*) Listen to others, like my workmates who have told me I am too thin and that I could do with another __ pounds. At first I thought, "No, I can't! I love being thin!" but now I can see in the mirror that I have bones sticking out that I should cover with a bit of flesh. I also realized that with another __ pounds, I'm not going to look fat. I would feel healthier.

David: What would have happened in your old anorexic days?

Tracy: I would have just thought it was all lies. But I have also started listening to myself.

David: What are you telling yourself now? And is it any different from your hospital experience?

Tracy: Oh, yes, I wasn't eating in the hospital. I was being tube-fed. It was all anorexia, anorexia, anorexia. They didn't want to know *me*, nor to make me realize there was my life. You have been so patient learning about me. You have made me realize there is a *me!*

David: That's great to hear! Have we established a you inside of you, put a person in your you, in a sense? And when it came to the showdown last weekend, were you able to make your choice?

Tracy: I have been living my life for anorexia for $3^1/_2$ years now. It is time I should make my own life.

David: Are you an advocate for your own life now? Do you feel your life is opening up again?

Tracy: (*laughing with some delight*) Yeah!

Chapter 10

I WANNA BE GOOD

A CONVERSATION WITH MARGARET

M argaret was a young adult who sought out therapy with me (RM) to address a number of problems, the most urgent of which was anorexia. During one of our first meetings, Margaret poignantly portrayed her predicament through a sandtray scene she spontaneously constructed. At the center of the sandtray she had placed some food. She then placed a circle of soldiers around the food, guns pointing outward at a woman and child who were being prevented from getting the food. This graphic illustration of anorexia as something forcefully keeping her from something she wanted (as opposed to protecting her from something she didn't want) momentarily enabled her to see anorexia more clearly and resist it. Over the next couple of days she was able to eat. However, unbeknownst to me, the voice of anorexia soon returned with a vengeance, convincing her once again that "self-control" (starvation) was the only path she could afford to take. The voice of anorexia warned her that her meetings with me threatened to undermine her self-discipline and clarity of purpose and that for her own good she should never set foot in my office again.

A couple of days after that meeting, Margaret telephoned to see if we could meet sooner than our scheduled appointment. My own anti-anorexic excitement (and wishful thinking) had me assuming that Margaret was pressing for an earlier meeting in order to build upon the anti-anorexic momentum from the previous meeting. But I subsequently learned that anorexia had its own agenda for this meeting. Margaret later described to me the conflict she felt about coming to the meeting, feeling simultaneously pulled toward anorexia and anti-anorexia.

> On the one hand, I did find the way in which you spoke to me unfamiliar and frightening and I wanted to figure it out. I felt a lot of respect from you and that surprised and intrigued me. I wanted to know if you were tricking me or trying to trap me or what, and that did influence my decision to at least see what this was about. I also think anorexia itself had a large part in my going to see you too. Anorexia wanted to fight you and to show you how horrid I truly am, to show me that you really agreed with it, and to expose your "false respect." I think anorexia would have taken me there to see you if only to further convince me that I didn't deserve anything, that I was worthless. Anorexia failed.

When we met for the session, I quickly realized that anorexia had engendered in Margaret an urgent desire not to build upon what she had begun during our last meeting but rather to tear it down. The part of Margaret still loyal to anorexia wanted to convince me that the practices of anorexia she had engaged with were both necessary and righteous. Immediately upon entering my office, Margaret went over to sandtray and quickly created another scene. This one was very similar to the previous one, but with one important difference: Standing shoulder to shoulder with the soldiers was a girl whom Margaret said represented herself. She had rejoined the ranks of anorexia.

Rick: I noticed that this sandtray is a little different than the other one. There is a girl in the circle of soldiers.

Margaret: Yes. That's me. I don't want them [the woman and baby] to have their food.

Rick: Why is that? Why don't you want them to feel entitled to eat?

Margaret: Because I'm not. It's not good to eat.

Rick: Tell me more. Why do you think it's not good to eat?

Margaret: Because I will get way overweight. I *am* overweight.

Rick: You think you are overweight? (*Margaret nods.*) What makes you think your body is overweight? What are you comparing this body to that leads you to believe this? What is your standard, a skeleton? Women on the cover of *Cosmopolitan* and *Vogue*?

Margaret: How I used to look.

Rick: Do you mean the time when your heart stopped and you had to be shocked back to life? [Margaret's heart had failed when she was 17 due to starvation from anorexia. Fortunately this had happened while she was in the hospital and her life was saved.]

Margaret: Before that.

Rick: Around that time?

Margaret: Yeah.

Rick: You think that's a good weight? That's a weight that nearly killed you. In fact, my understanding was that you would have died if not for the intervention of doctors.

Margaret: It was still overweight.

Rick: According to who or what?

Margaret: Me.

Margaret's responses indicated that her thoughts and perceptions were substantially dominated by anorexia, though she could not yet recognize anorexia's influence. At this point, I had already recognized that I needed to mentally "roll up my sleeves" and gather all of my wits in order to find a way of bringing anorexia into focus for Margaret, so that its effects could be evaluated and its claims to "truth" could be questioned. I began by mirroring Margaret's manner of speaking about herself as one with anorexia (e.g., "Why do *you* think it's not good to eat?") while moving toward a more externalized language. I believed Margaret might have felt misunderstood, confused, or possibly manipulated if I had immediately questioned her with anti-anorexic language (e.g., "How has anorexia convinced you that it is not good to eat?") that presumed a distinction between herself and anorexia that she did not yet see. I had no reason to assume that such a distinction would be meaningful to her as I had not yet introduced an anti-anorexic language by reading from the archive, nor had Margaret articulated aspects of her experience that could expose anorexia's lies. But by not using externalizing language at the outset, I also ran the risk of anorexia translating the meaning of my words into pro-anorexic sentiments. This turned out to be the case. Margaret later reflected: "I vividly remember that anorexia had me hearing you so different than the way I hear you now. It wanted me to believe you were in agreement with it. When you asked me if I saw my body as overweight, it made me hear you as agreeing that I was overweight. I was at one with anorexia. When anorexia is inside it makes me hear just about everything through its ears. It takes your words and has me hear them as against me rather than as against anorexia and for me . . . . Anorexia robbed so much of my voice in the beginning. The voice you heard was not mine."

Although I felt it was important to be explicit about my anti-anorexic position, without Margaret's taking a stand herself against anorexia, my unilateral cries of protest against her incarceration and impending murder would have accomplished about as much as banging my head against a stone wall. I decided that the best way to help Margaret recognize anorexia's monumental betrayal was to shift my language and speak about anorexia as something external to her, creating an anti-anorexic platform from which she could begin to repudiate anorexia without simultaneously attacking herself. Additionally, this linguistic separation between anorexia and Margaret (if she took it up herself) would give me more latitude in expressing my moral outrage at anorexia without making Margaret feel attacked. This would also make it more difficult for anorexia to convince Margaret that I was in accord with it.

Rick: What is making you believe in a weight that is so low and represents so much self-deprivation, torture, punishment, and starvation that your heart actually stopped . . . you were literally being starved to death . . . I have to wonder what it is that is trying to convince you . . .?

Margaret: It didn't stop, it just went really fast.

Rick: Well, it wasn't beating in a way that could sustain life and that was because of malnutrition.

Margaret: I think it was because something was wrong with the heart.

Rick: Didn't the doctors and nurses tell you it was because of not eating and weren't you told that in order to save your life you had to eat?

Margaret: Because of not eating they put tubes down me.

Rick: Precisely. Who is telling you otherwise? Is the voice of anorexia telling you that it really wasn't the not eating that caused that—that maybe the heart just had a problem?

Margaret: I think it had a problem.

Rick: Did the doctors say it was from anorexia?

Margaret: The doctors said it was from not eating.

Rick: But wasn't it the anorexia that was starving you? That's what anorexia does, it starves people. I know that anorexia tells you it's your friend, but if you look at what has happened you will see that anorexia very nearly killed you. If it wasn't for the doctors stepping in it would have killed you. Is anorexia telling you that your body should be the body of a dead person, one incapable of sustaining life?

Margaret: It just tells me to lose some weight.

Rick: So many people have told me, Margaret, that if they obey anorexia and they lose some weight, anorexia will set a lower weight for them, and when they get to that weight, it sets a lower weight, and that it is never good enough. Even when you were dying, did anorexia tell you that . . .

Margaret: I still needed to lose weight.

Rick: Right.

Margaret: But I did need to lose weight!

Rick: But how did you know that you did?

Margaret: Because I felt horrid.

I evoked the perspective of Margaret's doctors and members of the League to contradict anorexia's lies and offer an alternative perspective to that of anorexia. Had I expected this alone to get Margaret to see through anorexia's trick I might have begun to feel exasperated at this point. Fortunately I had no such expectation. Insiders have told me that because anorexia relentlessly bombarded them with its perspective, it was helpful to be exposed to other perspectives even if they were unable to embrace them at that time. Anorexia's "truth" can become so absolute that just knowing other perspectives exist can preserve hope that there is a way out. Margaret later commented, "I did experience a momentary separation from anorexia when you evoked the perspective of my doctors and the League members, but it frightened me. It wasn't enough for me to grab on to at the time."

Margaret had begun to tentatively talk about anorexia as an external influence (e.g. "*It* just tells me to lose some weight") and I felt encouraged by this. I wanted to continue to voice my unequivocal opposition to anorexia so that Margaret would know she could trust me as an ally when she finally turned against anorexia. I also wanted to encourage her to continue to express to me those ideas that kept her chained to anorexic practices so that they could be critiqued on the basis of her own experience. I regarded Margaret's willingness to share anorexia's voice with me to be, in itself, an act of anti-anorexic resistance, because it allowed this voice to be contested. Margaret, in retrospect, agreed: "For me, speaking about anorexia's voice was a way out. I think if anorexia was aware of that at the time it would have fought harder to stop me from sharing what it was saying to me. I hope for people who may be reading this who are struggling with anorexia that it doesn't get an education and silence folks from speaking about anorexia's voice. If it tries to silence you, ask yourself, 'If anorexia is telling me the truth, why does it feel so threatened by others knowing what it is saying to me?'"

Rick: Can I ask you, Margaret, how did anorexia make you feel horrid and make you feel overweight when you weren't? (*There is a long pause and then a pained expression comes over Margaret's face.*) Margaret, are you hearing a voice in your head telling you that you are horrid, that you are overweight, that you need to lose weight? (*Margaret nods.*) I guess what I'm inviting you to do is to become just a little bit questioning of those thoughts. Because I think those thoughts are coming from the voice of anorexia and that voice of anorexia is a voice that wants to extinguish your voice and your life and it shouldn't be trusted. So I would ask you to ask yourself how will you know what is a good weight for you and how will you know what is healthy for you?

Margaret: What feels good.
Rick: Okay, that's a start, what feels good.
Margaret: It felt better.

Margaret identified an aspect of her experience—"what feels good"—as a potential guide to discern what is in her own best interests. However, it was a guide that, because of the subjectivity involved, could be easily co-opted by anorexia. The fact that anorexia can starve a person to death while convincing her it is making her better and stronger is a testimony of the power of anorexic rhetoric to cut a person off from her own embodied feelings and replace these feelings with a disembodied account of what the body is feeling. When Margaret said that starvation "felt better," I suspected anorexia was doing precisely that.

Rick: Did it feel better because it *felt* better or did it feel better because anorexia was praising you, saying, "Good job, you're looking better, you're on the path, just a little bit more"? Was it the voice of anorexia praising you that made you feel better or was it actually how your body felt? Because people who are being starved to death usually start to experience muscle cramps, weakness, they can't concentrate, their stomachs hurt, they can't warm up. . . . Did your body experience those things? (*Margaret nods.*)
   Does it feel good to have your muscles cramping up? Does it feel good to be so weak you can hardly walk? Does it feel good to be so weak that you can't think?
Margaret: But if I lost more weight I would feel better.
Rick: That's what anorexia tells you? (*Margaret nods.*)

As the conversation progressed, the intricate layering of anorexia's lies became more transparent. Once the fraudulence of anorexia's claim that Margaret "feels fine" was exposed, anorexia accedes this fact but then attributed her feeling unwell to excessive weight and eating rather than starvation, excessive exercise, vomiting, and so on. A/b's deceptions can be metaphorically described as spiderwebs of clever rhetoric. If the person breaks through one strand of the web, another adjacent strand binds her. Meanings are spun from a very small and select subset of "facts" and their credibility relies upon the person's overlooking all the other "facts" that stand in contradiction to them. A/b's "logic" appears logical only when one's field of vision is telescopically narrowed. Part of what I was trying to do was invite Margaret to pay attention to the aspects of her experience that anorexia blinded her to.

Rick: Okay, so I'm asking you to be critical of that, to be skeptical of that. What was your experience, Margaret, as you began to lose more and more and more weight? Did your body feel better and better or did your body feel worse and worse? And I'd ask you to think about not what the voice of anorexia was saying you felt but what your body was saying. Did your body feel stronger, healthier, more alive, more vigorous as you lost more and more weight or did it feel more tired, sore, weak, and painful?

Margaret: For a while it felt better.

Rick: When did it stop feeling better and start feeling worse?

Margaret: Around the weight of ——.

Rick: When you reached that weight what did you begin to experience?

Margaret: I became really tired. And I became sick.

Rick: And sick. Anything else? Were you having difficulties concentrating?

Margaret: I got headaches. And I felt dizzy.

Rick: Were you experiencing muscle cramping?

Margaret: My stomach was burning.

Rick: And did anorexia tell you that this would be a stage you would pass through as you lost weight?

Margaret: And that I would feel better.

Rick: And did you believe it? (*Margaret nods.*) What effect did that have?

Margaret: I ate less.

Rick: And as you ate less, did your body begin to feel better as anorexia said it would? (*pause*) Did your strength return? Did your headaches go away? Could you move around better? Did your stomach stop burning?

Margaret: It never stopped burning. I spent less time in my body and withdrew into myself more. Though I can't say I was really with myself. I just wasn't there, if you know what I mean?

Rick: Why was that, do you think?

Margaret: It felt like a reward.

Rick: It felt like a reward to go away?

Margaret: To go. That I wouldn't be such a failure.

Rick: Did you feel like you were a failure when you were in your body?

Margaret: I wasn't good enough.

Rick: Anorexia made you feel like you weren't good enough?

Margaret: I *wasn't* good enough. I couldn't always do what anorexia required of me.

Rick: No one is ever good enough for anorexia. It's always cracking the whip. "Feeling good enough" and anorexia don't go together. Anorexia can drive people to their death only if it succeeds in convincing them that they are not good enough and that anorexia's going to make them good enough. Is it possible that you refused to comply fully with anorexia and, for that, anorexia made you feel like a failure?

Margaret: But when I'm eating I'm not as worthy. You don't get it.

Later upon reading the transcript of the previous conversation, Margaret commented: "Your understanding here of how horrid I felt and how much anorexia was driving me, cracking the whip, and your saying that anorexia and feeling good enough don't go together established you as far more trustworthy than anorexia. You won my trust here and anorexia lost my blind trust in it. But the mere mention of the idea that I was somehow refusing to comply really frightened me. If I hadn't broken from anorexia, it would have thrashed me to the end with that idea. I now think that the 'anorexia answer' you got had much more to do with convincing myself and anorexia that I hadn't fought it, so that it wouldn't punish me later."

Margaret's comments point to the sensitivity that is required in this work and to the importance of staying close to the person's experience. When I asked Margaret if her "not being good enough for anorexia" constituted a refusal to comply with it, I presumed far more separation from anorexia than she was actually experiencing. Thus, Margaret had to retreat to a statement of loyalty to anorexia in order to avoid a "thrashing" for admitting to an anti-anorexic rebellion. Because Margaret had not identified explicit acts of anti-anorexic rebellion for me to explore further with her, I returned to my attempts to help Margaret justify and extend what I perceived as her embryonic distrust of anorexia.

Rick: I understand you felt that way, but I refuse to see it that way. I just believe that no person should be made to feel worthless and then have to endure aching deprivations and cruel tortures in order to establish their worth. In what way does anorexia render you worthy? Why would starving yourself to death be a measure of your worth? Why would anorexia reduce you to . . .

Margaret: You're turning things on its head.

Rick: That is the only way that I can see it. That anorexia wants you to take pride in your own execution. Why would it want you to take pride in the very things that are destroying you, have you base your pride in things that are erasing you as person? I know that I'm presenting a point of view that is really different than the one that you're used to. All I ask is for you to ask yourself if it fits your experience. Does talking about anorexia in this way ring any bells of recognition for you?

Margaret: It's familiar.

Rick: Would you like me to read something that someone that I was working with wrote about anorexia that might be familiar?

Margaret: No.

Rick: You don't want to hear it? Why is that?

Margaret: (*very quietly*) It will make it harder.

Rick: How will it make it harder? Will my reading this cause anorexia to become even more demanding of you? Will it punish you for hearing it?

Margaret: It will punish me.

Rick: Is anorexia threatening you right now? Is it threatening to punish you if you agree to hear it?

Margaret: It feels that way. (*after a brief pause*) It's rewarding me.

Rick: You said, "it feels that way." Did anorexia's voice then say, "No, I'm rewarding you"?

Margaret: Yeah.

Rick: Which way is right side up and which way is upside down? You said, "Don't read it to me because anorexia's going to make it harder." You didn't say, "Don't read it to me because anorexia's going to give me a reward." That's an important difference, isn't it? You didn't sound eager for anorexia's so-called reward. Would anorexia reward you by screaming at you that you can't eat, that you're bad and unworthy and the only way to become worthy is to deny yourself and your body its basic needs? Of course it's not going to say it that way—it might tell you that your body doesn't need food, that you could live on air if you are good enough.

Margaret: Water.

Rick: Water. Does it say that really good people can just live on water? Have you ever met a person who can just live on water?

Margaret: No.

Rick: It's lying to you if it tells you that. Not even a plant, not even a fly, could just live on water. Can I ask you a question, Margaret? (*Margaret nods.*) If anorexia is telling you the truth, why would it want to keep it from me, or keep you from the writing I was going to share with you? Why does it want to keep you away from other points of view?

Margaret: It tells me their point of view will hurt me.

Rick: Do you think it is protecting you or protecting itself? Do you think you should have the right to decide what's best for you or do you think anorexia should decide? I'd just ask you to think about what's happened to your body when you've taken its advice and accepted its standards of worth. If, as a child, you didn't have people to drag you to the hospital you would have died. I know I'm doing a lot of talking against anorexia now, and I know this might be inviting anorexia to do a lot of talking against me. And maybe you're feeling a bit defensive of anorexia. I know anorexia offers people a lot, makes them a lot of promises. You should know right now that anorexia and I are not friends. I hate anorexia. I know a lot of people anorexia has tried to murder while passing itself off as a lover and friend.

Margaret: It says it's my friend.

Rick: Do you think, Margaret, that based on what you know of anorexia—not what it tells you it's doing but what it's actually done to you . . .

Margaret: It's helped me too.

Rick: Has it? How has it helped you?

Margaret: (*long pause*) It helped sometimes with stuff that I didn't want to do.

Rick: Do you mind if I ask you what it helped you out with that you didn't want to do? Stuff that you didn't want to do but felt that you had to?

Margaret: Yeah.

Rick: Like what? Do you mind if I ask?

Margaret: Sometimes with stuff that my dad wanted of me. My dad wanted me to eat some stuff.

Rick: Would your dad have hurt you if you had refused to eat it?

Margaret: I still ate it. But I didn't want to. Anorexia made me not want to eat it.

Rick: Why was it important that you did not want to eat it?

Margaret: My dad wanted me not only to eat it but to want to eat it. Wanting to eat it would have meant that I was like him, that I believed the things he was doing were okay. I didn't want to become like him.

Margaret's father subscribed to a pseudoreligious doctrine that justified his acting in ways that Margaret felt very opposed to, including the harming of children physically and sexually. In fact, Margaret herself had been physically and sexually abused as a result of these doctrines and practices. Margaret was denied food and water for several days in order to induce an intense hunger that her father hoped would destroy her inhibition against eating and drinking substances specified by the doctrine (substances that I can safely say would have revolted anybody). Wanting to eat the items selected by her father would have symbolized Margaret's acceptance of these ways of being and been an endorsement of her own abuse. Anorexia appealed to Margaret's desire to hold on to her identity as "good" by giving her the means to embrace her hunger and not succumb to her appetite.

Although the particularities of Margaret's situation were unusual, to say the least, a/b's knack for appealing to and then co-opting the values of girls or young women is extremely common, if not ubiquitous. Margaret believes this next portion of our conversation contributed significantly to her turning against anorexia: "Anorexia convinced me that, without it, I would have wanted to do things I didn't want to do. Anorexia took credit for the values I had all along and made me believe that without anorexia I wouldn't have been able to hold on to them, and that simply is not true." It is very common for a/b to help a person achieve something (e.g., survival, admiration) at a very high and hidden cost by convincing her that such an achievement would have been otherwise impossible. It is also common for a/b to take credit for achievements that it had nothing to do with and perhaps made more difficult (e.g., good grades).

Rick: Did you think without anorexia's help you would have wanted to eat that stuff ?

Margaret: I was hungry. You're talking about my best friend.

Rick: I think this is a friend who will kill you if given half a chance. Your desire to not eat that stuff and to not be like your dad must have preexisted anorexia, or why would you have called upon anorexia to help you resist in the first place?

Margaret: But I would have wanted to eat it. I wanna be good.

Rick: Okay. It sounds like you experienced a real dilemma. On the one hand, you wanted your dad to see you as good, to be accepted, to be protected, and the only way to get that was to eat and drink what he wanted you to. And you were also very hungry. On the other hand, you wanted to be true to your own sense of right and wrong, your own values, and you believed that required you to not want to eat and drink it. It sounds like eating and drinking those things was something that you never wanted to do, anorexia or not, but was something that you had to do if you were going to please your dad, to feel safe, to be approved of. If you had other ways of getting those things you wanted, wouldn't you have chosen that? If you could have pleased your dad by drawing a nice picture, would you have rather done that? Or doing a somersault ?

Margaret: A cartwheel.

Rick: A cartwheel. From what you've told me today I gather that you didn't want to eat that stuff because eating it would have been viewed as accepting your father's ideas and ways of acting that you knew were bad and hurtful. Is it possible that anorexia made you forget your real purpose in refusing to want to eat it? Did anorexia make food and eating into the bad and hurtful thing rather than those things your dad and his friends were doing? Do you really think that without anorexia's help you would have become the kind of person who thought it was good to hurt other people? It seems to me you already were the kind of person who would never want to hurt others. Could the fact that in your desperation to not *want* to eat it you appealed to anorexia for help be evidence of the strength of your values? I think anorexia is taking credit for something it doesn't deserve credit for. Quite the contrary, it betrayed you by trying to get you to forsake the very values you turned to anorexia to help you uphold. Is it okay if I just talk a little more before we stop? Could you listen or would anorexia punish you too much if you listened?

Margaret: I'm willing to listen.

Before the "spell" of anorexia was broken, my inclination was to pose questions without expecting or even making space for Margaret to answer. Although this practice may appear to the outside reader as brow-beating, rude, or disrespectful, the person to whom these questions are being addressed usually finds this a relief. I was assuming at this point that the power of anorexia's voice would make it too frightening for Margaret to openly express outrage at anorexia, thereby inviting its retribution. These questions were not, however, intended as merely rhetorical. I hoped that the questions I asked would ignite the spark of an anti-anorexic rebellion that would eventually supplant the anorexic monologue with internal dialogue and debate. This initial resistance to and questioning of anorexia may need to remain hidden until the person feels that her anti-anorexia has enough strength and support to withstand anorexia's counterattacks.

Margaret later made the following comments about the previous portion of the conversation: "Anorexia's first and last attempts to get me to follow it always involved trying to get me to see it as a friend. It claims it is a friend and even emphasizes the obligations friends have to each other, though it is not a friend but evil. This part of the interview was critical to my separating from anorexia. It shows just how despicable anorexia is that it took credit for what I achieved. It confused me so much about what I wanted that it made think anorexia was what I wanted when what I really wanted was to be good and accepted and protected by my dad, and to continue to know that it's not okay to hurt and disrespect others or to be hurt or disrespected oneself. That's way different than wanting anorexia."

Rick: Did anorexia give you some hope for the future, something that you felt you could control and be good at?
Margaret: I can be good at it.
Rick: But I think there are a lot of things you . . .
Margaret: There is not another thing I could be good at. There's nothing.
Rick: Anorexia wants you to believe that the only thing you could be good at is starving yourself?
Margaret: But I'm not good at anything.
Rick: Margaret, I'm sure that either you are or you can be. Can you do cartwheels?
Margaret: (laughs) Yeah.
Rick: If you feel that you aren't good at anything, is that something that we could talk about? I could either try and help you overcome that belief because it's not true, or help you become good at things that really

are meaningful to you. If you could choose to become good at something meaningful to you, why would you choose to become good at your own self-execution? Why would you want to become good at starvation? After you were dead, no one is going to say, "Boy, she did a great job at starving. We are going to vote her into the starvation hall of fame and speak of her to our children and grandchildren." If you wanted to be good at something, wouldn't you want to be good at something else, something that contributed to your own life and the lives of other people? You can. And if you think you can't we can talk about that—about why you think that you can't and how you got the idea that you can't. But you don't have to accept this idea that the only thing you can be good at is your own demise, your own death, denying yourself food to the point of death.

I had gained an understanding of how anorexia insinuated itself into Margaret's life at a time when she was desperate to hold on to a sense of herself as morally "good." But anorexia, over the years, had also given Margaret something that she could feel good at and made her believe that that was all she could be good at. This idea also needed to be critiqued. By expressing my genuine conviction that there were other things she was or could be good at, I hoped Margaret would begin to question anorexia's assertion that without it she would be a failure. I wanted to let Margaret know that I would be there to help her identify her own skills and abilities and to develop them further if she wished so that she could entertain some hopeful possibilities associated with a life apart from anorexia. Margaret had never before considered that she might have some skills and abilities that would allow her to achieve things that were more meaningful and less destructive. She commented: "Until you said this, it never occurred to me that I could talk about this with you and that I didn't have to accept the idea that anorexia was the only thing I could be good at. These ideas were foreign. This opened up some possibilities inside my own thinking that just weren't there before."

Rick: What kind of achievement is that [her demise]? It is difficult.
Margaret: Then it must be good.
Rick: It must be good if it's difficult? A lot of things are difficult. Sleeping on a bed of nails is difficult but I don't see much purpose in pursuing that as an achievement. Breaking a bottle over my head would be difficult. I'd have to put up with a lot of pain and injury. Why would I want to?
Margaret: But then you get treated badly if you are fat.
Rick: Unfortunately, there is some truth to that. Fat people get treated badly in this society, get oppressed.

Margaret: Skinny girls get everything.

Rick: Well, no ... they don't. (*I was thinking to myself about many "skinny" women I knew who had suffered their share of indignities, and for whom happiness and self-appreciation were not forgone conclusions.*)

Margaret: Yeah, they do. They're sure shown that way.

Rick: Well, they do get certain privileges. Anorexia might appeal to that, try and seduce you with that, but it is going to try and get you to go way beyond that. It did get you to go way beyond that. But if anorexia is telling you that you have to be thin to be considered beautiful, to be happy or to be successful, it's not true. If you look around you will see women who are not paper-thin who have good jobs, who have good partners, who are happy. It is often the skinny women who are constantly dieting and working out who are not so happy. If you have a concern that you are not going to be happy or achieve this or that, we can talk about it, just like if you have a concern that you can't do anything well. Anorexia preys upon those kinds of fears and concerns and seduces people with the promise of delivering something while at the same time it creates and supports the fear that they won't get it without anorexia's help. I want to read you something, a part of someone's diary.

Margaret: Do you have her permission? I wouldn't want you to read from someone's journal if they didn't say it was okay.

Rick: Right. I received her permission through my colleague David. (*I read from the anti-anorexic diary.*) I could read you fifty things like this that people have written about their experience. Did any of that fit for you? Could you relate to any of that?

Margaret: Yeah.

Rick: Do you think you may have stumbled into a similar kind of trap? Did anorexia make promises and leave out the details of the suffering? (*Margaret cries quietly. I pause before continuing.*) Is it a bit like signing a contract with someone who says, "I agree to deliver this but you will have to do whatever I ask of you but I won't tell you what that is. Please sign here."? And then you sign and find that enormous things are being asked of you, demanded from you, and all the while none of the promises are being delivered. It keeps on telling you, "Just wait, be patient, just do a little more of this, a little more of that and pretty soon I'll pay up." And *you* end up doing all the paying, and the ultimate price, of course, would be your life. Would anorexia then say, if it could speak to the dead, "Well I would have paid up but you died first. I'm sorry, I guess you just weren't good enough to live on water"? It's pretty evil, isn't it? You can have a good life, but anorexia isn't the way. If you trust anorexia you will be badly disappointed. I never met a satisfied customer. (*pause*) You're kind of crying a bit and ...

Margaret: I'm sorry.

Rick: No, no, that's fine, you don't have to apologize for it. My guess is it's like finding out that the person you thought was your best friend wasn't who you thought she was and there is a certain amount of loss about that. I'm sorry that has happened to you. You've experienced more than your share of people using you or hurting you in the name of love or caring.

Margaret: When I hear it [anorexia] I know that it's not right.

Rick: That's really great. Do you think this is perhaps the first step in getting free from anorexia, hearing that voice in your head and stepping back from that voice and saying, "Hmm, is this the voice of anorexia? Do I really want to trust that voice? Is that voice really looking after me or is it seducing me into something I don't really want?"

Margaret: It doesn't want me to listen to my own voice.

Rick: Would you rather be listening to your own voice or the voice of anorexia? Which do you think is more trustworthy?

Margaret: My voice.

Rick: It's going to fight to keep you from your own voice. It can be hard to get some distance from anorexia's voice and be able to recognize it as distinct. Rachel [a member of our local anti-anorexia and bulimia league] has been talking about how she's finding ways of seeing through it. You might want to talk with her about this. We need to stop for now. Would you be open to receiving some support from other people? Because when you leave I think anorexia is going to try and tear you down. Be prepared for that. As you begin to consider the possibility that you could have a good life without anorexia's help, and to trust in your own values and abilities, it may try and convince you that you are dreaming, that you are worthless and present itself as the only hope for you.

Margaret: Uh huh.

Rick: So you might need some support to help you know that that is not true. If anorexia begins to argue with you, would you want to be able to call upon other people for some support? Do you think it might help to hear what some voices other than anorexia's have to say about it?

Margaret: They won't want to.

Rick: If they wanted to, would you be open to it? Could we ask them? It is up to them. No one would make them, it would be totally voluntary and they'd have no reason to say yes if they didn't want to.

Margaret: I'd like to.

Rick: Okay.

Margaret: (crying out) No!

Rick: Is anorexia telling you that nobody would want to, that the only friend you have is it? Should we just ask and see if there are any people that would be more than happy to volunteer?

Margaret: It feels like you're asking me if I want to jump off a bridge! I'm afraid they will say no.

Rick: In any case, I'm always here. Do you think anorexia might be discouraging you from asking for support? Would you be willing to take this leap of faith and see what happens?

Margaret: Okay.

Following this meeting, several League members and other friends readily and eagerly offered Margaret their support, which was both surprising and deeply moving to her. Over the next several weeks this support took many forms. One League member offered to talk with her when she was struggling with her fears about embarking upon an anti-anorexic path. One friend encouraged her to consider taking a class in something she was interested in and enjoyed. Another friend made herself available to Margaret to just have fun together. Several League members joined Margaret in questioning where certain ideas lead. League members let Margaret know that by joining with her in these ways they experienced a strengthening and nurturing of their own anti-anorexic resolve and practice.

Part Three

RECLAIMING ONE'S
LIFE FROM ANOREXIA/BULIMIA

Chapter 11

UNMASKING AND DEFYING ANOREXIA/BULIMIA

B reaking the spell of a/b does not bring the person's struggle to free her life from a/b to a victorious conclusion but rather allows the person to initiate this struggle in earnest. The struggle *commences* when the person suspects for the first time that she may be in prison.

Similarly, a person can be said to be anti-a/b not just when she has become single-mindedly opposed to a/b, but when she has recognized that she is of two minds about it—one mind that has bought into a/b's promises and another that has begun to question and doubt those promises. Simply questioning a/b is a daring anti-a/b act, given a/b's insistence on unquestioning trust and devotion.

Taking one's life back from a/b often requires journeying along a winding road over shifting ground. For someone who has had a love affair with a/b, the progression from commitment to a/b to repudiation of it may be a very back and forth process. A/b's strategies provoke fear of living without it, doubts about one's worthiness, and pessimism about one's capacity to overcome it. Chloe, an 19-year-old, expressed her fear of turning her back on anorexia in this way:

> I was thinking about this recently (anorexia's allegation that "it is the provider of vital protection against my lacking self ") and I think it is one of the main reasons why I have remained under anorexia's grip for so long. . . .
>
> For me, anorexia is like a wall which I can hide behind. Anorexia may well be a prison wall but walls (even prison ones) serve their

purpose. For while walls keep one locked inside, a prisoner cordoned off from the pleasures of the world beyond the prison walls, they also keep things out. It feels safe behind a wall . . . you can hide behind a wall. No one need see you as you really are behind a wall. And while you miss out on the beauty and pleasure that lies beyond the wall, you feel secure behind the wall . . . you know the routine of the prison well, it is familiar. The world beyond the wall is unknown to you and somewhat threatening.

Fearing what lies ahead, the person may vacillate between a/b and anti-a/b. The oscillations can be dramatic and rapid, alternating daily or even hourly, and are greatly affected by the person's life circumstances, many of which may explicitly or implicitly support a/b (such as a belittling or disrespectful relationship). As these circumstances are addressed (for instance, by ending the relationship), the person will lean more consistently in the direction of anti-a/b.

When anti-a/b resolve develops, it is often born of the desire to end the torment and torture of a/b's prison. The person may not, as yet, have a vision of a life beyond a/b that seems promising, manageable, and realizable. Thus, initial opposition to a/b may be based more upon a hatred of it and a desire to escape imprisonment than upon the pursuit of an attractive and specific alternative. Chloe contrasted her later resistance to anorexia from her earlier, more conditional opposition, when life without anorexia seemed unimaginable:

> After seven and a half years, I have reached the point where I totally hate anorexia and just want to get better. That's not to say that I didn't want to get better in the past, but there were always conditions attached to it. For example,
> • I want to get better but am not prepared to gain weight.
> • I want to get better but can't see the point of life and have nothing to get better for.
> • I want to get better but am scared of what my life would be like without anorexia.

Without a clear vision of and belief in a future without a/b, every act of resistance represents a courageous leap of faith. As Rose, a 24-year-old, put it, "Often it seems like looking over my shoulder as a forest fire fast approaches, with my only possible escape being jumping into the 'deep end,' even though I have no idea I can swim but have to believe that I can because someone once told me that the body floats." These leaps of faith become easier to take when the person is surrounded by a community of concerned and loving people who believe in the person's ability to prevail, especially when the person has little faith in herself.

Anti-a/b can coexist with a/b and for a considerable time probably *must*, as the two worldviews clash and fight for the right to guide the person's life. Initially, anti-a/b may be a very small fish in the big pond of a/b, but this does not mean it is insignificant, as a/b is bound to claim. A/b will do its best to dismiss any effort to fight or resist it as trivial because it knows that revolutions always begin quietly and modestly, as passing thoughts of resentment or discontent and sentiments muttered under one's breath. It may also charge that though the person may have "won a round" with a/b, she has not yet "won the war," and therefore she is a failure in her attempt to overcome a/b.

One tactic a/b commonly uses to co-opt anti-a/b and make it serve a/b's purposes is to impose perfectionistic standards on anti-a/b endeavors. From the point of view of anti-a/b, one's anti-a/b actions need not live up to her anti-a/b words or intentions. Anti-a/b perfection, even if it were possible to achieve, would fly in the face of anti-a/b, which celebrates imperfection. If one attempts to step away from a/b perfectly, the "real gold" of anti-a/b is transmuted into the "fool's gold" of a/b.

Reclaiming one's life from a/b is often a two-pronged affair. One prong, discussed in this chapter, entails unmasking and defying a/b. This necessitates being able to see through and extricate oneself from the webs of meaning it has woven. However, seeing through and past a/b's deception does not immediately end a/b's assault. In fact, its assaults may intensify as it attempts to overcome the woman's newfound resistance. On the other hand, a/b will find that justifying such tortures is not as easy as it once was. The person's self-defense can now be founded upon a recognition of the immorality and injustice of a/b—a type of anti-a/b outrage—and can express itself inwardly as a passionate cry for freedom. In this prong of the fight, one must engage with a/b in order to disengage from it.

The other prong to the anti-a/b struggle, discussed in Chapter 12, has to do with constructing a life apart from a/b. For many, reclaiming one's life involves bringing one's attention back to the task of defining personal interests and passions and living one's life according to them, as well as attending to the dilemmas and fears associated with giving up hope for a/b's promised land.

In reclaiming their life from a/b, people usually move back and forth between these two poles. The prongs of anti-a/b work together and support each other: The person advances with her life when she can and turns to fight a/b when she must, like an army defending the rear (countering a/b's attacks, seeing through its threats, keeping it from co-opting anti-anorexia) as it advances and reclaims territory it has lost (connecting with personal desires and preferences and creating a life apart from a/b).

DISCERNING AND COUNTERING THE VOICE OF A/B

Discerning and countering the voice of a/b is an essential part of un-masking and defying it. This entails recognizing the camouflage a/b uses, searching for an anti-a/b path, distinguishing the voice of a/b from one's own preferred voice and those of caring and supportive others, and counter-translating a/b's translations.

The Camouflage of A/B

Contending with a/b means having to prepare for a prolonged struggle with a relentless and diabolically clever adversary. After glimpsing the deceptiveness and wickedness of a/b, one is not free to simply turn one's back on it and walk away. Little Red Riding Hood, after discovering the deception she had fallen prey to, still had to contend with the wolf. A/b is like the wolf who disguises himself as a loving benefactor. But unlike the wolf in the Little Red Riding Hood story, a/b is capable of shifting its shape and disguising its identity endlessly: in a blink of an eye, the wolf can cloak itself in sheep's clothing or appear as inviting as a cuddly teddy bear. Much of a/b's power is connected to this astonishing capacity for camouflage and deception. Chloe discussed the importance of being able to see through anorexia's camouflage in order to know how to fight it.

> I know that for me, coming to know the enemy was critical in being able to fight it. For the unknown is intangible . . . impossible to get a grip on because it keeps slipping through your fingers and vanishing into thin air. . . . Anorexia can so easily hide itself when one does not know what one is looking for . . . indeed, surely if one did not know what they were fighting against they could easily be looking the enemy in the eye without even knowing it. It is only in discovering the nature of one's opponent that one can carefully choose the weapons to enlist in one's fight.
>
> Unlike some of the other accounts I have read about how people had a clear moment or experience of "unmasking" the enemy, I have never had one particular moment that stands out like that. For me it has been more a process of painstakingly stripping the enemy to

discover what lies underneath. Thus, I cannot pinpoint any defining moment but, rather, lots of small glimpses I've had which have added up to a fairly clear picture of the enemy.

Searching for an Anti-A/B Path

Once a person can see where a/b is taking them, the next challenge becomes discerning the rhetorical tactics and strategies it uses. Trying to distinguish a/b from anti-a/b can be a bit like trying to discern down from up after being buried by an avalanche—you only have so much time before you suffocate, and if you start digging in the wrong direction, you will perish.

Furthermore, there is no one path out of a/b, no single anti-a/b voice or direction. Rather, there are many possible anti-a/b paths, each one as different and unique as a snowflake. One often must "make the road as one walks it."* The fact that there are no universal exit routes can be very frustrating for people struggling with a/b and for their therapists.

Initially, one possible way to discern whether an action, intention, or belief is pro- or anti-a/b is to ask oneself whether the action, intention, or belief would antagonize a/b or support or encourage it. As Chloe put it, "If anorexia stages a large protest, then you can be pretty sure it's an 'anti-anorexic' action that you are wanting to take." In other words, an anti-a/b path may not initially be defined by a well-articulated set of values and moral vision, but simply by whatever runs counter to a/b. This may involve refusing to go along with a/b even when one believes what it is saying at that moment. Chloe has resorted to such a practice of blind disobedience: "Even if I believe what anorexia says, I try to choose not to follow through with those thoughts. I have learned that by acting on those thoughts I wind up even further away from where I want to be and further away from my own values, goals, and aspirations. . . . I have to take the risk to go against those thoughts, even when I believe that what anorexia is saying about me is true, and try and create a life of meaning and worth."

Contending with Dueling Voices

Discerning the voice of a/b from other more benign and loving voices is an ongoing task, requiring constant vigilance with respect to the content of one's thinking and the effects of these thoughts on one's

---

* This is taken from the title of a book *We Make the Road by Walking* (Horton & Friere, 1990), about the work of the Highlander Center, an institution devoted to supporting social activism and change.

life. The following writings illustrate the intense jousting necessary to keep a/b's lethal spin from prevailing.

Monique, a 12-year-old, sent the following writing to me (RM) in the form of an e-mail message. In the subject line of the e-mail she wrote, "The voice that makes it hard to eat."

Hi,

I wanted to talk to you about that voice that makes it hard to eat because it won't shut up. I don't think it likes you because it sure argues with what you say a lot. It seems right, even though I like what you say better. Your voice doesn't give me a headache.

You said that I don't need to do anything to make my friends like me and you said I'm not just a body. The voice that makes it hard to eat says that's not true, that people do care about how you look and they won't like me if I'm not thin because people don't like and aren't nice to people who are fat. You said I wasn't fat. The voice says I am and that I would be happier, feel better, be healthier, and be liked more if I listen to it and not you.

It says it cares about me and is trying to help me. You said please don't lose weight and that I'm not fat. The voice says that you have to say that stuff to be polite and not hurt my feelings and that's not really what you think. The voice says I won't hurt if I listen to it because all I need to do is lose __ pounds and then I will be likable. It said if you were a real doctor you would help me lose weight and be lovable. You said I am lovable, and reminded me of people who love me.

The voice says to look at the people who are happy, lovable, and successful and they are all thin. I like you and the voice says that you are skinny and that's the one thing you got going for you. When I listen to the voice my stomach hurts. You say it's because I am starving. It says it's because I'm weak and, that if I listen more, I will be strong.

I want to be good. You say I am good. The voice says if I listen to it I will be good. My head hurts. The voice says everything that's good needs to be worked hard for and that's the way life works. It says that you don't know how life works and that I have to earn people's affection. It tells me, if I listen to you, I will be scared (I am scared) but, if I listen to it, I won't have to be afraid of them not liking me.

The voice says everyone listens to it and believes it except you and that all I need to do is turn on the television and I will see how right it is because everyone who is happy, lovable, and successful is thin. The voice says that feelings I had when my Dad called me "fatty" and when that stuff happened that made me want to hide and not be seen by anybody—it can make that feeling go away and I won't ever feel it again. I like that idea.

When I catch it in a lie, it says it lies to be nice to me and to not hurt me and it claims that those who don't lie to me are mean for not lying. It doesn't feel nice to be lied to. I've only talked to you two times now and I like you, you seem nice. The voice tries a lot to not let me talk to you, and to make you seem mean or wrong. I haven't caught you lying like I have the voice that makes it hard to eat. Seeing its lie hurts but I think it's a good hurt. Thank you for listening to me and talking with me.

Monique

The next writing was a journal entry made by Olivia, a 34-year-old woman. She titled it "Friend or Foe."

Dear Journal,
I'm confused. The voice of Anorexia claims to be my friend and yet other people are calling it my enemy. I know it doesn't always feel friendly to me. In all honesty it hasn't felt friendly to me in a long long time and yet still it seems to try to convince me of its friendship and I feel a bit defensive. I don't want to loose a friendship if it really is my friend so I figure, if I compare Anorexia to my other friends, maybe I won't be so confused. I don't know what else to do to figure it out.

My friend Anorexia	My other friends
You often offer to take my pain and anything bad in my life and make it better.	You don't offer to take my pain away or make the bad things better in my life, but you are there for me and listen to my pain.
My friend Anorexia	My other friends
You tell me that I will have friends if I listen to you and do what you say.	You plain and simply say I am your friend. I don't have to do what you say to be cared for.
My friend Anorexia	My other friends
While you tell me I will have friends if I listen to you, you don't let me go out with other people. You tell me they won't like me and will find me fat and ugly.	You support me in all of my friendships except with Anorexia. You don't focus on negative things about me and you encourage me to be with other people because it adds to our friends and gives us more to share.

My friend Anorexia
You don't let me eat when we
  are together and if I do you tell
  me to throw it up.

My other friends
You eat with me and often share
  and offer food to me. You don't
  ever suggest I throw it up.

My friend Anorexia
When you are with me you
  often tell me about all the neat,
  wonderful, fun stuff that I will
  be able to do if I listen to you.

My other friends
When I am with you we do a lot
  of neat, wonderful, fun stuff
  and, unless you feel I need to
  know something for my safety,
  I don't need to listen to you
  first.

My friend Anorexia
You lie to me and, when I find
  out, you tell me it is to protect
  me or it is my fault.

My other friends
You don't lie to me and when on
  occasion you have, you
  apologized and asked me what
  I needed from you to regain my
  trust.

My friend Anorexia
You always tell me the bad
  things about me and how only
  through our friendship can I
  somehow be good.

My other friends
You seldom talk to me about the
  bad things about me and, when
  I tell you about the things I think
  are bad about me, you often
  have a point of view that questions the validity of my view of
  myself or you help me see the
  possibilities to change, if I want,
  the things I don't like.

My friend Anorexia
You told me when I was
  pregnant that my baby would
  be ugly and unlovable if I made
  it fat and ugly like me. You said
  I shouldn't listen to my doctor,
  that he wanted me ugly and fat
  and my baby would be sick if I
  didn't listen to you. I believed
  and trusted you. My baby only
  weighed 2 pounds when she
  was born. My baby died.

My other friends
You told me both my baby and I
  needed to eat to be strong and
  healthy and that I and my baby
  were beautiful and you loved us
  both. I didn't believe and trust
  you and my baby died.

When I see this written down on paper in black and white there is no doubt you, Anorexia, are *not* my friend. You are a murderer and you have no heart whatsoever. . . . I think you are simply evil through and through and I don't want you in my life. Maybe that is one more big difference between you and my friends. If I decided to end my friendship with them, while it might hurt them, they would leave me alone. You, on the other hand, just keep harassing and intruding on me and my life, seizing every opportunity that you can to fuck with me. *Fuck off Anorexia!*

Olivia

For Olivia, as for most people struggling with a/b, anorexia and anti-anorexia coexisted, though not peacefully. In order to reject anorexia's assertion of friendship, Olivia compared anorexia's way of being her "friend" to her other experiences of friendship. Fortunately, Olivia had a reservoir of respectful, honest, and accepting relationships that formed the basis of her preferred view of friendship. Referencing this other set of experiences deconstructed anorexia's paradigm of friendship, making it easier for Olivia to repudiate it.

Counter-Translating A/B Translations

A/b also deceives people by twisting the meaning of others' words in order to create the impression that they support a/b. A/b almost always targets a woman's relationships with potential allies. When possible, it prohibits these relationships outright. If it can't prohibit the relationship, it will go to absurd lengths to twist the meaning of the ally's words or make fallacious interpretations of the ally's actions in order to paint them as pro-a/b. A/b tries to ensure that when the person casts her gaze outward toward her friends, family, and the larger world, she perceives only a/b reflected back. Failing this, it attempts to portray potential allies in the most negative light possible, misrepresenting their motives, assailing their honesty, and disputing their regard.

Therapy relationships have the potential to be among the most anti-a/b relationships. It is not surprising, then, that a/b often makes therapy one its prime targets. In the following letter to me (DE), Victoria commented on the manner in which anorexia attempted to distort the meaning of others' words, including my own. She also discussed the way she countered anorexia's "filtering" and considered a more plausible anti-anorexic interpretation.

When I first hear or read something, A. [anorexia] jumps right in and twists everything around to suit its needs. For example, a friend of mine said to me when I saw them for the first time in a while, "You are looking much better than when I last saw you." Enter A. and this gets translated into, "You look so much fatter than last time I saw you. It's hideous." If I then acknowledge that A. has filtered this message, I can stop, regroup, and then listen to the words again. It is also helpful for me to ask the person exactly what they mean at that moment. By doing so in this situation, I found out he had meant, "Last time I saw you, I was really worried about you. You looked very sick. Today you look more well."

So I guess "moving past" A.'s translation is just a matter of looking at things more than once. Due to so many years of practice, the first time I hear a statement, I hear it through A.'s ears—in the worst possible way. By reviewing what has been said a second time, I am much more objective in the interpretation. This is how I read your letters also. I am careful to expose A.'s twisted translations in my replies so as to allow you the opportunity to confirm or deny that this is what you meant. By doing this, I am having a conversation with David and not with David via A.

We have come to the conclusion that it is impossible for therapists (or others) to a/b-proof their questions and statements, no matter how knowledgeable they are about a/b's voice and tactics, although they should attempt to make their words as difficult as for a/b to twist as possible. But because their efforts will always fall short, we think it is a good idea to anticipate a/b's attempts to twist their meaning by inquiring about a/b's attempts to translate. Questions can be of a more general nature ("What was anorexia's take on what I said?"; "How did bulimia want you to hear what I just said?") or, if the therapist has a more specific idea about how a/b may have attempted to spin what he or she said, a more specific question can be asked ("Did anorexia tell you that what I meant was . . . ?"). Therapists are then in a position to speak for themselves and to counter a/b's translation of their words.

Resisting A/B Through Direct Engagement

We have never met a person who has won an argument with a/b. It doesn't yield to logic and has no compassion to which one can appeal. When we talk about "fighting" a/b, we do not mean fighting in the sense of defeating or conquering. A/b cannot be conquered, but it can be foiled. When we speak of fighting a/b, we mean resisting it, critiquing it, and eventually finding ways of escaping or disengaging from it. Laurie, a 14-year-old, discussed some of the benefits and drawbacks of resisting anorexia through direct engagement with its voice:

I think there are good things about resisting the voice of anorexia by engaging with it. When I battle anorexia, I come to a lot of knowing. For example, I come to know *why* I have a right to eat, to care for me. I come to know that when I'm hungry and I eat, I am caring for myself. Contesting anorexia is very useful if I want to have more of an articulated sense of entitlement to eat; words get put to my knowing.

However, when I get into resisting a/b through engagement with it, it sometimes feels like a feeding frenzy. The more of myself I present to a/b when I reply to its insults, demands, threats, or promises, the more food I give it to feed off. When I engage in battle with a/b, it learns how I resist it. Some new knowledge gets produced in the battle, but a/b picks it up too because the knowledge is produced in an engagement against a/b.

I supply anorexia with answers to the questions it asks me in order to challenge me. Then bam, it turns around and uses all of what I've given it against me. It will take my meaning for "entitled to eat" and strip it away and spit it back at me as something to do with being selfish or some other bad thing about me. My meaning for "caring about myself," which also includes caring for others, is thrown back at me by anorexia as some weakness or flaw related to the way I care. It learns from me how to fight me with the very things I used against it with even more power than it had initially. If, on the other hand, there is an opportunity to safely flee, I think that is the far better alternative.

A/b can trap a person (or her therapist) into endless back-and-forth debates, which allow the voice of a/b to become more sophisticated and tailored to the person's anti-a/b arguments. Many women find themselves so drained by these never-ending debates, or defeated by a/b's claiming the "last word," that they surrender and do whatever a/b says in order to stop the war in their heads. These endless debates with a/b are more easily sidestepped if insiders can find a way to honor their pre-anorexic knowing or the knowing that is more congruent with their values and purposes and allow this to serve as a portal through which they can disengage from a/b (see "Engaging with Other Kinds of Knowing" later in this chapter).

Laurie described another method that she used to resist anorexia by engaging with it. She referred to this method as *critique* and distinguished it from *battling*.

One word for a way I escape from anorexia rather than fight with it is "critique." With critique, anorexia becomes the focus, and I reveal less of myself. For example, you'll ask me what anorexia is saying to me and then I say it's telling me, "Your stomach is way fat and no one will like you if your stomach is fat, they will be mean to you." Then we take that apart and look at it. . . . I can speak about what anorexia says and critique it. When I do that, it misses most of what I reveal about my non-anorexic or anti-anorexic knowing. . . . It doesn't have the opportunity to speak back to me in the same way.

DISENGAGING FROM A/B

So far, we have discussed one kind of anti-a/b resistance, in which a/b is engaged with in some kind of battle or duel. This kind of struggle takes place face to face, so to speak. In this section, we discuss another form of resistance—one that is defined not by engagement with a/b but by disengagement. By *disengagement,* we mean "turning one's back" on a/b or "tuning it out."

Engaging with Other Kinds of Knowing

Breaking off the engagement with a/b and simply walking away from it is by no means an easy feat. From the point of view of a/b, a prolonged engagement is the next best thing to marriage. Breaking this engagement usually becomes possible only after a/b has been divested of its moral authority and legitimacy and the person becomes engaged with other kinds of knowing, perhaps a knowing that predated a/b's entrance into the person's life or one that is more in line with her life purposes and values.

Laurie referred to her pre-a/b knowing/feeling as the *ug*. Laurie described how she experienced the ug and the things that helped her connect to it.

> I don't know where my ug lives within me and I don't think it would be helpful to try and pin it down (my ug taught me that). I know it way deep in my stomach sometimes, and sometimes I experience it all over my body as tingles. I know it in my spirit, and I know it in my soul. I can connect to it through lots of things, like when kids laugh or sometimes in certain cries. I can find it when I'm doing things I enjoy or when I see something really pretty or moving. There are some people who help bring me back to the ug. I can come back to the ug with you [Rick], my kids, my sister, my grandma, Olivia, and some friends. All those things have a part in the ug.

This alternative knowledge may tend to be more experiential than intellectual and, initially, a person may not be able to put this knowing into words, though they may be able to feel it in their bodies as a gut feeling. We consider this pre-a/b knowledge (often experienced as moments of supreme clarity or flashes of insight) to be anti-a/b in the sense that a/b does not approve of it, and in that a/b's domination depends upon the supplanting or marginalizing of such knowledge. However, although we regard it as anti-a/b, we do not mean to imply that this knowledge was forged through an active engagement with a/b; the knowledge we are talking about is born from a domain of experience separate from a/b, though a/b may try to infiltrate this knowing and substitute it with "a/b knowing."

Although Laurie experiences her *ug* within her body, it is clearly something that is fundamentally relational. It is through her relationship with emotions, with beauty, with activities, and with people that she experiences this knowing. Other people have commented on the roles spirituality, safe places, and "seeing places" have played in providing a perspective or clarity that has enabled them to disengage from a/b. (See Chapters 12 & 18.) One women described how her Native American grandmother had taught her how to "ride the wind" as a means of gaining elevation and perspective, and this practice of "riding the wind" prevented anorexia from imprisoning her for significant lengths of time.

For Laurie, the *ug* opened up for her the possibility of disengaging from anorexia, which she referred to as "taking flight" or "fleeing."

> My voice of anorexia is always asking me questions. But they aren't real questions, they are accusing questions like "What am I doing eating that?" and questions that claim to know me. My ug knows at the moment of its asking that they aren't genuine questions that have my welfare at heart. When I listen to that ug at the moment of the question, I know that I don't have to answer. I know it's evil. I can simply leave, take flight from it, and I can keep my own knowing, my own ug, in flight. When I listen to anorexia and I hear the ug, I just know to take flight, to leave. I don't have a rationale for that, I just know it. I don't know why or how I know that but I do, and if I listen to it, which unfortunately is all too rare, I know to get the fuck out of there now.

Cultural Impediments to Disengagement

Why did Laurie listen to her *ug* only rarely? This culture highly values "rational" knowledge, and knowledge that is more intuitive or nonverbal is not considered by most to be as legitimate or trustworthy. Because her *ug* was "beyond words," she could not explain the foundation of her knowledge "rationally." As Laurie stated, "Because my ug isn't rational, I don't feel very supported in listening to it." A/b demands a rational explanation for a person's conclusions while securing its own conclusions by whatever means it can, rational or not.

Second, this culture has a "stand-and-fight" mentality and views fleeing as an act of cowardice. Therapists and treatment programs sometimes encourage women to remain engaged with the voice of a/b in the name of "dealing with your feelings" even when the person might experience the possibility of, and desire to, disengage from the voice of a/b. This disengagement is sometimes mistaken by therapists as avoidance. Laurie disputed the idea that she needed to fight anorexia or be rational in order to escape it.

> Anorexia makes use of ideas that seem all over the place. It exploits ideas like you have be rational, or have words, or fight for yourself. But I don't have to fight for myself, I can escape for myself too. I don't have to understand something that's trying to hurt me, either, or make sense out of the ug. I don't need to give a rationale for walking away from something that is trying to kill me. It's anorexia that is irrational and it doesn't make sense that I have to be rational in relationship to it. I can irrationally leave it and take flight.

Chloe concurred with Laurie about the limits of a rational and combative approach to a/b, as well as about the value of disengaging from it:

> Therapists often view direct confrontation as the only "true" or effective way of dealing with anorexia. In my experience, if one is not actively engaged in challenging the voice of anorexia through direct confrontation, they are often seen as seeking to avoid the problem or not being committed to recovery. For example, I have always been told that unless anorexia's voice or, in cognitive behavioral therapy's terms, the "irrational thoughts" are directly confronted and changed then it is impossible to ever recover. However, I have found that when I have taken up CBT [cognitive behavioral therapy] practices, anorexia's voice can always find a way to undermine or destroy outright any counter-argument I may put forward. This is extremely disheartening, especially when I am being told by therapists that this is the only way to "get better" and that my failure must be due to the fact that I am not trying hard enough or that I don't really want to "get better."
>
> One of the most powerful and liberating discoveries I have made is that I don't have to engage with anorexia, that I can allow its voice to be present without having to actively try to get rationality to triumph

over irrationality. Anorexia can tell me I'm an awful, fat, and worthless person and instead of having to rationally defend myself, which only incites anorexia all the more and leaves me feeling even more full of self-hatred, I can simply accept that this is the way I feel. But importantly, know that I *do not have to act* on those feelings. For me, this effectively takes all the power away from anorexia.

To accept its presence and choose not to engage with it leaves anorexia with little comeback. It is a bit like the schoolyard bully whose power is stripped when they do not get any reaction from those they seek to victimize. All anorexia can do is intensify the thoughts in an attempt to get me to act upon them.

I have spent many years in direct combat with anorexia, only to give up in despair as anorexia always came out on top. I really think that there is enormous value in the concept of disengagement. For me, disengagement is not a passive act of surrender but rather an active act of choosing *not* to engage with anorexia. I may not be able to change those thoughts but I can change the way I think about those thoughts. This has enabled me to reclaim more of my life than I ever was able to when actively engaged in battle with anorexia.

ENCOURAGING ANTI-A/B OUTRAGE

Connecting to feelings of moral outrage in response to a/b's violence and violations can be very sustaining of all forms of resistance, including critique and disengagement. Moral outrage is often an outgrowth of a person's realizing that a/b's "help" has not uplifted them as promised but, on the contrary, has resulted in a steady descent into a hell of increasing confinement and unrelenting tortures. It can fuel a woman's resistance to and ultimate repudiation of a/b and serve as a kind of anti-a/b shield, making the person more impervious to a/b's "slings and arrows." A person's moral outrage at a/b can give her the pluck to "slam the door" in a/b's face, refusing to give it an audience. Although a/b is very adept at finding ways of insinuating itself through cracks or prying open windows, over time instances of moral outrage build a foundation of anti-a/b suspicion and distrust and potentiate a more detailed clarification and elaboration of anti-a/b values, visions, and human rights.

Countering A/B's Claims to Moral Authority

For a woman to experience moral outrage, she often must first counter a/b's fraudulent framework of morality and assert an alternative moral framework. As discussed in Chapter 2, a/b claims that it possesses the moral authority to declare the worthiness or unworthiness of girls and women, and to pass judgment about whether or not they deserve to live. Anti-a/b manifests itself, among other things, as a rival moral authority. Anti-a/b, as a mode of life, is not fixed by any preexisting psychological or moral code. It takes its particular form through a contesting of a/b or through recourse to other domains of experience that have helped women clarify their own values (such as spirituality). It thereby allows a/b's declarations of what is good or bad and who is a good or bad person to be questioned and contested. In the absence of a rival morality, breaches of a/b's dogma and edicts can only be interpreted within a/b's moral framework as heresy, a sin that cannot be redeemed through penance but only expiated through torture and recantation. Without an anti-a/b counter-morality, freedom from a/b's jurisdiction becomes impossible.

Establishing a Counter-Morality

Such a rival morality often takes its shape by way of critique. Through this critique we aim to apprehend and undo the cultural assumptions that make it possible, for example, for a girl of eleven to believe herself to be entirely worthless unless she can subjugate her bodily desires and appetites until her body conforms to an elusive and lethal standard of beauty. Many, if not most, of the young people who become ensnared by a/b are (and have been) people of great moral integrity, desperately concerned with and distressed by the injustice they have experienced, witnessed, or have knowledge of. To use Gremillion's (2001) metaphor, these young people are often the moral canaries in the mines of contemporary culture, detecting toxicity before those less sensitive to injustice do. A/b appeals to their desire to put matters right by holding them responsible for everything that is wrong. Before they know it, they find themselves accused of moral crimes, convicted without knowing the specific nature of their wrongdoing or having any defense.

Reviving Alternative Moral Frameworks

Because a/b's prosecution takes place within the domain of its own moral jurisdiction, the person's defense can only be mounted within the domain of a counter-morality. Following is an excerpt from an urgent hospital consultation I (DE) had with Cecily, a life-threatened 17-year-old, and her mother. In the excerpt, I attempted to build a bridge back to a moral framework that had been overridden by anorexia.

David: How does anorexia talk you into torturing yourself? What does it tell you that gets you to violate your body and pull your hair out and make you seem a lot younger than you really are? What is it telling you?

Cecily: That I don't have the right to be happy.

David: Why do you think anorexia has forbidden you to have life, liberty, freedom, and happiness? Do you know the Declaration of Independence in the United States? Liberty and the pursuit of happiness. It's denying you your human rights. Why do you think it's doing this? Have you committed some crimes?

Cecily: I don't know.

David: Have you murdered anyone?

Cecily: No.

David: On what grounds is it denying you your freedom?

Cecily: I don't really know. I can't figure it out.

David: Say you were walking down the street in London and the police came and threw you in jail and said: "You can't have any freedoms!" What would you do? Would you say: "What are the charges against me?" Would you say you wanted a lawyer? Do you believe justice should operate in England?

Cecily: Yes.

David: Do you think this is just? You are being punished and tortured and you don't know what you've done wrong. I am wondering about it. To me that doesn't seem like a democracy. Do you believe in democracy?

Cecily: Yes, I do. But anorexia says I've done something wrong but I don't know what it is.

David: Where do you think anorexia got that idea from?

Cecily: I don't know.

David: Do you think you've had a fair trial? In my country, and I think in your country, you're told what you did wrong. Then there is a judge or jury. And then you defend yourself.

Cecily: She [anorexia] never tells me. I ask but she won't say.

David: This is even worse. This could drive anyone crazy.

Cecily: Yes, I feel like that sometimes.

David: Why do you think she would play such an insidious and cunning trick on a young woman? What purpose would she have in doing this? (to her mother) Would you consider Cecily a nice daughter or a nice person?

Mother: She has been nice to me . . . too nice to me.

David: Why do you think anorexia would take advantage of a very nice young woman?

Cecily: I don't know.

David: I don't think the answer is simple. I'm wondering why?

Cecily: I've asked myself that question many times and I haven't found the answer.

David: Maybe there isn't a simple answer. If you ask yourself why is there injustice, you may never find the answer but you may find a revolution to put things right.

Cecily: Mmm.

David: Do you sense there is some injustice here?

Cecily: (*with emphasis*) Yes, I do!

David: Well, I've got to tell you—so do I! Why do you think there is some injustice being done to you by anorexia? What's the nature of it? When did you realize anorexia was immoral? Did she tell you she was good or serving a good cause?

Cecily: Yes . . .

In this example, anorexia's morality was called into question rather than allowing it to condemn Cecily. Conversations that inspect the a/b morality from the perspective of a counter-morality can challenge a/b as the arbiter of the "good." Moreover, in time, these inquiries often reveal the perversity and malevolence not only of its judgments but also of the principles upon which these judgments are based. Under such anti-a/b scrutiny, a/b is defrocked. It is no longer viewed as the only means to improve a person's morals but, rather, as a manifestation of evil and one of the very violences these women oppose.

Chloe (see comments earlier in this chapter) wrote about wrestling with anorexia's moral authority. Through confronting anorexia, she was able to revive an alternative set of values that dramatically contradicted anorexia's moral authority.

> Anorexia most definitely implies—no, *states*—that I am indeed value-less. It claims its values as my own. For example, it claims that I have to be a certain weight (i.e., as low as possible). I have only recently seen the irony in this when I confronted myself with the question "What is so dreadful about gaining weight?" To which I got the answer "You'll get fat." I then asked myself, "What is more terrible, being fat and out of the hospital or losing weight and being in the hospital?"
>
> I could get no clear reply to that, but I was left, nevertheless, and still am left unsatisfied. When I thought further on the matter, I was struck by the realization that I am, and always have been, someone who despised society's emphasis on weight/shape/beauty, and to whom others' weight/shape/beauty is of no relevance whatsoever. What puzzles and angers me is that despite coming to this realization, I still hate every kilo that I am required to gain and not a day, or perhaps even an hour, goes by in which I don't long to lose weight.

So why, then, is my desire to lose weight so strong when I claim that weight is not important to me? Yet, in another respect, it is, or it certainly appears that way.

I feel so full of contradictions that it confuses me. For if you asked me what I value in others, I would list weight, achievements, and other superficialities last. Yet, why do I cling so fiercely to being underweight and why is it so important for me to achieve well in what I do? It was in discovering these contradictions that I started to question anorexia's values and found them very much at odds with my own. I still can't understand, if this is so, why I can't just reject anorexia's values and live by my own. I know I don't approve of anorexia's values yet feel compelled to live by them.

Chloe began her face-off with anorexia by confronting herself through a series of questions about what mattered to her, beginning with the question "What is so dreadful about gaining weight?" In the course of this self-interrogation, she was struck by the realization of a long history of despising the very values that anorexia sanctifies. Although these contradictions puzzled her, she was now in a position to evaluate anorexia's values through the lens of the moral framework she had resurrected. She was then able to pose another question: "I still can't understand, if this is so, why I can't just reject anorexia's values and live by my own." That question led to the exposing of anorexia's moral sleight of hand:

Anorexia does not so much try to devalue my judgments on what is important or valued in my life because it knows they are such entrenched, core values which reside in my heart of hearts. They are beyond anorexia's reach. What it does do to sabotage my values and judgments is to make me feel unable to live up to them. For example, if I was to claim that family and friends are important to me, anorexia would say I am incapable of being a good friend or family member. Or, if I were to claim that I value generosity, kindness, understanding, etc., anorexia would say that I have none of these qualities. Thus I am left with the feeling that I am unable to really live by my values or by what is important to me.

Because anorexia could never turn Chloe away from her "core values," its only recourse was to attempt to turn these these values into the nails for her crucifixion. It co-opted her own values and used them as the means by which it could assess her as a moral failure. Then, through its promises of reformation and redemption, it induced her, without her knowledge, into its own moral universe. She believed, at least initially, that by walking anorexia's path she could become a person who could live up to her values. Anorexia concealed from her the fact that, by striving through anorexia to realize her own values, she would ultimately betray them.

> I don't think I've ever questioned anorexia's authority to determine my "right-ful-ness" until very, very recently. I've always had a hard time arguing against anorexia when it comes to my rights and entitlements. However, I have tried to switch my mindset into that of a moral crusader and to look at it more impartially. When I did this, I found that anorexia was certainly very presumptuous in assuming it has the authority to preside over a person's "right-ful-ness." As a moral crusader, I don't believe that any one entity has the right to assume that it is the only voice of "true" authority. I don't think anorexia has the right to determine whether a person is worthy or not. I believe that all human beings are worthy and it is not something to be earned.
>
> As I write these very words, anorexia is ridiculing the idea of a moral crusade. It says that I am only trying to make myself feel better by deluding myself that I'm standing up for a moral cause. It says that even if I were on a moral crusade, my offerings to the crusade are so small and insignificant that I may as well not be a part of it in the first place. But by seeing every anti-anorexic deed as an affront to anorexia, not just my anorexia but anorexia as a whole, I am able to gain strength and bring more energy to the fight. I think it is important to know that your actions are a part of something larger than just your own personal struggle.
>
> I am so used to taking the rap, filling myself with shame and self-hatred. If I was to blame anorexia, I would probably convert my shame and self-hatred into anger against anorexia. I would get angry at it for the envy it provokes in me . . . I would get angry at it for taking hold of another person's life . . . I would get angry for it making me feel like I wanted to be even thinner . . . I would get angry at it for seeing thinness as a thing to be desired and aspired to.

Forbidden Anger and Moral Outrage

Those who struggle with a/b often find it difficult to connect with a sense of anger and moral outrage. This leaves them at a significant disadvantage when it comes to both turning against a/b and sustaining their resistance to it. Often the only anger a/b lets them feel entitled to is anger directed at themselves through self-blame. Needless to say, self-directed anger is of no use in combating a/b but rather becomes a weapon a/b wields against them.

Because one's moral outrage, when directed against a/b, can be a very powerful threat to a/b's domination, a/b has a very real interest in divesting women of their experience and expression of it. A/b's interests in this regard are abetted by patriarchal social institutions and cultural discourses that devalue and objectify women, delegitimize their experience of oppression, and pathologize their outrage.

This is, in part, accomplished through the upholding of a normative femininity (a cultural idea about what women are and should be like) that makes it less acceptable for women to be angry than for men. The Western feminine ideal encourages women to be caregiving, nurturing, and deferential. Girls and women who are drawn to a/b are often eager to excel and be acknowledged and approved of. Consequently, they often strongly conform to these dominant cultural specifications for womanhood.

In addition, some women who find themselves ensnared in a/b's web have been, as children, subjected to abuses of power that have left them feeling denigrated and out of control. They may have learned early in their lives that expressions of anger and outrage in response to these abuses would provoke even more violence. Thus, they learned either to conceal such responses or to adopt a story about what was happening to them that was incompatible with the experience of anger or outrage (e.g., that the abuse was brought on by them and they deserved it).

Furthermore, many of these women have been in contexts (family, school, sports, dance, and so on) where they have been subjected to high degrees of evaluation and judgment and where they have experienced the approval of others as highly conditional. As a result, these women often make other people's opinions of them the measure of their own worth and, therefore, are eager to please others. Becoming angry with someone whose approval you depend upon is a dicey affair, to say the least. Many women anticipate that others will ignore or discount their feelings of anger and annoyance and, rather than engage in a potentially painful, frightening, and fruitless confrontation, they dismiss their own feelings and try and "look on the bright side." This has the effect of further diminishing the likelihood of their connecting with their anger and outrage in situations where they experience maltreatment.

In short, for many women struggling with a/b, connecting with feelings of anger and outrage arouses strong fears of disapproval, rejection, and even physical retaliation, in addition to self-blame. Therapists should never assume that their clients have ready access to these feelings of outrage and the experiences connected to them. Because recourse to these feelings is often vital in turning against a/b and in clarifying one's own values and preferences, it is important that the therapist explore with the person what constraints might make it difficult for her to connect to feelings of moral outrage and make it more likely that she would accept and perhaps even welcome a/b's blaming her for whatever agony she is experiencing.

Linking to a Larger Struggle

A/b usually succeeds to some extent (and often entirely) in getting people to accept the pain and punishment that it inflicts, either on the grounds that it is good for them or because they deserve it. But although a/b can trick a woman into believing she deserves this torture, it has a much more difficult time persuading her that her friends and acquaintances who are also struggling with a/b deserve such treatment. Knowing others suffer at the hands of a/b often helps an individual step back and see through a/b's camouflage, perceiving it as a villain rather than savior. As a result, the first awakening of moral outrage at a/b often occurs in response to the suffering that a/b is inflicting upon others.

When attempting to find ways of reconnecting these young women to their own sense of moral worth and moral outrage, it may be helpful to keep in mind that they often find it much easier to recognize and validate their own experience of injustice when that experience is linked to the shared experience of others. When women feel that they are fighting not only for their own liberation but also for the liberation of others who are being subjected to the same injustices, their protest can take on a much larger significance; they feel they are not just fighting for themselves but for justice.* As Victoria put it:

> I would have given up a long time ago had I not realized the importance of fighting against anorexia for the sake of the liberation of others. If I had chosen not to begin to reclaim my life, I would have been a walking advertisement for anorexia. Considering the hundreds of impressionable young people I come across every week in my job as teacher, this would have been morally criminal.

---

* This idea of linking to other people's experience appears to have broader applicability. For example, one person who had been struggling with feelings of shame for many years found some release from those feelings only when she made a practice of forgiving herself not just on her own behalf but also on the behalf of everyone else who felt afflicted by similar feelings of shame. Her compassion for herself only became realized when she encircled others with her compassion.

This also seemed to be the case for Chloe, whose sense of a larger purpose was expressed through the notion of a "moral crusade":

> Ever since I was a child, I've felt powerless to make a difference to life/the world/others' suffering. I have always been so worried about what other people would think about me that I don't have the courage to state my beliefs, values, and opinions if they are contrary to that of the person whom I'm with. When I am able to think about being actively involved in a moral crusade, it is actually of quite substantial significance to me; it gives me the occasional glimpse of feeling like an active crusader rather than a passive on-looker. I feel a sense of empowerment, as if the life force within me grows and strengthens. It is a feeling of aliveness, of purpose, of excitement.

The sense of solidarity these women may feel with others who are resisting a/b and the forces in society that support it may be enhanced if they are given more outlets or avenues to publicly express their protests. These avenues of activism might include sharing one's anti-a/b knowledge and determination with other insiders through writing, audiotape, or videotape; writing letters of protest to advertisers and media outlets that give a/b a boost; speaking out against pro-a/b values and specifications (the equation of thinness with beauty, perfection, self-sacrifice, and so on) and standing with others who are attempting to live through a counter or alternative morality.

Creating Options, Avoiding Specifications

It is pointless and even potentially destructive to exhort a woman to become angry at a/b (or a person who may be mistreating her), especially before she has separated from the meanings that make anger seem "bad" or dangerous. This kind of pressure or expectation to get angry would only contribute to her feeling like a failure (either for feeling angry when she believes she shouldn't or for not feeling angry when she believes this is expected of her) and ultimately strengthen a/b's grip on her.

Instead, we propose that therapists attend carefully to meanings and ideas that have undermined the woman's sense of moral worth and capacity to experience moral outrage. These meanings may have their origins in past or present abuse, in internalized ideas about what it means to be a good or desirable woman, or in the privileging of the points of view of critical others over the views of those who are more appreciative and sympathetic. When the woman has been invited to examine the effects of these meanings and to understand the context that produced them, she often experiences the option of feeling outrage at others who are tormenting her. When the interactional, institutional, and cultural constraints against the expression of outrage have been lessened or removed, there is often a spontaneous welling up of anger and outrage at a/b, as happened with Margaret (see Chapters 10, 11, 13, & 15), who wrote the following letter to "the voice of anorexia."

> To the Voice of Anorexia,
>
> Tonight I spoke to my therapist about how I have never been angry at you and, as a consequence, I began to question the idea that I didn't have the right to be angry at you. It didn't hit me till after I got home how much you had influenced my thinking about anger and how much you supported the ridiculous lie that "good girls don't get mad." Well, I got some news for you, anorexia, I am mad. I'm more than mad. I'm outraged at your injustice! I hate you and everything you stand for. I wish for one second you could be solid and touchable so I could smash you with all my might. You took so much from me and almost took my very life. I thank god that doctors were there to revive me from your clutches. For years you had me believing, in spite of my doctors saying that it was your starvation of me that stopped my heart, that they were wrong and it was my very heart that was defective and bad. It makes me ill when I realize you actually made me believe that and think that if I continued to listen to you, you would make my heart strong.
>
> You are such a sick fucking liar. I now know why you never wanted me to be mad or angry. It had nothing to do with securing my good-ness but everything to do with not wanting me to see you for what you are—absolute and total evil. If I saw that clearly, I would have stood up to you long ago. Get the fuck out of my life and leave me alone! I don't have room for you in my life any longer.
>
> In absolute anger and hatred of you, anorexia,
>
> Margaret

Therapists' Expressions of Moral Outrage

Therapists who consider a/b an external influence or force (as opposed to an internal illness) will almost certainly find themselves connecting with their own sense of moral outrage as they speak with young people about the devastating effects a/b is having on their lives and the sinister means it uses to deceive them. It is important for therapists to have outlets to express their moral outrage and experience some sense

of solidarity with others.* These outlets can include talking with colleagues, family members, and friends, engaging in political activism,
teaching, and contributing to and circulating anti-a/b archives.

Therapists should also consider the possibility of sharing this moral
outrage directly with the people (and their families) on whose behalf
they are feeling it. This may seem like an egregious error to those
therapists who believe in maintaining a "neutral" stance towards their
"patients" and the problems with which they are contending. However,
expressing this outrage may have many positive effects and, in some
instances, may be crucial. The expression of this outrage communicates
the therapist's moral opposition to a/b and may hasten an alliance
with any resistance the person may already have to a/b's tyranny. The
expression of moral outrage may provoke more anti-a/b skepticism in
those who trust a/b. It may also incite anti-a/b moral outrage on the part
of the person and her family, and it may legitimize and even encourage
the claiming and expression of this outrage.

This is not to say that these expressions on the part of the therapist
are without hazards. For example, it is possible that such expressions
might alienate a person who has not yet begun to question a/b and
still views it as a friend and savior. It is also conceivable that a/b might
make some people feel guilty and responsible for the therapist's distress, thereby turning the therapist's moral outrage into a weapon of
a/b. Therapists need to consider the potential benefits and liabilities
associated with being transparently outraged, but these considerations
do not necessarily need to be solitary. Sometimes it is best to solicit
the thoughts of the person consulting them about the effects of such a
practice.

Several years after I (DE) began working with women struggling
with a/b, I received by fax a letter[†] from a young woman (Chloe, then
age 17) who had spent a great deal of her life up until then in hospitals.
In my reply to her I allowed my moral outrage at a/b to permeate both
the content and tone of my response. Four years later I asked her if she
could recall her reaction to this initial letter. She replied:

> I think at first I was a bit taken aback . . . I had never received a letter
> quite like it before (or for that matter, anything like it!). I was struck by
> the anti-anorexic passion that was contained within the letter and was
> amazed that anyone could possess such energy and moral outrage.
> At the time I wasn't really able to keep up with your questions and

---

* This may help them avoid the *secondary traumatization* (as some have termed it) associated with
  the witnessing of or hearing about violence.
† To read this letter, log onto http://www.narrativeapproaches.com

anorexia didn't allow me to dwell on them for long, but it touched me deeply and, despite the strength of anorexia at that time, I found myself compelled beyond all odds to write back to you. Of course anorexia dismissed all that you said to me but the spirit with which the letter was written ensured that it lived on despite anorexia's best attempts to make me forget about it.

Prior to this letter, Chloe had refused to talk with or meet any other therapist or treating professional, even when her family had traveled hundreds of miles to consult them. The fact that Chloe had been able to overcome all odds to respond to the letter, and that the spirit of the letter lived on for her, is a testimonial to the potential impact of the therapist's expression of moral outrage.

Following is an edited version of another such letter written by Ann Epston to Emma, age 13, and her family, whom she had met for the first time that day. In the letter, Ann summarizes much of what she had learned about the circumstances of Emma's life that opened the door to anorexia, and the tactics and strategies anorexia used to exploit these circumstances. Ann did not simply reiterate what the family had told her. Instead, she reflected on the moral implications of what she had heard and expressed these implications through her moral outrage, much of which was addressed directly to anorexia. By addressing anorexia directly, Ann clearly distinguished between anorexia and Emma so that Emma would not mistakenly conclude that Ann was angry with her. Addressing anorexia had the further advantage of making the distinction between anorexia and Emma more vivid and tangible right at the outset, facilitating Emma's ability to separate herself from it both conceptually and in practice.

Dear Emma, Sandra, and Brian,

It was good to meet you all last night and make a start on getting to know you. Thank you, Emma, for your frankness and bravery in talking and in answering so many questions asked by a stranger.

I woke up at midnight and couldn't get back to sleep for hours; my mind was boiling with a furious anger against anorexia. I thought, "Here we go again, anorexia! So you've sneaked into the life of yet another innocent young girl, pretending to befriend her at a time of big changes. How cunning of you to detect Emma's uneasiness with her developing body, and how unscrupulous of you to offer her an 'easy' solution—dieting! How neatly you insinuated yourself into her uncertainty, her longing for friends and boyfriends, promising her that thinness would ensure attractiveness and popularity, would win her admiration and make her the envy of all who know her.

Anorexia, did you tell her the price she'd have to pay? Did you warn her you'd eventually steal even her soul in exchange? I heard you actually convinced Emma she's your only victim, in a school of 1,200 girls!

"You vampire, anorexia, haven't you taken enough already? Aren't you satisfied with the stream of young girls you've preyed upon, stealing their fat, then their flesh, their strength, their energy, their enthusiasm, their sparkle, their humor, opinions, sports, games, friendships, social times, confidence, trust, creativity, originality, individuality—their very lives?

"I suppose Emma was an attractive choice: intelligent, friendly, humorous, a lover of animals, responsible, ambitious, prepared to study hard and train to be a vet. What a delightful tall poppy to cut down at the threshold of adolescence! What pleasure you must be taking in draining her energy, blurring her concentration, and alienating her from her own body.

"How did you do it, anorexia? How did you train Emma to criticize and reject her body instead of loving herself? How did you make her believe that some imaginary schoolboy's opinion was worth starvation? What vulnerabilities did you seize upon to convince her that thin, weak conformists are more desirable than strong individuals?

"I suppose you have lots of help: the movies, magazines, TV soaps, advertising, school girl culture—they all tell the same story, that less is best for girls' bodies and minds. Did you use your usual trick of comparing? Making Emma compare herself against friends and declare herself the loser, then offer your services in consolation, the perfect solution? Did you use the old drug dealers' trick of just a little bit at first? Did you slip smoothly from the oh-so-reasonable 'no junk food' to gradually defining all food as junk? Did you use secrecy and the pretense of 'specialness' to isolate Emma in subtle ways from the loving concern of family and friends? And of course I know you used fear, that despicable technique favored by tyrants and bullies the world over. Yes, you terrorized this 13-year-old into accepting your lie—that you offer 'control' and without you, Emma will lose all control and her hunger will be insatiable.

"If it weren't so vicious and evil it would be laughable, your threat that a healthy, active young woman will become the size of a whale just by the simple fact of eating ordinary nourishing food. This fear has tormented and tortured countless thousands upon thousands of young women into submitting to your hateful rule.

"But, anorexia, we will not stand for it. Emma has wise and loving parents who will not allow you to prey upon their beloved daughter.

They have chosen me as their anti-anorexic therapist, and with the help of Dr.—— and her dietitian and everyone who cares about Emma, we will fight anorexia and fear and drive you out of this family's life. We do this because we are perfectly clear about what is right and what is wrong. Take notice, anorexia, we will do everything in our power to free Emma from the spell you have cast over her. We are guided by two principles: unwavering support and love for Emma and unwavering hatred for anorexia and the harm it does."

Yours anti-anorexically,
Ann Epston

For many insiders (if not all), embarking on the path to reclaim their life from a/b will mean courageously taking the leap of faith that a fulfilling life can be constructed without a/b's so-called assistance. Through discerning and critiquing the voice of a/b, the "curtains" can be pulled back and a/b's "true face" can be exposed. It is our hope that by joining with us and others in this collective critique of a/b and the cultural discourses that support it, insiders and their allies will be able to see through a/b's fraudulent moral claims, and by doing so, bring their own moral commitments into sharper relief. Recognizing the discrepancy between one's own morality and a/b's immorality can give rise to moral outrage at a/b's violation of those human rights and values that one holds sacred. The act of disengaging from a/b is simultaneously an act of engaging or reengaging with those things you cherish: your own aspirations, values, rights, hopes, and dreams. It is these matters that become the foundation upon which your anti-anorexic/bulimic lifestyle can be constructed.

Chapter 12

CONSTRUCTING ANTI-ANOREXIC/BULIMIC LIFESTYLES

Lend your voices only to sounds of freedom/No longer lend your strength to that which you wish to be free from/Fill your lives with love and bravery/And you shall lead a life uncommon.

— Jewel

When people first realize that a/b is a mortal enemy and mobilize their outrage in order to unmask its voice, they cease living *for* a/b and begin, instead, to live *with* or *against* it. The subsequent construction of an anti-a/b lifestyle makes it possible eventually to live *apart* from it. Victoria (see Chapter 11) plotted her progress along an anti-anorexic path in terms of her identity vis-à-vis anorexia.

As a child, I was Victoria. Then, at the age of 13, I was transformed into Anorexicvictoria. I then decided that I wanted to "reclaim my life" and became Anorexicvictoria (who doesn't want to be Anorexic anymore). When I progressed to a state of war, I became Anorexicvictoria-Anti-Anorexia. The Anorexic prefix to my identity is fading more and more as time goes on. So I guess the next step will be Victoria-Anti-Anorexia. I hyphenated this name to indicate that Anti-Anorexia did not overtake me as Anorexia did. Rather, it is something I have chosen to embrace and integrate into my life. It now feels as if it resides in the core of my being.

ACCEPTING THE RANGE OF ONE'S EXPERIENCE

Constructing an anti-a/b lifestyle involves making choices that are based on what one wants to divorce oneself from as well as what one wishes to embrace. These choices are both a repudiation of one manner of living and an affirmation of another. Chloe (see Chapter 11) put it this way:

> For me, living an anti-anorexic lifestyle is about living a life according to my own values, beliefs, and dreams rather than those of anorexia. It is about actively choosing between the life anorexia would have me lead and the life that I envisage for myself. It is about taking anti-anorexic challenges and risks wherever possible and accepting temporary "defeat" when it is not possible (and most importantly— not letting that "defeat" stop me from rising to the challenge at some later date).

If women desire to forge a life of their own design rather than confine themselves to a prescribed and ill-fitting "off-the-rack" life, one of the first necessary steps may be to alter their relationship to their own experience. For people who have been ruled by a/b for years, discerning what it is they want and value in their lives may require listening to and honoring themselves and their own embodied experience. Under the regime of a/b, these feelings and appetites had become the enemy, to be scorned, purged, or otherwise overcome through self-discipline and willpower. But for the person who has turned against a/b and achieved some degree of separation from it, these feelings can provide occasions for the acceptance and appreciation of the full range of one's experience. Victoria described how definitive this was for her anti-anorexic style of living:

> I have come to a simple way of explaining my Anti-Anorexic lifestyle. Are you ready? . . . Just being!! "Just being" means to me just feeling like I am feeling at that precise moment. If I am tired, then I will be tired. If I am feeling sick, then I will feel sick. If I am happy, then I will be happy! It is living without unrealistic expectations of myself—like if I am sick, that I have to pretend I am fine and soldier on instead of taking a few days out to rest and recover. If I am feeling too tired to talk on the phone, then I will ring them as soon as I have had a rest. If I am feeling too overwhelmed to respond to any correspondence, I wait and take another look at it when I am feeling more on top of things.

DISCERNING ONE'S PREFERENCES

The acceptance of oneself and one's experience without the imposition of unrealistic expectations is, in itself, an enormous anti-anorexic lifestyle change, but it also paves the way for the discerning of one's preferences in all areas of life. A/b can make it difficult for a woman to identify these preferences by provoking fears about new steps and initiatives. This was certainly Chloe's experience as she attempted to challenge anorexia's confining prescriptions and prohibitions as she went about improvising her life. In struggling to define and fashion her own life, Chloe developed a practice of asking herself questions designed to ferret out her own interests and desires by bracketing out anorexia-incited prescriptions and fears.

> Something I find useful in distinguishing whether a challenge is anti-anorexic in nature is by stopping to think about whether it is something I would like to do *if* I didn't have fears around it. For example, would I like to go out with my friends *if* I wasn't scared that we might go out to a cafe? For me, if the answer is "yes" then I can be sure it's an anti-anorexic challenge. Sometimes it is difficult to ask myself such questions because anorexia tries to make me forget what I really do or do not like. In these instances I tend to ask myself, "Is this something I would have liked to do *before* anorexia invaded my life?" For example, "Would I have liked to eat this particular food prior to anorexia's invasion of my life?" Again, if the answer is "yes," then it confirms that it is an anti-anorexic challenge and one well worth embarking upon.

WALKING THE ANTI-A/B PATH

The a/b lifestyle, like a fast-food hamburger, is prepackaged and guaranteed to be the same every day. Because anti-a/b is antithetical to prescriptions and prohibitions, every person will invariably construct an anti-anorexic/bulimic lifestyle that is uniquely her own. Women's anti-a/b lifestyles are one-of-a-kind, fashioned against the particular ways in which a/b spoke to them, and according to their own preferences and heart's desires. They will vary from day to day because of their responsiveness to the fluidity of mood, whim, and desire, and their openness to the vulnerability inherent in journeys without pre-ordained destinations. But while the destinations will ultimately be different, it is likely that the journeys themselves will share some characteristics. Below, we present some of the practices that can assist a person, moment-to-moment, in constructing an anti-a/b lifestyle and life.

Embracing Risk

Discerning one's particular anti-a/b path can be difficult; actually walking it can be terrifying. Forsaking a/b's fraudulent security and "perfection" for a path with an unknown destination means cultivating one's capacity to take risks and be undeterred by fear. Chloe found that opening herself up to vulnerability allowed her to take risks.

> For me, one of the most important aspects of paving the way for an anti-anorexic lifestyle is opening myself up to vulnerability and taking risks. Anorexia is so regimented, controlling, and restricting, always demanding that one knows (as Phoebe put it) ". . . the best path even before you walk it." For me, anorexia is all about having guarantees—e.g., if you don't eat anything then you won't put on weight, or if you don't take up this new hobby then you are guaranteed not to fail at it. So anti-anorexia, by nature, is about taking risks; about opening myself up to new experiences where the outcome might be unknown. It is about choosing to take the risk that you might not get perfect grades if you choose to study a subject you don't know much about but choosing to do it anyway because you are interested. It is about choosing to fight against anorexia in every possible way you can even though there are no absolute guarantees that you will ever be completely free from it but continuing to fight anyway in the name of hope and moral outrage. For me, anti-anorexia is about knowing the value in the journey rather than focusing on the destination. It is about forging your own path rather than searching for the "best path" down which to walk.

Although, undoubtedly, everybody will experience some fear in turning away from the regulated life of a/b and toward her own unpredictable choice-filled future, each person will have her own particular reasons for taking these risks and her own particular way of managing the fear. Chloe's determination to fashion her own life and push through this fear stemmed from her moral outrage at anorexia, her recognition of the costs of anorexic enslavement, her sense of being obligated by love to all those who had fought for her over the years, and perhaps most importantly, her desire to live a life filled with meaning, value, and "sparkling moments."

What enables me to do this is knowing what my life looks like when I don't take risks and don't open myself up to vulnerability and instead live only by anorexia's guarantees. I have discovered over the years that such a life is decidedly bleak and desolate. It is a life without friends, because in order to have friends, one must take the risk that your friends don't really like you and are just being nice to you out of sympathy or the goodness of their heart. It is a life lived on the sidelines because to join in would be to risk not performing to standards or making a fool of yourself. It is a life without learning and growth, for in order to learn and grow one must risk making mistakes and not being perfect straight off. It is a life without connectedness to family because to open up to family relationships you have to risk finding out they wish that you weren't part of the family and care for you only because they feel duty-bound to do so. It is also a life of complete isolation because to be in the company of others means that you have to risk whatever they may think of you or how they may judge you. Most of all, it is a life of nothingness, of mere existence—devoid of all the "sparkling moments" that make life worth living.

I am able to take anti-anorexic risks because I realize that, despite often being painful, they are necessary if I am to create a life of meaning and value. I take them because of the hope I see they elicit in those around me who have fought so hard for my life over the years. Hating anorexia and all that it stands for also enables me to take such risks and challenges so that I may live out my values and renounce those of anorexia.

Embracing Choice

Whereas Chloe described taking risks as a hallmark of her anti-anorexia, Victoria emphasized *choice* as a central feature of her anti-anorexic lifestyle.

Anti-Anorexia is very much about choices for me. For so many years I was trapped into various commitments, career choices, and routines and I feared I could never get out of them. Anorexia offered me an escape route when I felt I had no other choices. However, as I gradually learn to leave Anorexia behind, I am discovering that I have so many options and choices ahead of me. Anorexia had my life fully mapped out for me. Thinking Anti-Anorexically has allowed me to say, "Anorexia, I don't know if I want this life you have decided I'm going to have," and to start looking at what else the world has to offer. I can also enjoy the idea that I can choose to go in whatever direction I want to, and that if it doesn't turn out the way I'd hoped, I don't have to stick it out, suffering. I can change direction anytime I want to, and that does not mean that I am a failure at all. By embracing and integrating Anti-Anorexia into my life, I am embracing choice. I know what will happen if I keep buying into Anorexia's crap. I don't know what might happen if I fight Anorexia and reclaim my life, but the possibilities are endless and exciting.

Of course, with choices come risks. Victoria's approach to risk was to engage in a cost-benefit analysis of sorts.

I have always found it useful to look at both sides of a situation that appears risky and to pose the following questions: What am I risking? Is protecting myself from the possible negative consequences that may occur worth missing out on what happens if the risk pays off? Every single time the answer has been "no way!"

When the person begins to separate from a/b, small anti-a/b acts will begin to multiply. The focus of therapy can then shift away from the deconstruction of a/b and its tactics and strategies, and take up these anti-a/b developments. There are many things about these initiatives to explore and understand, including their anti-a/b significance, what made them possible, what effects they had, what they say about the person's hopes and dreams and preferences, and the relationships that support them. We find these inquiries to be occasions for profound joy, great fun, and subversive mischief. Invariably laughter and smiles abound in these conversations. Witnessing the client's coming-to-life during these meetings can be similar to watching a time-lapsed film of a tree leafing out and blooming.*

Remembering that the Small Stuff Counts

Even seemingly small anti-a/b actions can have powerful anti-a/b repercussions, both on a physical level and on a symbolic level (or meaning level). Consider the following story from Chloe:

It occurred when I was 10, several months after discharge from my first hospitalization the previous year. Anorexia had me strictly regulating my meals—not only what I ate, but when I ate it. It was set against this background that I remember making one of the most unexpected and delightful anti-anorexic actions. I was at school and it was lunchtime. A bag of chips was broken open by a friend and chips were duly doled

---

* See the transcript of David's meeting with Amy (Chapter 14) for an example of one of these meetings.

out. When my turn came to receive my chip, I automatically shook my head, which didn't come as any surprise to anybody as they were used to my changed eating habits since I'd "got sick." I didn't even give it a second thought. But then my friend said, "go on Chloe, have a chip" and all of a sudden I found myself reaching out my hand, accepting the one potato chip and eating it of all things! I remember being absolutely stunned because it was something I hadn't even considered doing... it just sort of happened. At the time, although I realized the significance of the event, I couldn't really put a finger on what it was that was so amazing and have never told anyone else what I did that day.

For those looking on from the outside, it may seem insignificant ... "she ate one single chip—so what?" But for me it wasn't about the chip...it was about breaking free of anorexia's imposed regulations and doing something on the spur of the moment just for the "hell of it." It was about regaining my sense of autonomy rather that being driven and dictated to by anorexia.

The physical ramifications of Chloe's eating a potato chip were inconsequential but the symbolic significance of the action was enormous. The significance of this act lay not in the extent to which it nourished her body but in the degree to which it strengthened her heart, buoyed her spirit, and reaffirmed her as a person.

Not surprisingly, a/b will try to minimize and dismiss anti-a/b initiatives in the hope of supplanting these efforts with discouragement and resignation. It is vitally important that people allow themselves to place their faith in these actions and their slow but inevitable progress towards freedom. Chloe discussed the importance of "the small stuff" to the construction of her anti-anorexic lifestyle:

My anti-anorexia is also about knowing that the small stuff counts. It is about knowing that every anti-anorexic action you take or challenge you set for yourself erodes anorexia's stranglehold over your life. Anorexia would tell me that, because I was unable to take big anti-anorexic leaps forward and push anorexia totally out of my life, that I was a failure and there was no point even trying to fight it. For example, when it came to a mealtime and I was agonizing over whether to push myself and take that extra mouthful, anorexia would say, "What's the point? Just taking one extra mouthful isn't going to get you anywhere, it's nothing. I (anorexia) still control so much of your life and one additional mouthful isn't going to change that." My parents urged me to take an anti-anorexic challenge, but I would invariably frustrate them with my replies of "What's the point? It's not going to get me anywhere or do anything to change the big picture." It was hard enough to endure the vicious nature of anorexia's backlash when anti-anorexic challenges were taken up without the added "bonus" of anorexia convincing me that those were pointless. This made taking any anti-anorexic action quite impossible.

So for me, a really important step in moving towards living an anti-anorexic lifestyle is accepting that every little anti-anorexic challenge and affront to anorexia counts and makes a difference. I still find this hard to remember sometimes, but I try to remind myself of something David wrote in one of his original faxes to me—"How do you think the steady drip, one drop at a time, finally cracks the largest rock?" This is a reminder to me that every drop of anti-anorexia is slowly but surely chipping away at anorexia's seemingly rock-hard surface. After a year and a half of taking small counter-actions against anorexia, I find myself at a place where I never imagined I would get to. Is this proof that all those seemingly pointless anti-anorexic actions I have taken, and all the feelings of extreme guilt and self-loathing that I have endured as a result of challenging anorexia, have in the end been worth it? Slowly but surely, I am coming to believe that the answer to that question is *yes!*

Just as a/b claims that the smallness of actions testifies to their insignificance, so too will it disparage the pace of progress. It might make pronouncements such as "If it were going to happen it would have happened by now" or "You are getting nowhere." Victoria had this to say about an anti-anorexic time frame:

> It is really important to highlight and keep highlighting the fact that it takes a long, long time to hew out an Anti-Anorexic lifestyle. This lifestyle is going to be unique to the individual and worthy of celebration. This, I believe, is a part of the beauty of Anti-Anorexia. It has been helpful for me to keep in mind the length of time Anorexia has had control over my life and to realize that this 9 years cannot be reversed in a day. Sometimes I think it would only be fair to allow myself at least 9 years to develop this Anti-Anorexic lifestyle. On the other hand, while my Anorexic lifestyle is fading out, I don't think there is ever going to be an end to my Anti-Anorexic lifestyle, which I find exciting.

Living According to Feelings and Preferences

A/b attempts to number a person's days, both literally and figuratively. Below, Victoria discusses the importance of refusing to live by numbers as a means of measuring and ordering her life, and instead, allowing her embodied experience to guide her actions.

> One significant Anti-Anorexic step has been to reject weights and measurements. This has had a huge influence on my Anti-Anorexic lifestyle. A short time ago I was obsessed with weighing and measuring everything—the duration of exercise I did, the kilograms I weighed, the percent of effort I was putting into any activity I took part in, how many friends I had, how many grams of fat I ingested in a day, how many hours I spent sleeping . . . the list goes on. As I try and look at my life Anti-Anorexically, these measurements have become less important. I now try and exercise until I have had enough, eat when I am hungry and until I'm full, sleep for as long as I need to, etc. My life has become much less regimented and much less bound up in routine. To me, this is very Anti-Anorexic.

> I think I never truly understood just how much time I spent obsessing about food and weight and numbers. It is only now that I wonder how I remembered how to tie my shoes or work the telephone while under that much Anorexic pressure. I had a hard time perceiving how total my preoccupation was when it *was* so total. By continuing to fight against Anorexia's demands and by exposing it every chance I can, the routines and rules it made me live by have faded in their intensity. I am finding out that the world is more interesting than what the scales say.

Welcoming Spontaneity

Another seemingly ubiquitous feature of an anorexia lifestyle is the mindless routines and rituals that can dominate nearly every waking moment. These rules, and their manifestations as obligatory rituals and routines, can turn a person into a "zombie" (as one insider put it), physically alive but spiritually deadened. Embracing risk and choice, and living life from the inside out (according to one's own preferences) are all means by which a person can refuse to be confined by the order(s) of a/b. Chloe, in her correspondence with David and Victoria, described another means by which she defied anorexia's attempt to regiment her life.

> Lately I've been able to be much more spontaneous, which is one of the things anorexia had taken away from me. However, anyone looking in at my life would conclude that I'm not in the least spontaneous and they would be right. However, I am, nevertheless, more spontaneous than I have been (which was regimented to the extreme). For example—previously I always had to walk exactly the same route each

day (when I went out for a walk) so that I could be sure I was burning the same amount of calories each time. I could go for longer walks but never shorter. Not only that but it had to be at the same time each day. Now I go for a walk whenever it fits in best with my day, and sometimes when I start out on my walk I am struck by the desire to challenge myself to disobey anorexia and so I go off in a completely new direction and just go wherever my feet take me without knowing if I've walked for the equivalent distance or amount of time. This is a very small act of spontaneity in the grand scheme of things but it is at least something.

Venerating Imperfection

Maintaining an anti-a/b lifestyle often necessitates a vigilant contesting of the ideal of perfection in whatever quarter of one's life it might appear. The ideal of perfection is one of a/b's most powerful allies. Brian (age 12) opined, "Anorexia and Perfection are like a married couple." Perfection and a/b exist symbiotically, both supporting and upholding each other as they parasitically feed off their human prey. Both a/b and perfection assess people as "deficient" and institute "rules" for proving themselves "worthy."

Chloe spoke about the influence of perfection on her efforts to construct an anti-anorexic life and how it made her feel like she was in "no-man's-land" and then tempted her with the prospect of once again becoming the "perfect anorexic."

> I have recently come to realize that a large part of what I find so difficult about gaining weight is that I become a nobody. What I mean by this is that by complying with anorexia's demands and losing weight, I am being, if you like, the "perfect anorexic." When I gain weight and disobey anorexia then I lose that. It would be okay if I could replace that by being the "perfect anti-anorexic" (as if such a thing were even possible) but I am unable to achieve that status because, while I may gain weight and take small anti-anorexic actions, my life and habits are still very much dominated by anorexia. Thus I feel like I'm in a no-man's-land—neither a successful anorexic nor anti-anorexic. And while I have come to realize that I'd much rather be the perfect anti-anorexic rather than the perfect anorexic, I must be a perfect *something*. When I see myself falling short of being the perfect anti-anorexic the temptation is to fall back to that of being the "perfect anorexic" because I know that I can achieve some success when it comes to being "anorexic."

In the hospital, I found that the idea of there being no middle ground was reinforced. I always felt that whatever achievements I made against anorexia, they were never good enough because I was not "normal" yet. "Normal" was held up as an ideal... a person had to be a "normal weight," be able to eat "normally," be able to eat what "normal" people eat, think like "normal" people think. Often I found perfection within me strengthened by the way "normal" was held up as an ideal. I felt like I could never achieve "normal" and so I may as well achieve "abnormal" (anorexic). Perfection has always tried to make it very clear to me that it is better not to try at all than to try and to fail.

Chloe's hospital experience speaks to how any norm opens the door to self-surveillance, evaluation, and judgment. This can be problematic in any situation, but when perfection interacts with these norms, success and failure become absolutes.

THE ROLE OF SPIRITUALITY IN RECLAIMING ONE'S LIFE

Spirituality can provide a significant platform from which to both fight a/b and construct a life apart from it. As many insiders have shared with us, spiritual knowing powerfully contradicts a/b's view of the self and the world. Spirituality can profoundly link a person to herself and to the world around her, whereas a/b cuts a person off from herself and disengages her from the world. Spirituality can cut through feelings of isolation and alienation and leave people feeling connected to the web of life. It honors and sanctifies life, whereas a/b dishonors and profanes it. Spirituality can connect a person to her heart and provide a moral and ethical framework for action, whereas a/b disconnects people from their bodies and imposes a punitive and perverse morality. Spiritual *spaces* often provide emotional respite and comfort for those who have been subject to abuse and oppression or have been recruited into self-abuse and self-criticism. These spaces promote gentleness, love, and acceptance and do not easily admit harshness or meanness. A/b, on the other hand, opens space for criticism, condemnation, and coercion.

Gaining Perspective Through Spirituality

Connecting to one's spiritual knowing can provide a person with an elevation from which she can survey her life and her world with a refreshing perspective. This connection can make it possible for a woman to gain clarity about her most cherished values and commitments and, on the basis of these, rediscern her preferred direction in life. Perhaps many of the qualities associated with being "spirited" or having a strong spirit—courage, determination, valor, heart, daring, verve, fight, and sparkle—are simply manifestations of the knowing that has come through the "elevated" perspective associated with the spiritual. And perhaps this very knowledge of one's most profound values and visions is one of the things that that can fortify the spirit and make it indomitable.

Another feature of the spiritual perspective is the experience of the interconnectedness of things. This awareness of a person's connection to a larger totality can allow her to experience the ultimate smallness of her own life in relation to the vastness of being and of time. This perception of smallness or insignificance can, paradoxically, lead to a profound sense of belonging and "place." This sense of smallness, humility, and belonging is in sharp contrast to the sense of belittlement, humiliation, and disconnection that results from a/b's spirit-breaking.

Victoria, in her correspondence with David, described how an experience of the power and beauty of nature helped her regain a perspective that allowed her to get some distance from anorexia.

> To succeed in its ultimate seduction, Anorexia must convince me that *it* is the single most important and most influential thing in my life. Although I may have felt totally defeated, to sit out on the edge of the jetty with the entire lake spread out in front of me was just too strong to be blocked by Anorexia. The crystal-clear water, the calm flat surface, the surrounding cliffs covered in bush, the pink glow of Mt. Tarawera, and the sheer size and power of the rawness of nature broke through all the crap that was going on in my head. I felt so humbled in that I felt very small and insignificant in this environment. I felt privileged to be able to sit here and appreciate nature's beauty. I concluded that if I felt small and insignificant, then Anorexia, in turn, must be even smaller and more insignificant, as it was inside of me.
>
> I will always remember this very moment as I believe it was a turning point in my life and in my relationship to Anorexia. On one of those days, as the sun was rising, I stood on the jetty, in the exact place that I had experienced that "telling moment," and took a few photos in sequence to put together to give me a panoramic view. It is a magic photo and if I look at it and shut off everything around me, it feels as if I am back in this place. This reenergizes me and puts things back into perspective again.

Spirit-Nourishing

For people who identify *spirit* as something that allows them to achieve a perspective that separates them from a/b, it is important to consider what has (in the past) or might (in the present) nourish their spirits. Spirit-nourishing experiences may be solitary endeavors such as meditation, prayer, awe-provoking encounters with nature, or warm baths. The spirit might be nourished by engaging (either as an actor or spectator) in artistic or cultural experiences such as music, dance, painting, writing, and so on. For some, spiritual nourishment might come through efforts to assist others and work for social justice. Spirit-nourishing activities might involve collective expressions of spirituality and religiosity such as singing, prayer, and ritual, or they may rely upon day-to-day interactions with significant others, including parents and other family members, friends, lovers, therapists and other helping professionals, pets, stuffed animals, and so on. There are really an infinite number of experiences that might be potentially nurturing of one's connection to spiritual knowing.

Chloe reflected on her spirit and the role others played in rekindling it after anorexia had succeeded in nearly extinguishing it:

> I have come to the conclusion that in my heart of hearts there dwells such a thing as the essence of my spirit, my will to live, my wonder and amazement at life, my ability to be touched by others' kindness, and a wish to reach out and touch in turn. When I think about it . . . I think anorexia has actually managed to displace that which calls my heart of hearts its home. How can one live when one's essence is destroyed, you may ask? Well, the simple answer is that I have always been surrounded by those who would not let me give up. Imagine, if you will, that within everybody's heart they have a flame burning which symbolizes their life force, their spirit, etc. Well, anorexia has time and again reached out with its long black fingers and extinguished that very flame which resides within me.
>
> However, there have always been people (e.g., my parents) standing by, waiting to relight that flame by using the light of their own flame within them. Like the way a candle can be used to relight another candle. They keep on trying over and over again until the flame finally catches alight and burns once again of its own accord. When anorexia extinguishes it again, they are back, to repeat the process all over again. I am grateful for the extent of their love and kindness. However at times I have longed to let the flame die and to be allowed to fade away from life itself. It is so painful to be kept alive when

the flame in one's heart is gone. I have no doubt that if it weren't for my family, my flame would never have been rekindled on so many occasions.

Chloe spoke of the way in which anorexia "time and again reached out with its long black fingers and extinguished that very flame which resides within me," necessitating the "rekindling" of her spirit on many occasions. In the next chapter we discuss the virtually inevitable *comebacks* staged by a/b and how these comebacks might best be viewed and responded to.

Chapter 13

COMEBACKS AND RETREATS

Insiders often describe the process of disentangling from a/b as a horrifying roller coaster ride. When a person progresses in her pursuit of reclaiming her freedoms from a/b, it is likely, if not inevitable, that a/b will try to "cut her off at the pass." Forging an anti-a/b lifestyle means, almost by definition, inciting a/b's wrath. As a/b begins to lose its grip, it ratchets up its rhetoric. Its seductions become more perverse, its logic more preposterous, its rebukes more vicious, and its warnings more dire. A/b never concedes a battle or unconditionally surrenders. In fact, the weaker it gets, the harder it fights. Perhaps that is why Victoria (see Chapters 11 & 12) would have run from anti-anorexia if doing so would not have almost certainly resulted in her death:

> I have found that the most powerful and painful punishments from Anorexia have followed closely behind a significant Anti-Anorexic action or series of actions. This is very difficult at times. In fact, it is *such* hard work that I would not recommend it to my worst enemy. When I compare being Anti-Anorexic to being Pro-Anorexic, it is, in many ways, harder. Yet, I know that as one of Anorexia's pawns, you have to work really hard. You have to work to resist all attempts to help you, and make you eat, and draw you away from death's door. One thing is guaranteed by the work you do for Anorexia—a painful death. Anti-Anorexia, on the other hand, provides you with limitless possibilities. So why not put that same amount of fierce determination

into Anti-Anorexia instead? Then, instead of earning yourself an early death, you may earn yourself a life.

A/b typically finds ways to make a comeback in the life of a person who has succeeded in putting some distance between herself and it. This distance can be large and sustained over a long period of time (even years), or it can be a recent and small distance achieved in the day-to-day tug-of-war with anorexia. We are using the word *comeback* to refer to those times when a/b mounts a counter-offensive and is able to regain some of the influence it had lost. The experience of a comeback can be very sudden and terrifying, perhaps akin to being abducted and assaulted, leaving one in fear for her very life. Lorraine, a 21-year old, described such an assault:

> When I got home, it grabbed me. This was not so much a romancing, but an assault. Although I had only been back into a pattern of restriction and purging for a week or two, I felt as if I could not get out of it *ever.* And I panicked. It literally felt as if I were heading rapidly downhill and that there was no stopping. It was hard for me to describe my panic to people around me, especially when I seemed so healthy having just returned from a vacation from Anorexia.

Although comebacks can be triggered by many things, we wish to distinguish between those which are precipitated by the person's taking an anti-a/b step (or steps) that threatens and antagonizes a/b and those which result from a/b's exploiting difficult circumstances in a person's life. These "rough spots" can include experiences of abuse or denigration, difficult transitions, losses of valued relationships, work stress, and examinations and evaluations of any sort. Any of these circumstances can throw the door wide open to a/b, which doesn't hesitate to kick a woman when she is down, and to do so with unprecedented malice.

Although comebacks can be both terrifying and discouraging, they are both predictable and surmountable. Despite what a/b might proclaim, comebacks say nothing about the person's ultimate capacity to escape from a/b's prison. Over time, as a person gains more experience dealing with comebacks, they tend to become less alarming, less frequent, and more manageable.

PRO-ANOREXIC/BULIMIC "SPINS" ON COMEBACKS

It is not unusual for comebacks to repeatedly thwart a person's progress toward the reclaiming of her life and keep her mired in a/b indefinitely. When this occurs, it is usually not the comeback itself that is the culprit, but the manner in which a/b spins the meaning of the comeback. As Victoria stated, "Anorexia will do anything to turn a relapse into a trip on a train that has come off its tracks and is speeding on its way to self-destruction." Following are some of the strategies a/b uses to derail "the train" and turn comebacks into a destructive descent.

Claims that the Woman Is Back to "Square One"

In a typical fight, as the adversary weakens, the strength and effectiveness of his or her assault also weakens. A/b defies this logic by fighting more viciously and deviously as it grows weaker, and this potentially gives a/b an advantage over its unsuspecting adversary. When a/b makes a comeback in a person's life, it fraudulently claims that this is evidence that, despite all her hard work, a/b has only grown stronger and more dominating. The woman is often convinced that she is back to "square one" or worse. Furthermore, a/b may argue that not only is she worthless, but that her therapy is useless as well.

Claims that the Woman Is a Failure and Encourages Her to Give Up

A/b's spin on the comeback can result in the woman's experiencing not only a sense of panic at being once again overtaken, but also a devastating demoralization and sense of failure. A/b has a vested interest in labeling comebacks as failures so that it can convince these young women that they themselves are failures, something a/b has gone to extraordinary lengths to persuade them of in the first place. By labeling these women as "failures," a/b further diminishes their belief in their value, making them even more open and vulnerable to a/b's claims of betterment or more accepting of its tortures.

Claims that A/B Is Part of the Woman's "Nature" and Destiny

If anti-anorexic/bulimic acts of resistance have been instrumental in helping a person see that she is separate from a/b and not defined by it, a/b very often attempts to use these comebacks to reinscribe itself onto the person's identity. A/b might claim at this juncture: "You *are* anorexia, and any effort you make to go against your 'nature,' even when it seems you are succeeding, is just a sham. You are destined to, deserve to, and need to suffer this lot in life." A/b may try to obscure the fact that, even in the midst of a comeback, a/b's intensity varies, as does the person's ability to resist it. A/b leads the person to believe that every day's struggle will be the same, and that it will be as difficult as the hardest day.

Exploits the Traditional View of Relapse and Healing as Polar Opposites

The conventional way of thinking of a/b as an illness may also play into its hands because *illness* and *health* are conceived of as polar opposites, as are *relapse* and *healing*. According to this way of thinking, a person cannot be healthy if she is ill, nor can she be in the process of healing if she is relapsing. These constructions are so taken for granted that it is difficult to imagine the possibility that relapse can be a part of healing. The ups and downs of moods and the back and forth of meanings that occur during the prolonged struggle to reclaim one's life from a/b are perhaps better thought of metaphorically—as akin to changes in weather or seasons, or to the ebb and flow of a tide.

ANTI-ANOREXIC/BULIMIC WAYS OF VIEWING COMEBACKS

When a/b asserts its own demoralizing spin on comebacks, it is important that insiders, parents, and therapists all have recourse to some alternative means of viewing comebacks. Below, we present two ways of viewing comebacks (though there are undoubtedly more) that seem to fit the experience of insiders better and promote hope rather than despair.

Comebacks as an Inevitable Response

How can these comebacks be viewed, if not as failures, as evidence of the futility of resistance, or as manifestations of nature and destiny? First, they can be viewed as an inevitable part of the journey toward reclaiming oneself. It is inconceivable to us that a person could begin to break free from a/b's prison without antagonizing a/b in the process. If a/b has found it necessary to "turn up the heat," perhaps it is because the person has been defying it in ways that a/b finds unacceptable. Because a/b's antagonism to anti-a/b developments can be very forceful, the person may find herself temporarily ensnared once again in a/b's web of meaning.

Comebacks as a Sign of A/B's Desperation

Chloe (see Chapters 11 & 12), when asked what she considered to be an anti-anorexic way of looking at comebacks, offered the following reflection:

> Perhaps comebacks could be a sign of anorexia's desperation—that anorexia is losing its grip. When a tyrant's power is threatened, it

resorts to lashing out in desperate attempts to cling to power. Thus, I'm wondering if comebacks might be viewed as desperate acts by anorexia. If comebacks were viewed in this way, I'm wondering if some of the shame, disappointment, and sense of hopelessness could be taken out of them.

I know that it would be asking a lot for comebacks to be worn with a "badge of pride" because they involve pain, suffering, and deprivation. And I do not wish to glorify comebacks because they are terrible to have to endure and can pose very real dangers of pulling the person down so much that they slip back into anorexia's embrace to the point that they find themselves trapped once more. However, maybe the pain of such an incarceration would be easier to bear if it were known that it was a sign of the person's gains and anorexia's subsequent desperation.

PREDICTING COMEBACKS

Because comebacks of varying degrees are likely to occur, we believe that by foreseeing and predicting comebacks, therapists and other treaters may be able to partially inoculate the person against the sense of failure and hopelessness that so often results from them. These predictions reassure the person, in advance, that the therapist will not in any way view a comeback as a failure or a disappointment and that, on the contrary, comebacks are often indirect testimonials to the force of the person's anti-a/b and the extent to which she provoked a/b's wrath and viciousness through her disobedience.

Although we believe that predicting comebacks is advisable, it is not without its hazards. A/b is very likely to twist the meanings of these predictions, so it is very important that the therapist leave as little ambiguity as possible for a/b to play with. It is possible to anticipate a/b's twist by asking something like "Is anorexia telling you that I think you are are going to fail or that escape is impossible?" An alternative approach—one that might be better when the therapist finds it difficult to anticipate a/b's twist—is to ask a more open-ended question like "What did anorexia try to make of my comments?" If the therapist learns that a/b has indeed twisted the meaning of his or her words, he or she can insist on setting the record straight. A/b may still claim that its interpretation of the therapist's words is true, but the young woman will now have access to two competing interpretations, making it possible for her to discern which is more reliable or trustworthy.

RESPONDING TO COMEBACKS

When a/b renews or intensifies its hostilities, leaning a little more heavily on the care and regard of others can be crucial in slowing down the "speeding train" and getting oneself back on an anti-a/b track. If one is rapidly sliding or tumbling down the side of a steep hill, reaching out for something anti-a/b to grab on to can slow and even arrest the fall. Perhaps that is why a/b usually insists that the person must go it alone, on the grounds that seeking any help whatsoever is a humiliating show of weakness and that being a winner means being able to succeed on one's own. Friends, partners, and parents may serve well as "handholds" or "footholds" if the young woman can reach out to them or can grasp hold of the hand being offered. Chloe spoke of the importance of seeking assistance from others in addition to doing things for oneself:

> I guess that for me, having people around me that are able to retain their hope and faith in me during a comeback increases my chances of being able to not give in to the despair and sense of failure that anorexia would try to engulf me in. I think that when engulfed in anorexic quicksand it is important that one recognizes the need for help from someone who still has their feet firmly planted on dry land; that a cry for help is not a failing but rather an imperative. This is not to say that the person can only lie helpless, waiting for outside assistance with ropes to pull them out—there are most certainly things one can do for oneself to prevent further sinking but ultimately one needs backup support in order to pull oneself free.

Any experience that can help a person recover a sense of her own goodness and remind her of who she is can provide an important lifeline during such times. Some people may choose to seek relief or recover perspective through spirituality, be it through prayer or meditation, singing, listening to music, or spending time in nature. Others may choose to "batten down the hatches," "lower the sails," and try to weather the storm. This defensive posture might also involve trying to tune out a/b as best as one can, e.g., by "turning down the volumne."

What can therapists do when they see someone losing her anti-a/b foothold and being dragged back into the concentration camp of a/b? Following are some guidelines for responding to comebacks. These are derived from what insiders have told us about the types of therapist responses they have found most helpful or unhelpful. Obviously no "off-the-shelf" guidelines are as reliable and trustworthy as the feedback a therapist gets from the insiders he or she is allied with.

Acknowledge the Struggle

Unless you are an insider yourself, avoid claiming to understand what the person is going through, as such an understanding would be virtually impossible to obtain unless you have lived through it yourself. The most you can reasonably expect to do is to make space for the person to express her anguish and to commiserate as best you can. Lorraine spoke of the trap many therapists fall into when they fail to grasp the counterintuitive logic of anorexia—that the weaker it grows the harder it fights.

> I don't think that many professionals have conceptualized this part of the recovery process. I don't know how many times I have felt completely invalidated in my struggles when those who have been aware of my process negate the power of that very loud Anorexic voice by the seeming normality of my body or my success up to date. I guess their logic makes them really want to hear that the "voice" has disappeared or has become more superficial when in fact the reality is that the "voice" can take on an extremely abusive tone at this point. Of course, the danger [in the therapist's trivializing the comeback] is that Anorexia is given fuel in its wish to "prove" how loud a voice it is.

Maintain a Posture of Compassionate Concern

Comebacks can pose real dangers, and when a person's very life is at stake, it can be difficult to avoid or contain one's alarm. Any expressions of annoyance, disappointment, or panic are likely to confirm what a/b is already telling these girls and women—that they are failures and, as a result, are doomed. Therapists need to try to counterbalance this tendency toward alarm by reminding themselves that the person has both the intention and ability to regain whatever ground she has lost and continue on the path of reclaiming her life and freedom from a/b. Never is it more important for the therapist to maintain faith in the person then when she herself is likely to have lost it. And there is little to be gained by "losing your mind" just when you need it most.

Be Unrelenting in Your Efforts to Help

When a/b has a tight grip on someone, it will often do its best to isolate her from those people who are a threat to it. Under a/b's influence, the woman may insist that she neither wants nor or needs your help, and tell you to "get lost." Don't be daunted by the person's rejection of support or even attempts to drive you away, and don't take it personally.

In Spanish, the expression "dying from starvation" translates to "dying like a rabid dog," a reference to how ill-tempered starvation can make a person. You may have to endure some "biting," so you might as well grow a thick skin. Later, when apologies are offered and forgiveness sought, they should not be accepted, as such apologies are not warranted in the first place (e.g., "If there is anyone who owes me an apology it is anorexia, and I know all too well that anorexia never apologizes for anything").

Inquire Into the Circumstances that Precipitated the Comeback

A/b will deflect attention away from the circumstances that provided the context for the comeback. In fact, we have found that many people are blind to circumstances that seem obvious to us. If circumstances have led a person to feel belittled, demeaned, or traumatized, a/b will invariably run with that, blaming her for whatever happened, no matter how unjust or undeserved this blame may be. The therapist needs to assist the person in unraveling these indictments and accusations by recontextualizing the conclusion about herself that a/b has insisted upon and by re-viewing these events through a more compassionate and just lens—one that allows her to entertain her own innocence. The therapist must persist in posing the questions "How have you ended up here?" and "How did this comeback come about?" It is very important to normalize the comeback under the circumstances so that the person does not feel blamed or judged for the comeback itself (e.g.,"If you are hit by a car, can you expect to walk away uninjured?").

Deconstruct A/B's Tactics and Strategies

Whether the comeback is a result of some recent anti-a/b initiatives or a result of difficult external circumstances, therapists can attempt to expose a/b's voice, invite reflection on its effects, and raise questions regarding the morality of its assault. For examples of how this kind of inquiry can be conducted, refer to Chapters 8 and 11.

Recount the Earlier Anti-Anorexic/Bulimic Progress Made

Recalling the history of the woman's anti-a/b progress and its various themes (e.g., standing up for yourself), even if that progress was brief, can be enormously helpful in dispelling some of her hopelessness and getting her back on track. These recollections have the potential to rapidly reconnect her to her original anti-a/b purpose and remind her of her preferred direction. Recalling the "right track" has positive effects on the therapist as well, helping to bolster his or her faith in the person and in the therapy. Such anti-a/b reminiscing is almost as important for the therapist as it is for the person experiencing the comeback. It is important, however, to refrain from adopting a "cheerleading" posture or from attributing anti-a/b strength to the person when it may not fit for her. Either of these practices can leave the girl or woman feeling as if the magnitude of her current difficulty is being trivialized or invalidated, or that her therapist is not available to hear about or help her deal with a/b's onslaught.

THE RHYTHM OF "RECOVERY"

The battle between a/b and anti-a/b is an epic one. The conflict between these two antagonists mirrors those between the grand themes of Western civilization: life versus death, good versus evil, freedom versus tyranny. The tension between these classic polarities will never be resolved through something as definitive and final as victory or "defeat," just as the struggle between a/b and anti-a/b cannot be adequately rendered through terms such as *cure* and *relapse*. Comebacks can be viewed as a/b's desperate attempt to reverse a person's anti-a/b momentum. And although a woman's forward momentum may be temporarily halted while she turns around to defend herself against a/b's assault as best she can, such a reversal should not be viewed as a setback but rather as an inevitable part of the back-and-forth rhythm of "recovery."

As noted earlier, the dynamic interplay between a/b and anti-a/b is better captured through nonlinear metaphors such as the ebb and flow of tides. Interestingly, the same metaphor is often used to describe battles and wars—"the tide of the war has turned"; "the offensive came in waves." Tatiana, a 23-year-old and the first woman to consult David about her struggle with anorexia, used the metaphor of waves to chart the trajectory of her struggle with anorexia:

> Overcoming anorexia came in waves. Low periods, when I felt miserable (or nothing) without knowing why, were followed by equally intense high periods. I started to like myself and felt increasingly confident—which was a good feeling—but in waves. I think these waves may have been related to a continual struggle between what anorexia had in mind for me and my efforts to discover what I wanted and needed rather than what other people wanted and needed.

Negotiating a comeback can be a bit like trying to swim through ocean swells to return to the beach: one moves forward with the waves to near the shore while simultaneously resisting the inevitable backwards pull of the water as best one can.

STRATEGIC RETREATS

In life-or-death struggles with an adversary, there are times when it may be necessary to retreat in order to live to fight another day.* We consider these "strategic" retreats. By *retreat*, we mean a period of time when active resistance to a/b is suspended and replaced with passive resistance. Retreating can take many forms: refusing to fight, avoiding a confrontation, allowing others to take up the battle for a time, or temporarily going along with a/b until one is strong enough to resist actively again.

What distinguishes a retreat from a surrender? For Olivia, (see Chapter 11) the key distinction was the capacity to know anorexia as "the enemy."

> When I retreat from anorexia, as opposed to surrendering to it, I'm able to continue knowing that anorexia is my enemy. Even though I might end up going along with anorexia and, at some level, agreeing with it, on another level I continue to know that it is the enemy and maintain some determination not to let it kill me. I simply can't take it on directly or counter its assaults. When I retreat, on the outside it might look similar to a surrender but on the inside I know it's not my friend and that it's out to kill me.

Insiders who have always regarded retreats as surrenders or defeats might want to consider whether such "surrenders" might, in fact, have represented a form of passive and covert resistance.† For example, did they find a way of safeguarding the knowledge that a/b was their mortal enemy so that they could actively oppose it when it became possible to do so? Did they sequester their hatred of a/b to a place in their soul beyond a/b's surveillance? Resistance and hatred must be well hidden and well disguised if they are to survive under the nose of a/b.

---

* The French phrase *reculer pour mieux sauter* ("to retreat to leap forward better") describes this time-honored tactic.

† To fully appreciate the significance of planned retreats or passive resistance, read Scott's *Domination and the Arts of Resistance: Hidden Transcripts* (1990) —particularly Chapter 6, "Voice Under Domination: The Arts of Political Disguise." Scott surveys historical and cultural circumstances of the "powerful" and the "powerless" and how the latter enact resistance "offstage" and through "hidden" means. He quotes Balzac: "Mes enfants, you mustn't go at things head-on, you are too weak; take it from me and take it on an angle.... Play dead, play the sleeping dog."

Chloe concluded, upon reflection, that her retreat contained within it an enduring but hidden hatred of anorexia:

> Retreats can include overtly going along with anorexia but inwardly and covertly detesting it. I think that this is a very anti-anorexic form of retreat. I must say that my retreats never feel very anti-anorexic. Most of the time I feel like I'm not only going along with anorexia overtly but covertly as well, but I think this is largely due to what anorexia would have me believe. I'm sure that there must have been a part of me that was still inwardly despising anorexia. Sometimes perhaps that part even had to pretend it wasn't despising anorexia in order to avoid taking a further battering from it, but it must have been there somewhere.

If circumstances have conspired to knock the wind out of someone, the person may not have the ability to make headway against a/b at that time. Attempting to persevere would only invite further aggression on a/b's part, antagonizing an enemy who, at the moment, is much stronger. Chloe commented on the anti-anorexic wisdom of knowing when to retreat:

> Is there not anti-anorexic strength in realizing that the "enemy" is stronger for the moment and not throwing oneself in direct "enemy fire" but rather waiting for new arms and reinforcements? Imperative in this realization is the fact that the enemy's position "on top" is only temporary—I can't emphasize enough the importance of the person being reminded of this because it is something that anorexia will do its utmost to make them forget or disbelieve.

In some cases a person's anti-a/b efforts end up strengthening a/b's hand. For example, a woman might take an anti-a/b step in asserting her worth and her needs, only to have a/b use her resistance against her by persuading her that she is selfish for doing so. At these times it is better to retreat in order to figure out a way to sidestep a/b's sabotage.

Bending So as Not To Break

Being able to recognize the need for retreat and to honor these retreats as part of the anti-a/b ebb and flow can be difficult for women who have come to depend on their sheer force of will and self-discipline to see them through. Importing the a/b values of discipline and willpower into anti-a/b practice can undermine that practice by denying it the suppleness and flexibility that is needed to deal with a/b's tactics. Like an umbrella, double-jointed so that it can bend in the opposite direction when a strong gust of wind gets underneath it, an anti-a/b practice built on flexibility allows a woman to survive by temporarily being moved by anorexia and then once again, resuming her resistance. Without such flexibility, the force of a/b would rip the fabric of the anti-a/b umbrella or tear it from the grip of the person holding it. Flexible resistance also upsets a/b's requirement of perfect success, in that strategic retreats are something of a success-through-failure.

Retreat as an Anti-Anorexic/Bulimic Choice

Retreating purposefully in the face of an a/b onslaught can mitigate the feeling of having completely lost control and the sense of despair that often accompanies this. Choosing to retreat for an anti-a/b purpose can allow a woman to maintain some control and feel less violated and dispirited. Rhoda, a 39-year-old, articulated this particular benefit of her purposeful retreat:

> I kind of resisted it [bulimia] for a while and then I decided to give in and said to it: "You can have me for a while." I was in control and it hadn't taken me over. I had given Bulimia permission. I had not been assaulted. I kept a dialogue up with Bulimia and said: "This time you can have me." The next morning I felt strong enough to take my life back and got on with it.

Lorraine put it this way:

> With every temporary retreat we afford ourselves we must not allow ourselves to believe its lie that "this violation is just like the other times" because *it is not.* What I think I am getting at here is the element of choice. If there was a way to hang onto the element of choice in some way, then it would certainly feel much better. This does not in any way negate the pain of the current violation, nor the pain of past violations, but if the pain can be transferred into conviction not to be vulnerable for another attack, then that is of great benefit.

MANNERS OF RETREAT

There are times when the tide of a/b can be very powerful indeed. Trying to fight a/b when one is overmatched can be like trying to swim against a riptide that has knocked one off one's feet and is carrying one out to sea. Victoria elaborated upon this riptide metaphor:

> A riptide is very much like Anorexia in that it sneaks up on you and you often do not know that you are caught in it until you have drifted

a fair way out. It also mirrors the way Anorexia works in that a rip is the calm spot in a surf beach—the spot where the unsuspecting often go to swim.

If you are caught in a rip, swimming against it is exhausting and will eventually take all of your energy until you are too weak to keep yourself afloat. The sea then swallows you up, only to spit your body back out onto the beach at a later date. However, if you do not struggle against the rip, you have a much better chance of making it back to shore in one piece. If you swim sideways in a rip, you will eventually get to the edge of it and then you can swim back to shore.

Surfers often use the rip to get out behind where the waves are breaking to the place where the water is calm. There they can then have a rest, and prepare to catch the next good wave. I mention this because I think this could be compared to an Anti-Anorexic way of dealing with relapses—riding Anorexia's rip out to the calm waters beyond it and then preparing to come back in when it suits you—when you have rested and gained strength.

Conscientious Objecting

One variation of retreating is what Ali referred to as *conscientious objecting*. For her, this practice was rooted in a moral objection to her own further victimization, which she understood would be the outcome of antagonizing anorexia at those moments.

> I have used the tactic of biding my time until I have felt stronger or more supported to fight back. In some cases I believe anorexia bene-fits from engaging people in battle—no matter what the outcome—because the fight itself does so much damage. In the situations where I felt like I had gotten knocked to the floor over and over, I often de-cided it was wiser to just *stay down* because I knew if I got back up again I was just going to get trashed. So at those times I adopted the strategy of refusing to fight. In a way, it was like conscientious ob-jecting. I refused to engage in the battle knowing that I didn't agree with the fight itself and that it was not in *my* best interest.
>
> For instance, for a long time I *knew* looking in a mirror would bring nothing but pain. I always ended up believing anorexia's insults about my body which, in turn, made me feel terrible and more vulnerable to anorexia's promises from that point forward. So instead of trying to contest its claims, I covered my mirror—for like a year. I just didn't give anorexia that chance to hit me. I just tried to hold on to what I had and believed that, even if I couldn't do it then, at some point I'd be able to see myself and be okay.

Entrusting One's Physical Health to Others

Temporarily putting the responsibility for the safeguarding and nourishing of one's body in the hands of others may also constitute a form of retreat, as Chloe discussed:

> I know that, for me, one form of retreat is having nasogastric tube feeding. At the time it has always felt like a "giving up" rather than a retreat (which are often hard to recognize at the time because often anorexia will trick the person into believing that they are surrenders). However, when anorexia is just too strong and I don't have the energy left to fight it anymore no matter how determined I might be, then sometimes I need to give up fighting for a while and let others take over the responsibility for nourishing my body. While being tube fed and not nourishing myself could be seen as giving up or going backwards, it sometimes allows the fight to be taken out of my hands for a while, allowing me to regroup myself and wait until I feel strong enough to press forward once more. Although it almost always feels like I'll never have the strength or will to launch another attack against anorexia, that time has always come.

Temporarily Letting Someone Else "Carry" One's Anger and Outrage

When a/b's influence has become nearly absolute, harboring hatred of a/b within one's mind or consciousness can feel too unsafe. Margaret (see Chapters 10, 11, 13, 15, & 18) and Rick discovered an alternative way of harboring feelings of outrage.

> Recently anorexia made a comeback that left me unable to find the spirit and energy to counter its attacks and accusations. Anorexia was attacking me for anything and everything: for having feelings, for eating, for existing. During one of my meetings with Rick, I mentioned that I didn't feel I could afford to be angry with anorexia at the moment. Rick asked if it was okay for him to be angry at anorexia on my behalf. I consented and said "thank you." His being angry on my behalf allowed me to retreat without this becoming the grounds for anorexia to make me feel like a failure for not being able to fight it. I was continuing to fight it by proxy, through Rick. This shielded me from anorexia's attacks while at the same time safeguarding my outrage for me to return to when I felt stronger. This assisted me in gaining some strength back. It allowed me to retreat and to still know anorexia is not my friend.
>
> At times when I need to retreat, it is vital to know that there are anti-anorexic allies out there who have strong anti-anorexic spirits and that

there exists communities of concern such as the Anti-Anorexia and Bulimia League. It is helpful to know that, at those times, others have energy to fight anorexia and be angry with it. Without an awareness of other allies out there, I don't think I could have prevented my retreat from becoming a complete capture.

Margaret's reflections speak to the importance of a repository of anti-a/b sentiment in the larger culture. These repositories serve as lifelines for those who find themselves behind enemy lines. Like beacons, these individuals and communities beckon the besieged to come home and remind them that there is a home to come home to.*

---

* This is the purpose of the "Archives of Resistance: Anti-Anorexia/Anti-Bulimia." This archive can be found at http://www.narrativeapproaches.com.

Chapter 14

LIVING LIFE FROM THE INSIDE OUT

A CONVERSATION WITH AMY

T his chapter and the one that follows it illustrate many of the means by which women separate themselves from a/b and construct alternative lives and identities. Recounting the stories of two women, Amy and Margaret, these chapters show how therapists can assist women in the reclaiming of their lives.

The edited transcript that follows is from my (DE) third meeting with Amy, a 40-year-old who had been suffering from a/b for 23 years. Six years after this meeting, I asked Amy to review the transcript and comment on it. These comments appear in italics in the text. Throughout the chapter, I have interrupted the transcript to discuss the intention behind my questions. These discussions are more theoretical and technical and therefore may be of less interest to nontherapist readers, who should feel free to skip over these parts if they are so inclined.

David: How's it going for you?

Amy: I don't know what's happened for me lately. No, I do know what's happened, but there's just such a lot happening for me, and I so much want to get well!

David: Yeah, I can see that. Something about you tells me that. But now you have to be aware of perfection. It has to be slow. It can't be an overnight thing.

Amy: No, it can't. It's good that you reminded me of that.

I acknowledged Amy's excitement about some recent developments but heard in her exuberance a sense of urgency and impatience, which could allow anorexia to divert her anti-anorexia. In a previous meeting, we had coresearched the manner in which anorexia can promote perfectionistic expectations that inevitably lead to a sense of failure. My warning to Amy about perfection helped remind her that if anorexia could create perfectionistic expectations with respect to her progress, it would use her imperfect anti-anorexia and the necessarily slow pace of this work as another opportunity to reproach her.

That was a really good reminder. It's a process. To get from A to Z, there is an alphabet in between. I know people want it overnight and I did too, but it just doesn't work like that. The more you fight it and think, "I've got to be over this tomorrow or right now," the more you are fueling the anorexia. Anorexia is trying to make you make haste so that it maintains control. So you are feeding it! If you just say, "I'm going to do it my way and I'm finding out my way!" and allow that process so you are not doing it from a perfectionistic/anorexic point of view, the less likely it is that anorexia will infiltrate.

Amy: I mean it's been really up and down for me the last few weeks. Yesterday and today I'm feeling pretty good. Yesterday, I was awakened by the phone. It was relatively late and Jo phoned me and said jokingly, "Ah! You should be out of bed by now!" and it really sort of went (*bringing her hand to strike her abdomen*) like that. Yes, I should have been dressed and up and out the door to aqua-aerobics, which would have been in a half an hour, and I thought, "No! This is the anorexia talking." So I phoned someone and spoke with her about it, and that was really great. She said, "No you can't go, it's too late anyway. What are you going to do?" And I said, "I'll probably stay in bed a bit longer!" (*laughing*)

David: Oh! Amy, this is pretty radical, you know. It's not something that anorexia would think kindly of you for, taking your own pleasure. Would you be surprised to learn that other people have told me that being able to stay in bed is one of the first signs of anti-anorexia? I mean, it sounds odd, but would that make sense to you?

Amy had just shared an instance where she identified the voice of anorexia and then made a conscious choice to defy it. By labeling Amy's decision to remain in bed a bit longer as "taking your own pleasure," I introduced a more general anti-anorexic theme. This theme, if it resonated sufficiently with Amy's experience, had the potential to become an important element in an alternative narrative through which Amy could live—one that included her right to both value and claim her own pleasure in life. The expression "taking your own pleasure" had more subtle anti-anorexic implications: The words *your own* implied that she had the right to claim ownership of her pleasure. The word *taking* juxtaposed this anti-anorexic theme of taking her own pleasure with the anorexic theme of having her pleasure robbed from her.

That is one of the things I have been slowly able to chip away at. I no longer swim, walk, or cycle madly. I've been on my bike three times in the last 3 years, whereas in the past it would have been three times a day. I can now sit down and watch TV or just lie on the floor. I still have an exercise regime but it's not as arduous, because my body physically couldn't take it. In a sense, it was a blessing that I physically couldn't do it anymore. Otherwise my health would have suffered. Anorexia wouldn't have cared about that, but I was able to listen to that wise part of me—"I don't want to be bothered anymore!"—a part of me that has wanted to change so much. I don't let the anorexia mind beat up on myself for not swimming or cycling or walking. I still walk but it is no longer a forced march.

Amy: Yeah, I actually meditated, but in bed.

David: Was that something that was a pleasure to you, not a requirement?

Amy: Well, it was both. I mean I really enjoy meditation but I am compelled to do it also.

David: Yeah. Is your mediative space a space for you or a space for anorexia? When you create that space does anorexia intrude there?

Amy: Sometimes, yeah. . . . Especially in the obsessional part of it. I'd use my mind power practice and I'd be rigidly sticking to that, and I would say, "Ha! I better watch this too."

David: It can be subverted by anorexia, can't it? Taken and put to anorexia's use?

Amy: Oh yes, it's like, I've got to do X amount of this every day. . . .

David: Yeah, and that you're not doing it good enough or . . .

Amy: Sometimes, yeah.

David: Or your mind really isn't as good as you think it is, and . . .

Amy: That's right.

I no longer am doing a lot of the things I was compelled to do. And in a sense, it means you have to dump the lot and find what you really want to take back. And to come from a new point of view saying, "This is what I choose to do because I want to do it, not because anorexia is telling me I ought to do it. And that makes a whole new ball game! A whole new life! It's like the difference between freedom and imprisonment.

A number of distinctions and metaphorical descriptions related to the differences between Amy's preferred lifestyle and anorexia's lifestyle were brought forth: exercise versus torturecise, walking versus forced marching, doing things because you want to versus doing things because you have to, freedom versus imprisonment. These distinctions disentangled the voice of anorexia from what Amy regarded as her own voice and highlighted some of the effects anorexia's voice had on her life. Not surprisingly, this way of speaking about anorexia strengthened Amy's determination to free her life from its strangle-hold. She then shared a recent experience that spoke to this anti-a/b determination.

Amy: One time I was setting myself up for a binge and . . .

David: How could you tell that?

Amy: Well, if I'm going to the supermarket to pick up some muesli or some-thing like that. It's real picky stuff and I love it. It can be a bit of a binge. However, I chatted with God about this, and I really felt I didn't want to do this anymore. It is just killing me, literally, and I stopped!

David: Really, is it a bit of a first for you to be so resolute?

Amy: It's not the first, but it's embryonic.

David: Embryonic of what? What is it a precedent for?

Amy: Being free! Being free because there have been times when I've been okay, but now I really feel that not only do I want to stop throwing up, but I don't want to even have to think about it. I just want to get on to a normal course of living. And I feel there's been a big shift within me.

David: That sends shivers up my arms when you say that. Can you help me understand that?

"Getting well" doesn't mean that you stop bingeing and throwing up, they are only the superficial manifestations. "Getting well" means that you are not caught up with food. There is a lot of underneath work that needs to be done. It would be nice if that was instant and overnight but it isn't!

This foundational work involves getting back the self-worth and feeling connected to yourself. The bingeing stuff is superficial. It is really about getting back to finding out who I am, what I want, and how I am going to live my life. And the food stuff, which is symptomatic, will resolve without you trying. Anti-anorexia is living your life from the inside out; anorexia is living your life (if you can call it a life) from the outside in. That's it in a nutshell!

Amy: Yep. It's a shift about really wanting to be on this planet, about really be-ing human . . . getting real. I mean, I just have these words running through my head going: "Get real, woman. Get real, and get honest."

David: (*writing*) "Get real, get honest."

Amy: Because the anorexia won't, or hasn't, allowed me to get honest.

David: Is it a form of deception?

Amy: Oh, yeah, and a liar. And I just really want it to get out of my life. It has to get out of my life. I can fight it by not giving it power.

David: Yeah, yeah. That's a true kind of fight, isn't it? To give yourself value, rather than giving it value?

Amy: Right!

David: Can I just read to you what someone else wrote to see what your thoughts are?* I just got this from a colleague. It's from Allison, who has been hospitalized.

> Dear Anorexia,
> I'm writing to you because you have just about won, almost but not quite. It has come to be dangerous and life-threatening. If it continues, you will kill me. It is so bloody hard to fight you. I'm terrified to put on weight, because my body shape (lack of it) is so much a part of me wanting to disappear. (It had been so important to me unconsciously for years, but now I'm well aware of how good it feels and that's the battle.) The last 2 or 3 weeks I have spiraled down so unbelievably quickly and you think you've got me. But you haven't. You haven't. You can't offer me anything but death. Yes, I will then have disappeared totally, but that's not what I want. The euphoria I feel is scary. Yes, it's real (not imagined) but it's wrong. I want control of my life, but you have it. The battle is not over. I am going to keep on, keeping on battling you as impossible as that seems. As you know, joining your name to anorexia's dotted line is like signing your own death warrant. But you haven't got me, not yet, and you are not going to because whatever is left in me, which you are well aware is almost zilch, I'm going to battle you. I have support, and let me tell you, it's all against, anti-you, anorexia.

And then she wrote:

> Dear Anti-Anorexia,
> I am writing to you because I have chosen life. I have stated it before, and I'll say it again: "I want to make something of my life." As you well know, anorexia is out to kill me. I don't want it to but it is bloody hard. I know in my head that it can offer me nothing, but it doesn't help how it is. There has been a tremendous cost to have come this far, but it isn't going to be for nothing, because in making the decisions I have, there has come the start of finding myself, and that is what you are into—letting me be me. No, I don't mean my body, but me, you know, the inner me—my feelings, emotions, values, intellect, ideas, thoughts, spirituality. To find happiness and joy in living life.
> I have a goal, an achievable goal, and that is to get a one-bedroom flat of my own, and you and I can do that together. Can't we? You see

---

* For a discussion of the various uses of the archives, see Chapter 8.

that's an exciting prospect for me, because I'll be able to do things the way I want, when I want, for the first time, without the dread of being pursued. Together, me and you anti-anorexia can make a go of reality by taking small steps, one at a time.

And then she wrote several weeks later:

Well, anti-anorexia, the goals have become a reality. I have a flat but it has been hell to get to this place and, as you are well aware, it is not over even yet. The battle and struggle still goes on. And you, anti-anorexia, are winning. Although at times it doesn't seem I am getting there, you will one day be on top to stay. Life is what I've chosen, and life is what I'm starting to find and experience for the first time. And there is plenty of living to do, and enjoyment to be found in it. The flat is exciting as it represents my future, but scary also, as it involves many changes. But with the support I have, which is all on the side of you, anti-anorexia, I will be okay.

David: Did you like that, Amy?

Amy: Great, yeah.

David: She adds some more thoughts to anorexia, three days later:

You think you are cunning, but I'm willing to be more cunning than you . . . to outsmart you, because that is the only way I will beat you, by finding every trick in the book and using it against you. You keep saying, "Tomorrow, put it off till then." But that is your way of attack because that would undermine today. I'm becoming wise to you. But I will tell you again, that is not what I want. I want life.

Well, you so nearly won the battle, but you didn't. Let me tell you, anorexia, I am getting there and I will beat you and it will be permanent. You see, over the last month, I've come to the understanding of why you became an integral part of me from a very early age. But that is changing. You have been with me so long you are a part of me, or a part of the old me, the past me. But slowly and surely you are disappearing until one day you will be no more. You will have all but died, and I will lead a constructive way of life that you will not be able to take from me.

Amy: Is there a spare copy of that?

David: I'll get you one. What struck you about that? What did you value in that?

Amy: Just seeing her perspective of looking at anorexia and the anti-anorexia and the energy that she got in her wanting to be well. This is really important, this is something that I find. My energy is coming through . . .

David: You've got more energy in you?

Amy: Yes.

David: You know anyone watching this videotape wouldn't be aware of how you were when I first met you. Would you be willing to describe how you were feeling then?

Amy: Oh, a hell of a lot worse than I am now.

David: What shall we say? You didn't want to live or you had those sorts of feelings as though you were losing your life rather than gaining your life as you are now?

Amy: Oh, I was once suicidal, and the last suicidal thoughts were quite prevalent...

David: Yeah, I remember that...

Amy: But since that first meeting I haven't wanted to kill myself.

David: What was it at that first meeting that brought you back into a desire for life?

Amy: Well, you... you had an understanding and you were saying I could get better and I suppose anorexia was telling me that I could never get better.

That really did help because I realized there was hope. And that something could be changed. I didn't know what or how but just the knowledge that I didn't have to be an "anorexic" for the rest of my life. I didn't know where to turn. All the avenues I had tried didn't provide any help. You saw me for me and then I knew there was a chance for my resurrection!

David: What did it say? That everything's hopeless? What if it had spoken to you at that particular point and you were to enter into a debate and said: "Hey look, I've really got to get over this"? What would anorexia have replied?

Amy: It would laugh at me and make fun of me—"Look at you, I'm denying you being who you really are."

David: If anorexia had a purpose or if you could impute its purpose, why do you think it was trying to talk you out of your life and to refuse to allow you to have any pleasure in your life? What's behind that?

Amy: It's truly self-destructing... soul destruction.

David: Why should Amy's soul be destroyed by anorexia?

Amy: Because she's not worthy.

David: I see. And can I ask... how do you think it was that anorexia's affected your sister? Do you think that there's some commonality between her experience of her life and your experience of your life? And how was it that your two other sisters escaped, or one and a half were able to escape? How was that possible? What sense do you make of that? Do you know?

I invited Amy to consider what anorexia's driving her to want her life to end might say about anorexia. I was interested in assisting Amy in ascribing an intention to anorexia, one that would be consistent with the effects of anorexia she described. Because a/b so predictably presents its own intentions as benevolent, it is important to help a person draw conclusions about its intentions based on her actual experience of it. If these experiences are regarded by the person as highly undesirable (as they almost invariably are), this can lead her to view a/b's intentions as malevolent rather than benevolent. This helps to undermine a/b's tactic of getting people to dismiss their to-date experience of the effects of a/b by telling them that they eventually will be rewarded if they continue to obey a/b and just try a little harder.

Amy characterized anorexia's motives as "self-destructive" and "soul-destroying." When I asked, "Why should Amy's soul be destroyed by anorexia?" I conveyed my own belief in Amy's innocence and expressed my anti-anorexic outrage. But the question was not merely rhetorical. I knew from prior conversations with other women that, once the guise of anorexic benevolence has been shattered and anorexia's rules and requirements are no longer perceived as helpful suggestions but torturous demands, anorexia still does not throw in the towel. Exposed as a punisher and torturer, anorexia's fallback position is often to persuade the person that she is deserving of punishment. I anticipated that anorexia would propose a justification for its attempt to destroy Amy's "self" and "soul." Thus it was no surprise when Amy responded, "because she's not worthy."

The question "Why should Amy's soul be destroyed by anorexia?" was both asked and responded to in the third person. This allowed Amy a little more distance from which to observe and comment upon anorexia's tactics. It also depersonalized these tactics. Asking Amy about her sisters' experience of anorexia challenged the idea that there was something in particular about Amy that rendered her unworthy. Instead, it focused attention on the broader social and familial circumstances that might have contributed to feelings of worthlessness and that anorexia then appropriated for its own purposes.

Amy: Well, they didn't have anorexia, but they overate. Perhaps everyone in our family has some sort of eating disorder. I mean, two sisters are overweight. And my two brothers are very scrawny. You know, very thin and I'm sure one of my brothers is an alcoholic. And he monitors his weight . . . you know, it's not very healthy.

David: So what was there in the family you came from that put a special value on weight or food or whatever? What do you make of that?

Amy: I've been puzzling that. My parents were large and were concerned about weight. I'm the oldest and when my mother was pregnant with me she put on 30 pounds and never really lost it. And for a while I felt guilty that I was the one who made her fat.

David: Is that something that you picked up all by yourself or construed yourself?

Amy: Well, I probably construed it myself, but I've spoken to my mother about that and she said, "Oh, I certainly don't see it as your fault. It's just the way it was." I think I may have heard her saying when I was a little girl that when she was pregnant . . . I mean, I destroyed her self-image by making her fat. Here I am talking about my mother.

David: Was your entry into this world, according to you, at your mother's expense? Is that something worth thinking about?

Amy: She doesn't actually . . . there's no animosity there. . . .

David: No, no, it's just how a little girl, a little girl Amy, construed that.

Amy: Mmm.

David: Did you think that by working so hard, getting so busy, and looking after your Mum that you would make it up to your Mum for what you construed you had done to her?

Amy: Yeah, it could have been. I mean, I could have been maybe giving her the time to do what she needed to do. I mean, I took on so much because I just hated to see her cry. She had six kids and a busy husband. I wanted to relieve her, you know. And I felt guilty that I couldn't make things better for her.

David: No, you couldn't. Did you try to exceed your Mum in terms of giving?

Amy: Not consciously, but it probably ended up being like that. There were times when I had to look after the whole family when she went to the hospital and her admission went on longer than had been envisaged. It was really quite difficult to give up the reigns afterwards.

David: Were you sort of like an acting Mother?

Amy: Mmm, oh yes, or a substitute.

It is easy to see from the preceding dialogue how the circumstances of Amy's early life led her to take on an overriding sense of responsibility for the well-being of other family members and to adopt an ideal of self-sacrifice. Of course, no matter how hard she tried, she could never make everything okay for everybody. This opened the door to feelings of guilt and worthlessness, which anorexia exploited, first by promising to make her a better person, and later by telling her she was a worthless person and deserved its punishments. Often when a person who has taken on these ideas comprehends the context and circumstances that led to them, they lose their status as truths and consequently, no longer have as much power to shape the person's identity.

David: You mentioned you were letting go of some things when we first talked today. Is it possible in any way that some of the letting go has to do with this guilt about your mother?

Amy: Do you think I feel guilt?

David: Ah, I don't know. I just wondered. You seemed to be talking to me today with a bit of detachment about it, like it's over and done with or . . . it didn't seem to live for you as much as it might have?

Amy: It just has to go. I don't know but it reached a point where I can't take any more without not being here. And I don't know but it just seemed like this is where I can just think "stop." I don't want to do that anymore. I've gotten bored with it.

David: Ah, yeah.

Amy: I mean, anorexia's been boring!

David: Oh, it is. I don't mean to dismiss you or your experience in any way, but anorexia is so redundant.

Amy: Yeah. It really is boring. And you know it's boring.

David: Do you think it's bored you half to death and there isn't much of you left?

Amy: Yeah, that's it. You've got holes bored in you (*laughter all round*) and everything goes straight through.

Speaking about anorexia as an external force or entity rather than as something residing within her permitted Amy to more clearly see the effects that anorexia had upon her life. This often leads to opportunities to speak against anorexia rather than merely about anorexia or the "anorexic." Typically it is anorexia that speaks against the person, who is silenced and made an object or specimen to be picked apart, brutally criticized, and then "reformed." In this anti-anorexic way of speaking, anorexia was rendered into an object that could be criticized, belittled, and scorned by Amy, who, for the moment, had escaped subordination and was now in a position to ridicule and demean anorexia. As can be seen in the following portion of transcript, these opportunities to engage in anti-anorexic conversation provide some sense of redress and vindication and can be great fun.

David: What is the most boring thing about anorexia? It's almost really subversive for us to even talk like this, isn't it? I mean, it's a bit cheeky.

[Talking about anorexia in that way] helps lighten the atmosphere because anorexia is so heavy! Boring! Dull! *And a pain in the proverbial. . . . Laughter sort of breaks the energy of that and helps* me *stand back and say, "I can lighten up here!" It stops me being consumed, subsumed, and taken over by the anorexia. It puts me into an observing position, detached,*

and I don't like being laughed at so I am quite happy to laugh at anorexia because I know it won't like it. It helps put it back into perspective.

David: Give me an example of the most boring thing about anorexia.

Amy: Well, it makes everything into a ritual and an obsession and it has to be done 150% perfectly. And it's very easy for negative patterns to be set.

David: They sneak up on you don't they?

Amy: Uh, huh! Yeah.

David: What do you think about what Tracy said, which I thought was fascinating? She was 15 going on 16. What she said was that "anorexia is rituals and anti-anorexia is creativity."

Amy: Yeah, lovely.

David: Rituals couldn't be more uncreative. Doing the same thing over and over again must be the least creative act that you can do. Why do you think it wants to render you kind of stupid in a sense? What would be its purpose there?

Amy: It's got an ego so big it doesn't want someone to say, "f—— off."

David: What this one young person said was that it was like a corrupt power, and once it took you over it had to continue to run you, otherwise you would no longer put up with it. So it had to act absolutely tyrannically. He said for a long time the only way out was to do whatever it demanded, which was to do perfection. The only way to get it off his back was to do this. He now believes you need to fight it and oppose it, and not go along with it. He actually inadvertently went along with it thinking that it would give him some peace. Did you find that in any way?

Amy: Yes, I was writing about that yesterday, where you think acquiescence is the line of least resistance, and maybe if you don't fight too much, then it might go away. But in actual fact it encourages it.

Anorexia does need to be fought so that anorexia doesn't get empowered but the self does. Pro-anorexia is to just keep on being bored, to keep on walking, running, cycling, whatever you are doing, to keep on letting yourself be brainwashed. In order to stop that you have to do something different. I might walk and I have to go around that corner in a certain way and I have to go up a hill X amount of meters and come back, blah, blah. I let the anorexia think that's what it is going to make me do and I'll suddenly just turn around and go home! Or I'll suddenly just sit down on a bench. It has to be that quick so the anorexic mind doesn't have time to cut in. You have to take little steps at a time so you can make chinks its armor and its footings can be eroded. While you are eroding anorexia's footings you are laying your own foundations.

The most important part of it is separating your mind from the anorexic mind, even if you don't know what your own mind is, even if it is just giving yourself space to feel space. One tool that really helps sometimes is to say, "God, this isn't really me! Something else is taking over here." But now I can take back control by saying, "Be quiet! I want to listen to me!" It can be frightening to pull your mind back from anorexia. Anorexia will say, "You are feeling this" or "you don't know what you are feeling so I had better come back and take you over!" It is really important to allow yourself to feel whatever it is that is going on that is disconnected from the anorexia. You won't know what it is like. *It is just having to experience it day by day. Some of the feelings are painful. For me, that's what anorexia has been there for—to bury all the sadness, grief, the hurt or whatever it is.... Just allow yourself to feel them. There is no right or wrong feeling.*

David: In what ways do you think you've given rise to some sort of opposition to this force called anorexia?

Amy: By deliberately changing and just doing different behaviors.

David: Give me some examples of your resistance that anorexia would certainly disapprove of.

I now shifted the focus of the conversation to recent anti-anorexic actions Amy had taken. In the language of narrative therapy, these questions are referred to as "unique outcome" questions because they inquire about actions that would not have been predicted or expected if the problem were wholly dominant. These questions bring to light a person's agency and influence with respect to the problem. The actions and events these questions illuminate become the basis for an alternative story about the person (White & Epston, 1990). Because I had learned from Amy and others that a person can believe she is acting anti-anorexically when in fact her actions are inadvertently encouraging it, I asked about examples of resistance that "anorexia would certainly disapprove of." I was implicitly proposing a possible criterion for discerning whether a given act was anti-anorexic or pro-anorexic. According to this criteria, acts such as appeasement or acquiescence, even when performed with the intention of getting anorexia off one's back, would not constitute anti-anorexia because anorexia would no doubt approve of them (purposeful retreats notwithstanding—see Chapter 13).

Amy: Well, like not going for that swim, not being forced to exercise. I mean, normally, I've had to do two or three swims a week.

David: Mmm. Like a lot of people tell me that anorexia says they're really no good unless they do so much torture. You know, they have to do so much torture before they can start to have the rest of the day.

Amy: And doing penance, penance, penance . . .

David: Yeah, for the rest of their life.

Amy: God! (*laughing*)

David: You're living life as free now? Isn't that wonderful? You don't have to pay for it.

Amy: And I think I'm making positive affirmations.

David: About you?

Amy: Yes. Part of it is building up the trust in myself and being loving to myself.

If one has only a narrow conception of anorexia (e.g., fear of eating and getting fat), the anti-anorexic significance of something as seemingly small as getting out of bed in the morning 2 minutes later than usual would certainly be missed. Yet the regimentation imposed by the regime of anorexia is so all-encompassing that any stepping out of line can constitute an outrageous or terrifying act of rebellion. My acknowledgment of Amy's anti-anorexic insurrection was vital to conveying my appreciation and support of these difficult steps toward an untested anti-anorexic vision of a new life.

As the consultation continued, we explored the anti-anorexic practices that had fostered Amy's self-trust and self-love. These practices had not been prescribed by me but rather were developed by Amy based on her own anti-anorexic strivings. Consequently, they fit nicely within her own framework of meaning.

Amy: I mean, if I say I deeply love and trust myself, even if I don't believe it, I say it.

David: Yes, yes, yes.

Amy: And rather than having one, I can have about four or five affirmations that I'm using at the moment.

David: That's good.

Amy: But I've ended up singing them in my head when I'm busy. It's been part of my creativity. I say them in my head or when I'm walking on the street or something.

David: Really?

Amy: During the day I'll have these tunes running through my head. . . .

David: Wow!

Amy: So I've got the tunes with the affirmations, instead of all the other shit going on. I was really delighted when I discovered all these little tunes I was singing! (*laughing*)

David: That's probably a lot better tape to have running in your mind than an anorexic tape.

Amy: Right.

David: What if anorexia was running through your mind, what would it be saying?

Amy: You should be doing it this way. You haven't done enough exercise yet, or you haven't beaten yourself up enough yet . . .

By asking the question "What if anorexia was running through your mind, what would it be saying?" I invited Amy to place side by side the two categories of tapes that run through her mind—those associated with self-affirmation and those associated with anorexia. By bringing the two genres into a collision with each other, the contrasts between the two become more evident.

Author Barbara Kingsolver once said, "The role of art is to reconnect an act of violence to its consequences." The same could be said of the "deconstructive" or "unmasking" aspects of an anti-anorexic therapy. But an anti-anorexic therapy is also eager to explore the other side of that equation by reconnecting anti-anorexic acts of self-love and self-acceptance with their consequences.

In the transcript that follows, I wondered aloud about the consequences of Amy's self-affirmations and asked about the effects those positive affirmations were having on her life. Rather than posing the question in an open-ended, general way, I asked specifically: "Tell me, as the positive affirmations start entering into your life, in your mind, and your spirit, have you found that you're, in a way, more eligible for pleasure and joy?" Asking the question in this way reflected my understanding of one of the negative effects of anorexia's words; the eradication of joy and pleasure from her life. In addition, this question wove back into the discussion the thread of the new story identified earlier in the meeting—that of Amy "taking her own pleasure." This question contributed to the filling out of this new story by connecting the more external actions associated with "taking her own pleasure" with the internal events associated with the positive affirmations. Questions that knit together these inner and outer landscapes contribute significantly to the realization of an alternative story and an alternative life.

David: Tell me, as the positive affirmations start entering into your life, in your mind, and your spirit, have you found that you're, in a way, more eligible for pleasure and joy?

Amy: It's beginning.

David: Like what? Tell me about the first beginning. I always like to hear the very beginnings of your anti-anorexia. It's very touching, actually. What was the first joy that you had?

Amy: Hmm, well gosh! I don't know, but what comes easily to mind is just that I'll allow myself to sit and watch a TV program.

David: Oh, my God! Hey, you know I was just talking to Lana and she said what she'd actually do was watch soaps on TV. And she really felt good that she could watch junk on TV just for fun! She really felt this was subversive and anti-anorexic (*laughter all round*). And you don't have to backlash yourself with guilt or be tortured for having done so?

Amy: No.

David: Really? What were you watching that anorexia wouldn't have allowed you to watch?

Amy: Oh, something, just . . . I have a program that I particularly enjoy.

David: You did it. You used the word enjoy!

Amy: Yeah, right. *Quantum leap.*

David: I've heard of that one. What else? Any other programs?

Amy: Let's see, . . . *Brides of Christ.* Actually that was quite good for me to watch that. It hit quite close to home.

David: Yeah, I imagine it would.

Amy: And I managed to watch that.

David: Anything else you've been able to watch that you enjoy?

Amy: I went to a movie the other day. I just said, "Oh well, I want to go to a movie."

David: What would have happened in your anorexic days?

Amy: I wouldn't go. I wouldn't have been allowed to go. I do enjoy movies.

David: Anorexia wouldn't have allowed you to go and have fun?

Amy: No. That's because he didn't want me to save energy. Anorexia says: "No, no, no. Don't sit down. You've got to be serving me. You've got to be flat out burning up energy, or, you know, hell-bent on self-destruction."

In the previous dialogue, my questions traversed first the anti-anorexic landscape and then the anorexic one. This zigzagging course of questioning is characteristic of our style of anti-a/b interviewing; it sharpens the contrasts between the two landscapes and, if the woman is occupying the anti-a/b landscape to greater and greater degrees, like Amy, it heightens the distinctions between past and present experience and generates a sense of progression towards a preferred destination. Because Amy had suffered with a/b for over two decades, I was interested in undermining whatever sense of hopelessness, frustration, and futility a/b might have engendered.

The question that follows (below) was asked with the same intention—to help Amy mark her anti-anorexic progress. However, it should be noted that when you enter the realm of numbers—percents, weights, calories, minutes—you are entering a/b's ballpark. When the body or one's experience is quantified, a/b can use this number as a means of goal-setting, goading, comparing, and evaluating. Thus we rarely invite people to measure anything in such concrete terms, and when we do it is with extreme caution. Only Amy could say whether or not, in this instance, anorexia used my attempt to quantify her anti-anorexic progress against her.

David: Can I ask you, since we first met to where you are today—we haven't spent a long time in terms of clock time—but what percent do you feel you're starting to make good your escape from anorexia?

Amy: About 35%. But I do have from within me energy, a new energy that's really my own. My own self-energy because anorexia really tried to destroy my soul. Nearly got me but not quite.

David: No, it wasn't total or you wouldn't be here. How is this soul energy different from the fake energy of anorexia by which you were being driven? It's like a person with a whip, whipping you on. It's being driven! When you refer to soul energy, what's different about that?

Amy: It's my true energy. This is something really crucial for me. I'm beginning to find out who I really am.

David: Wow!

Amy: My soul being. The pure essence of me, instead of. . . . I mean, anorexia just sort put a glossy layer over it. It's like I was blinded by this layer that anorexia put there so I couldn't see what was underneath.

David: Look, tell me about the Amy that you're uncovering. Who is this person and what's she about and what's she for . . . ?

Amy was using expressions such as "essence," "real self," and "true self." This way of thinking about the self is rooted in the philosophical tradition known as "modernism" or "structuralism." This tradition understands a person's behavior as stemming from an essential or real self that lies at the center of the person. It is this tradition that has given rise to universal models of what it means to be psychologically "healthy" and, simultaneously, to the pathologizing of people when they violate these socially constructed norms. Narrative therapists typically subscribe to a *poststructural* or *social constructionist* view of the self. This view understands the "self" to be something that is not internal and true but rather an identity or identities that are constructed through interactions with others and informed by larger social and cultural meanings.

When Amy used the words *essence* and *true self*, I understood her to be describing a version of herself that better fit her experience and led to her preferred possibilities for her life. Because she found the distinction between anorexia and her "true self" to be an enormously helpful one (as do so many people trying to reclaim their lives from a/b) I did not feel a need, at that moment, to provide her with a poststructuralist account of "the self." Instead, I continued the conversation within the framework of meaning she had identified as anti-anorexic. I could, if needed, help her develop a more relational account of her preferred self during subsequent meetings.

Amy: You know what's really amazing?

David: What?

Amy: I've actually felt like a woman today. I felt feminine and had these feminine feelings because I've actually put on a bit of weight. I'm scared but I've just got to go with it and I actually feel a bit softer and a bit more ordinary.

David: Does that sit with you okay now?

Amy: Beginning to, yeah.

David: Good, good, good.

Amy: I'm not fighting it. I literally don't have any energy to fight anorexia anymore. I mean it's a matter of accepting who I am and not to feed anorexia.

David: Would your life be a lot easier because you're going with your qualities, rather than anorexia demanding you go against yourself?

Amy: Mm-hmm! I mean . . . here's me, somewhere, but where? How do I get ahold of it? Because anorexia's held it away from me. And you just go that way because there was no way I could make that link between anorexia and what was really me.

David: Did anorexia separate you from yourself?

Amy: Totally!

David: Did it divorce you from your feelings, appetites, desires, and spirituality?

Amy: I think so.

David: Are you feeling like you are becoming more substantial as your person, rather than less substantial as anorexia's person?

Amy: Yeah.

David: What are you finding out about yourself that you can enjoy, appreciate, or cherish?

Amy: It's really simple stuff. Being in the present, just enjoying being, and exploring what that feels like. And there are no strings attached, no guilt attached. There's this new energy in me, that's just like coming from the inside out.

David: Oh, that is the difference, isn't it? Coming from the inside out, rather than being an external power, and being tyrannized by that?

Amy: And also me trying to find other ways of healing myself working from the outside in, trying to repair my body. My body has said to me just these last couple of weeks that I've nearly lost it. I've got to stop. I'd been going dizzy and passing out. (*ironic laughing*) Maybe my body's just saying, "Ha, ha, ha! You've got to drop to the floor, kid."

David: Or "Be more generous to me and value me because I'm a part of you, I'm not separate from you?"

Amy: Yeah.

David: Amy, do you think anorexia's real intention is to separate women's minds and spirits from their bodies, and separate you from your mind and spirit?

Amy: Mm-hmm, and total disintegration.

Anorexia is totally possessive. It wants all of you and all your attention and anything else is competition. I can now do these anorexic things and stop and laugh. It is my opportunity to have some derisive laughter and express my anger at anorexia. Sometimes by laughing at something it shows your anger. I was taught that it is not okay to hate anybody or anything. It is not okay to be angry at anybody or anything. Anorexia feeds on that. It exploits that. But anorexia is just a thing, an energy, so I can get cross with it and laugh at it. When I think about it it would have been almost inconceivable to laugh at anorexia when I was in the thrall of it.*

David: You've really assisted me in understanding a lot of things. Would you have believed it was possible for you to have made such headway in such a short time? I think anorexia had really ruled you and tyrannized you for about 23 years?

Amy: That's right! Twenty-three years!

David: What do you think about the fact that you've made so much headway so quickly? I'm merely asking that. I'm not putting you under any obligation whatsoever of making any more headway or getting there any more quickly. By asking this question I am not intending to set any goals or deadlines. That would be a very anorexic thing for me to do, wouldn't it? I would just like us both to take pleasure in this fact and enjoy it and understand it as best we can. So what's it all about?

Amy: Laugh at it and have no compunction about it. *Do it!*

David: Is that laughter like the holy wisdom of some Oriental religions? They talk about the cosmic joke of seeing through some stuff? Have you heard of that? When you see through things, you just have this resounding laugh?

Amy: Yeah, because I cracked it. I mean anorexia is really dumb, God!

David: It's really ridiculous, isn't it? It's stupid! (*both laughing together*)

---

* Amy's ability to laugh at anorexia is a manifestation of her degree of separation from it, an expression of her anger at and defiance of its "doom and gloom." Because this laughter emerges from Amy, I feel free to join her in it, and delighted in doing so. I would never, myself, initiate laughing at anorexia unless I knew for certain that the insider could join with me in this laughter. If my laughing was premature, chances are good that the insider would experience a lack of empathy for her suffering or an urge to defend anorexia. There is also the very real danger that anorexia would persuade her that I was laughing at her.

Amy: Yes, it is, and I see it. It's a laughter of relief, and of joy, and flipping it that way. It's not making light of it, but it's making the situation lighter. I mean literally energy-wise. Anorexia is so often doom and gloom and heavy, you know, but to laugh and laugh at it straight in the face. Because I can now do these anorexic things and I can stop and laugh at them. Oh my God! (*laughter from both*)

David: I think your anti-anorexia has gone a long way when you can do that.

Amy: Yeah.

David: Anorexia is no longer so terrorizing. When you were in anorexia's thrall, could it terrorize, frighten, and panic you?

Amy: Mm-hmm. There's so much darkness and black spaces. That really does tell you so much . . . to laugh at anorexia at such times, that would be too scary.

David: Yeah, yeah.

Amy: Now I have a strength within me that I can call upon.

David: Well, where to from here? Or is there a case for consolidation? If you're fast or in a hurry is there enough time for just consolidating your anti-anorexia so you don't overburden your resources? You don't want too much on your hands.

Yes, it is important to consolidate, especially when you are shifting foundations. I know you want to go forwards quickly without experiencing the journey. The journey is important, not the destination. Otherwise you are missing so much. It is really about staying in the present moment. If you go too fast, it is like quick-setting concrete, it won't last. When you set new foundations, you have to season the cement. If you go too fast, it is like building your house on sand. You have to build your house on the rock.

Amy: Well, believe it or not I actually sat and did some writing and I actually got a really clear sign of what I need.

David: What was the clear sign of what you need?

Amy: To accept my needs. To allow that it's okay to ask for my needs to be met. In fact, it is vital that they are met. Let me give you an example of something that happened. Chris rents an apartment in my house. Well, at first Chris wanted to park his car behind mine. But I need to know that I can get in and out of my drive anytime. It blocks my freedom. And I would be feeling encroached upon and really uncomfortable. And I spoke to a couple of people about it who told me you have every right to say he's not going to park behind your car. So I went downstairs and did it. (*laughter*)

David: What did he say?

Amy: He said, "Oh, fine!" (*laughter*) And then the other day I went over and I just wanted to clarify a few things. I thought he wouldn't appreciate this. I told him I wanted him to pay the rent on time. No big deal, I just did it.

David: Can you be a little bit proud of yourself ?

Amy: Yeah, and I actually allowed myself to be proud of myself. Whoosh! I even patted myself on the back.

David: Not only were you proud, but you allowed yourself to feel that pride.

Amy: Mm-hmm.

David: In the past, did you think that feeling proud was a vice?

Amy: Oh, yeah. I wasn't allowed to feel good or proud or pleased that I'd done something. And that is one of the triggers—"Oh, I'm feeling good now but I'm not allowed to"—that would set me off on a binge.

David: How could it be that you could go against 23 years of considering that feeling good and proud of yourself were vices, to allowing yourself to feel such pride? I don't want you to make light of this because it's a quarter of a century here. Am I right?

Amy: It's an awful long time, isn't it?

David: You've turned a corner here but it's a mighty long road, a 23-year road to change. What advice might you have for anyone else who might watch this tape, feeling hopeless and despairing? How would you explain to them how it was possible for you to change the course of your life?

Amy: It's really difficult to put it in a nutshell because it has taken a long time for me to get where I am.

David: If you were to look backwards down your anti-anorexic road, were there some milestones that had already been laid before today?

Amy: Yes. One of them, and this one's the one that comes to my mind immediately, is that deep down somewhere I knew that anorexia was not the way I had to be for the rest of my life. Anorexia would have totally obliterated me had I not believed that there is a shred of my being that anorexia cannot touch.

David: Okay, what is that?

Amy: It's my soul. It's what I understand to be my essence which anorexia cannot touch or contaminate. Through all this shit, I have managed to hang on to it.

David: Amy, do you think anyone else has noticed that you have more than hung on to your soul?

It is hard to sustain claims about oneself if those claims aren't authenticated by others. Thus, when Amy identified something about herself that she regarded as positive, I evoked the experience of others that might serve to substantiate these claims.

Amy: I haven't got a lot of friends yet. They're all in my head! (*laughing*)

David: No, of course.

Amy: But my Mum has.

David: What's your Mum say?

Amy: My Mum said she could see that I have a lot softer energy and that I sound stronger.

David: I'd agree with that. You do sound stronger. There's more strength in your voice. I don't mean volume. I mean more substance.

Amy: And more power.

David: (laughing) Yes. Well, it's possible with your permission that people could look in on this. Anything you'd like to say here to someone who's just beginning to see and to oppose anorexia?

Amy: I'm quite convinced that the most important anti-anorexic things for me were being really honest with myself about my feelings, and trying to sort out the difference between my feelings and what anorexia demands I feel. And ultimately, being true to myself by no longer believing anorexia.

Chapter 15

ANOREXIA'S SOLDIERS

ANOTHER CONVERSATION
WITH MARGARET

In Chapter 10 we presented a conversation I (RM) had with Margaret, who, at the time, was very much under anorexia's spell. That conversation helped to open Margaret's eyes to some of anorexia's treacherous deceptions and offered her some hopeful and credible alternatives to achieving what anorexia had promised but not delivered—some ability to keep herself from being harmed by others and an opportunity to feel successful, competent, and worthy. In this chapter, we meet with Margaret a few weeks after that conversation.

Although Margaret had encountered some recent circumstances that heightened her vulnerability to anorexia's voice and made its messages seem more credible, she had miraculously been able to maintain a critical and suspicious vantage point. Her anti-anorexic skepticism had enabled her to avoid becoming reenchanted with anorexia. The following two interviews illustrate one form early anti-anorexic conversations can take once anorexia's spell has been broken.

Just prior to this meeting Margaret had left a few messages for me about her distress regarding some Internet chatroom conversations she had engaged in. Several of the members of the Internet group had disparaged homosexuality and argued that gay and lesbian couples should not be permitted to raise children. The gay, lesbian, and bisexual members, including Margaret, decided to retreat to their own group for a while to support each other and discuss how they wanted to approach the larger group. Margaret felt devastated by the homophobic remarks and by the way in which several of the individuals, whom she had come to regard as friends, supported the right of the other members to express these disparaging views. Anorexia, she confided, was using this instance of homophobia to attack her sense of moral goodness and worth and was then offering to make her a better person.

Margaret appeared uneasy and a little jumpy as she walked from the waiting room to my office. She immediately sat down on the floor in front of my sandtray and rapidly made a scene in the sand. By the time I had readied myself in my chair, she had already stood back up and settled on the couch, covering all but her face and head with a thick chenille throw. She appeared listless and subdued.

Rick: Hi, Margaret.

Margaret: Hi.

Rick: We talked the other day about whether you thought you should disappear or remain visible. Have these hateful conversations on the Internet invited anorexia back into your life and perhaps convinced you that it is better to disappear and become invisible?

Margaret: (*nods her head*)

Rick: How is it speaking to you? How is it using what the Internet listserve members are saying for its own purposes?

Margaret: It's making it really hard to feel entitled to anything. It's telling me I can't change.

Rick: Is anorexia implying that you should change?

Margaret: It's telling me I can't eat, for starters. I've been told that I'm so bad in so many posts because of my support for the gay and lesbian people in the group. Anorexia then amplifies and generalizes these negative messages. It tells me that someone like me doesn't have the right to do anything.

Rick: It's joining that chorus of voices telling gay and lesbian people they don't deserve to raise children, then it takes this to a different level and tells you that you don't even deserve to eat, that you are just bad?

Margaret: Yeah. But through weight loss somehow I can be better. If I'm hungry I can be better. I don't get it. But it sure carries a lot of weight.

Anorexia once again was trying to exploit interactions that devalued Margaret and left her feeling unsafe. In this instance, anorexia found a tremendous ally in homophobic and heterosexist discourses. The beliefs associated with these discourses are readymade to instill self-hatred and shame. Anorexia was fully capable of twisting and distorting things to make Margaret feel "less than." In this instance, the moral condemnation of gays and lesbians associated with the discourse of heterosexist supremacy had already gotten the ball of self-hatred rolling. All anorexia needed to do was encourage this self-hatred to encompass the totality of Margaret's identity. Anorexia could then offer itself as a response to self-hatred, a golden opportunity for redemption.

Any form of dominant discourse that establishes a hierarchy of moral worth is inherently empowering of a/b. A/b is directly dependent upon the dominant Western discourses that elevate thinness as an aesthetic ideal, attribute moral virtue to those who achieve it, and devalue and discriminate against people who are fat. But other discourses such as racism, classism, sexism, and heterosexism are indirectly supportive of a/b because of their powerful potential to leave some people feeling inferior and unworthy. It is extremely difficult to resist these discourses because, like the aesthetic of thinness, they receive so much support from the institutions of our culture—schools, the media, the workplace, the military, and so on. It is easy to see how tempting a/b's promises of control and moral redemption can be to people who are subject to these forms of devaluation, disenfranchisement, and attack.*

Margaret had managed to remain somewhat separated from anorexia insofar as she continued to suspect its motives and did not eagerly embrace it. Thus, there was less need for me to focus on the potential effects of anorexia on her life as I did during our previous meeting. My primary interest was to help Margaret continue to identify the means by which anorexia was trying to regain her allegiance. I attempted to do this by asking questions that aimed to expose anorexia's tactics and strategies and make it easier for Margaret to resist them.

Rick: Does anorexia want to carry all the weight of authority and you to carry none of it?

Margaret: Yeah. It feels that way to me, but that's not the way it represents itself. It tries to convince me that it is actually giving me more voice and protecting me.

Rick: Anorexia's saying to you, "You are bad and if you really want to be better, don't eat"?

Margaret: Basically. My head hurts.

Rick: From not eating?

Margaret: Yeah. That's the kind of stuff it's doing. It tells me it hurts because there is something wrong with me, but I know it hurts from not eating.

Rick: Do you think anorexia wants to weaken you in order to make it harder for you to think?

Margaret: Yeah, it wants to make it hard for me to think, but it's also making me stronger.

---

* See Thompson's *A Hunger so Wide and so Deep: A Multiracial View of Women's' Eating Problems* (1994) for a more in-depth discussion of the relationship between institutional oppressions such as racism and anorexia.

Rick: How's it convincing you of that? In what sense are you becoming stronger, Margaret?

Margaret: I'm not hurt as much by the stuff on the Internet list. I don't feel it as much.

Rick: People are beating you up emotionally and anorexia steps in and offers to help you not feel it. Does it encourage you to numb yourself and become less alive rather than to resist these ideas about who you are and find ways of holding on to your own knowing?

Until this point in our discussion, Margaret had been repudiating anorexia. Now she identified something anorexia was doing that she believed was positive. By weakening her physically and distancing her from her bodily sensations, anorexia provided some anesthesia from the emotional pain she had been experiencing. As anorexia encouraged Margaret to become increasingly disembodied, it drew upon the common societal discourse that equates strength with stoicism and emotional detachment to portray this emotional anesthesia as "becoming stronger." In doing this, anorexia cleverly exploited the value Margaret placed on strength to spin this as a positive development.

Rather than engage in a deconstruction of anorexia's definition of *stronger* and explore the present and future effects of this definition, I wanted to stay focused on Margaret's belief that anorexia would take her pain away because I believed that she would be drawn to this emotional anesthesia regardless of whether it was defined as *strong.* I was interested in exposing the ultimate price Margaret would have to pay for anorexia's emotional "relief" and helping Margaret find alternative responses to her hurt. My inquiry with Margaret at this point resembled the "breaking the spell" conversation presented earlier, because Margaret was enchanted by anorexia. It is always essential to follow the person's experience and remain fluid and flexible from moment to moment.

Rick: Margaret, haven't you been down this road before?

Margaret: Yeah, but it's not all that clear. Anorexia's making it hard to remember what happened.

Rick: If anorexia has helped you out so much in the past, wouldn't it want to make the memory of its help very vivid? If it is really your friend and has so much to offer you, why would it want you to forget all that it's done for you? Do you trust the voice of someone who says, "Oh, let's just forget about the past and focus on the present. That's all water under the bridge. Let's just stay focused on what I can do for you now?"

Margaret: Normally, no.

Rick: How much are you trusting that anorexia, by starving you to death, is going to take your pain away and make you better and stronger?

Margaret: Taking my pain away is pretty tempting. I want to trust that.

Rick: Would you want to lie down in bed next to your murderer and think he or she is your lover?

Margaret: It seems like we talked about something similar to this recently.

Rick: We did? It's interesting because as I said those words I was reminded of your method of coping with your father's abuse of you as a teenager. You actually had the ability to turn him into a boyfriend in your imagination, and doing so did make it feel less painful in the moment. Do you think that is what is happening now in a sense?

Margaret: (*laughs*) Yeah.

Rick: This is something I've been talking about with some other people who also found anorexia's offer to take away their pain tempting. They told me these claims ultimately never came true. Some people felt better immediately after throwing up but everyone eventually felt worse. If the more pain a person is in the more tempted she might be to take up anorexia's offer of pain relief, then anorexia actually has a vested interested in people being in pain. Can you see the work of anorexia in the pain you are now in? Do you find that anorexia is insulting you, telling you that you are worthless and bad?

Margaret: Yeah!

Rick: So what does it mean for anorexia to tell you, on the one hand, "I will take your pain away" while simultaneously sticking it to you? Is it a bit like someone sticking a knife in your back and then saying, "Look, I'll pull it out for you and then you'll have me to thank"? (*Margaret laughs.*) "Don't pay attention to how I'm sticking it in, I'll just take credit for removing it." Do you think that's what it's doing with you?

Margaret: Yeah, that's what it feels like.

Margaret realized, at least for the moment, that anorexia was not only a temporary reliever of pain, but also an inflicter of pain. This understanding was critical, for it suggested that diminishing her hurt might be better achieved by opposing anorexia rather than befriending it. But anorexia, until now, had prevented her from seeing how it instigated or exacerbated the pain it promised to save her from. I wanted to co-research with her this tactic of anorexia in order to further undermine anorexia's credibility and to help inoculate her to this tactic in the future. As you will see, Margaret anticipated this line of questioning and readily took it up.

Rick: Does anorexia try to keep the two apart in your mind?

Margaret: Yeah.

Rick: What is it doing, on the one hand, so it can try to . . .

Margaret: (*anticipating the rest of my question*) . . . seduce you on the other? (*pause*) It silences other voices. It uses things on the Internet list to tell me that things are just too big. It makes everything feel like it is too big and hopeless. Then it tells me it can take away the pain because it is so huge.

Rick: Does it tell you it can take away the pain of heterosexism and ignorance and callousness by cutting you off from your body, from your feelings, from your voice, and ultimately from your life?

Margaret: It doesn't say it that way. It says it's giving me life. (*laughs*) It makes it hard to see how it's making me feel bad.

Rick: How does it make it hard? How does it disguise its abuse?

Margaret: Like Stella [an Internet list member] does. "It's good for you."

Rick: "It feels bad but it's really for your own good." Something like that?

Margaret: Yeah, that kind of thing. It presents itself as caring. It says it's in my best interests.

Rick: Just based on this conversation so far—and I know it's been a short one—are there sufficient grounds to make you think it would be good for you to question its motives and intentions towards you a bit more before blindly turning your life over to it?

Margaret: To question it, yeah.

Rick: There are a lot of things it's doing that are pretty suspicious, like "forget about the past," "don't listen to other voices" . . . saying, "I want to take your pain away" while simultaneously putting you down.

When I asked Margaret if there were sufficient grounds on which to question anorexia's motives and intentions, I hoped to invite her to move from the position of passive respondent to that of critical interrogator. If Margaret were to keep herself from becoming imprisoned again by anorexia, she would need to engage in ongoing and vigilant questioning of her thoughts in order to ferret out anorexia and evaluate its pronouncements and promises. Unfortunately, I defeated the purpose of the question by elaborating on Margaret's affirmative response myself, rather than asking her what she now believed those grounds to be.

Margaret: Putting me down feels supported by a lot of people.

Rick: By the group members, you mean? Do you think anorexia is kicking you while you are down? That the verbal abuse on the Internet got you down and made an opening for anorexia to come in at a weak point, thinking that maybe, in this weakened state, it could sell you some of what it's saying?

Margaret: It came in as a support when I was feeling weak.

Rick: Do you think anorexia and self-hate go hand in hand?

Margaret: Anorexia and self-hate, but with the illusion of self-love.

I was intrigued by Margaret's phrase "self-hate with the illusion of self-love." It concisely captured one of the most significant and lethal deceptions of anorexia. I found myself wondering that if self-hate was the handmaiden of anorexia, genuine self-love might be a pillar of anti-anorexia for Margaret. So far during this meeting we had focused on the circumstances in her life that anorexia had been able to leverage in its attempt to seduce and ensnare Margaret. Now I sensed an opening to explore what might lie on the anti-anorexic side of her life. Self-love, it seemed, might be a part of that landscape. Of course, self-love does not occur in a vacuum any more than self-hate does. I wanted to know what community of concerned and caring others might be implicated in this self-love, and what Margaret might see in herself when she looked at herself through this lens of self-love.

Rick: That's a really interesting way of putting it. When you've really been loving yourself and feeling loved, has anorexia ever gotten itself through the door at those times?

Margaret: (*laughing*) It makes attempts.

Rick: What do you know about yourself at those points that enables you to slam that door shut, if that's what happens?

Margaret: I know that I'm good. I have more spaces in my life where I can *be*.

Rick: Where you can be yourself? Where you feel accepted? Do you feel this [gay/lesbian/bisexual/transgendered] caucus will be an anti-anorexic place, a place where you will feel you can be?

Margaret: Yes. But there's a voice that is trying to convince me that I shouldn't participate. It tries to turn what is said there against me. It sows doubt and distrust.

The conversation had quickly returned to anorexia and the means by which it attempted to negate Margaret's connection to others' love and concern. Despite my enthusiasm for exploring the anti-anorexic side of her experience, it was important that I follow her back to anorexia. A better understanding of the means by which anorexia was denying her the nurturance of others was needed before she would be able to push anorexia aside and take in the respect, care, admiration, and love that others held for her. She would then have recourse to an identity informed by the experience of others who appreciated her and to an experience of genuine self-love rather than anorexia's counterfeit self-love.

Rick: It disqualifies whatever support you could get? Does it ever do that by putting down other people in the caucus?

Margaret: To me? Yeah. It's also trying to cut me off from you.

Rick: How is it doing that?

Margaret: It's trying to disqualify you, trying to argue against you. And worst of all, it makes me hear the things that you say differently than the way you intend them.

Rick: Is that what happened last time we met, when you jumped up in alarm when I said, "You haven't disappeared"?

Margaret: It made that into a challenge and wanted me to hear it as "you should disappear."

Rick: So is this any way for a friend to behave?

Margaret: It doesn't feel very friendly.

A long pause followed, during which Margaret seemed to be engaging in some internal struggle. Knowing that Margaret had just spoken against anorexia, I suspected that anorexia had been provoked and was now rebuking her.

Rick: Did anorexia fight back when you said it didn't feel friendly?

Margaret: It said it's the only friend I have. Everyone else will only hurt me.

Rick: It sounds like its argument right now depends upon the idea that life is hopeless, futile, and that without it you are doomed to live a life filled with pain. Something like that?

Margaret: Yeah.

Rick: (attempting to discredit the picture anorexia has painted) Hey, did you enjoy at all the day where you just took a break and went over to your mom's and swam and played with the kids?

Margaret: No. I was dizzy. I experienced the drawbacks to playing. That's part of the problem when you're not eating.

Rick: It's not the drawback to playing, it's the drawback to being starved. Do you want to keep on submitting to starvation or do you feel entitled to eat something?

Margaret: I'm afraid to answer.

Rick: What's the fear?

Margaret: That anorexia will fight even harder.

Rick: Okay, all right. So you don't have to declare your position if you think that will draw anorexia's fire.

Her initial reluctance to openly express an anti-anorexic position seemed to be motivated by a desire to avoid provoking anorexia further, and I believed that at this moment she was motivated by anti-anorexia. But in an instant anorexia co-opted her anti-anorexic stance and asserted a pro-anorexic rule.

Margaret: I'm not allowed to talk about it with anybody.

Rick: I don't know if there is a way of avoiding a confrontation with anorexia if you are going to have your life back.

Margaret: Neither do I!

The arising of the question of whether or not Margaret could free herself from anorexia without a confrontation seemed like an opportune moment to look at the sandtray scene she had constructed upon entering the room, as it very graphically portrayed her predicament. The sandtray was very similar to one she had made during a recent meeting: food in the center, surrounded by soldiers whose guns pointed outwards at a girl and a baby. The difference between this sandtray and the last was that the girl was no longer standing arm in arm with the soldiers but rather faced them in opposition.

Rick: Can we look at the sandtray you did when you first came in? Does the girl with the gun pointed at her represent you?

Margaret: Yeah. I feel like that person, the white one standing there.

Rick: Well, I'm sorry that you're having guns pointed at you, but it's good to see that you've deserted the army of anorexia. I'm sure anorexia would want you standing with its soldiers rather than against them.

Margaret: You're right. She can go either way.

Rick: Right. That's the way it goes. It's not an easy thing. (*returning to the theme of open confrontation versus covert resistance*) Do you think anorexia will be angry with you for acknowledging, both in words and in the sandtray, that you are hungry? (*a long pause*) What are you thinking?

Margaret: I am a bit angry.

Rick: (*I imagine that anorexia is really making Margaret pay for her open opposition to it.*) Do you wish we never had this conversation?

Margaret: (*clearly distinguishing anorexia's voice and desires from her own*) That's not what I wish. That's what I'm hearing in my head.

Rick: Is that anorexia speaking?

Margaret: It's saying that whether I eat or not is none of your business. It's a personal thing. (*sounding bewildered*) But you're my therapist, aren't you?

Once again, anorexia had deviously attempted to distract Margaret from its violation of her fundamental right to physical sustenance by turning its attack against me as well, insisting that I was violating her hard-won right to privacy.

Rick: Yes. Isn't it interesting how anorexia will try to speak to a right that you had to fight for—a right to privacy that you were denied by your father? Anorexia will sidle up to you and harmonize its voice with a voice that's been a good voice for you, one that helped you stand up for yourself and set limits with others. But is it protecting your privacy or its privacy? It seems more like what your father said to you to keep his abuse of you a secret: "How dare you write about what goes on in this house in your journal and show it to a teacher!"

By pointing out the parallels between anorexia's tactics and those of her overtly abusive father, I hoped to access the skills she had previously developed in discerning abuse and claiming her own rights.

Margaret: Anorexia doesn't say it that way.

Rick: I know, but when you look at the effects of what it tells you, what does it most resemble?

Margaret: It more resembles what my dad would do.

Rick: Is it you that doesn't want to talk about it or is it anorexia? Is it protecting your privacy or is it putting a gag in your mouth in order to cut you off from other people's help and support?

Margaret: It says it can give me more support because it knows me better.

Rick: Well, since you've been the recipient of anorexia's so-called support, have you found the quality of your life improved? Have you found yourself smiling or laughing much? Have you been in good moods?

Margaret: No. (laughs)

Rick: Anorexia will probably say, "Well just wait."

Margaret: Yeah.

Rick: "You have to work hard first and then you'll reap the rewards after hard work. The rewards are just around the corner." But you've told me that, in the past, no matter how hard you tried, it was never good enough for anorexia.

Margaret: There are moments when it is good enough.

Rick: Like you get a pat on the back? You might have some anorexic sense of accomplishment, some sense of anorexia-pride?

Margaret: Yeah.

Rick: Do you think there is a difference between anorexia-happiness and . . .

Margaret: . . . my own?

Rick: Yeah.

Margaret was referring to another aspect of anorexia that she experienced as positive, namely those times when she had fulfilled anorexia's requirements and received a pat on the back for a job well done. I wanted to deconstruct anorexia's version of happiness and contrast it with what, in Margaret's experience, might be an anti-anorexic experience of pride or happiness. The fact that Margaret chose to contrast anorexia-happiness with "my own" (rather than with "anti-anorexia happiness," which was what I was going to say) indicated the extent to which she was experiencing herself as separate from anorexia. The remainder of our meeting was spent juxtaposing anorexia-happiness and Margaret-happiness and elaborating on the distinctions between them. The elaboration of these two visions of life enabled Margaret to clarify her own desires and more wholeheartedly align herself with those desires.

Margaret: You're *more than* and *better* with anorexia. You feel better and above other people. The other way you're just a person.

Rick: Which kind of happiness do you prefer—the "better and above" kind or the "I'm just a person" kind?

Margaret: The "I'm just a person" kind.

Rick: Why do you like that one better?

Margaret: My experience has been that being just a person can be more human. I don't have to be perfect.

Rick: It doesn't demand perfection from you? Do you think that the other kind of happiness is demanding?

Margaret: It's a perfection-driven happiness.

Rick: Which is something that can be pretty fleeting, I would think, because no one can be perfect. Does it end up being more the hope of happiness than happiness itself?

Margaret: Yeah, but in a way it's also "Look at how good you are." There is that kind of happiness.

Rick: Is that the kind of happiness that has to do with becoming less of a person, less of a self . . .

Margaret: You don't look at it that way. (*pause*) Yeah, kinda.

Rick: Less feelings, less of a mind, less of a body? Does it just boil a person down to willpower, self-control, obedience? Is that all that's left of them?

Margaret: (*with conviction*) Obedience!

Rick: Saying no to oneself and yes to anorexia?

Margaret: After a while there is nothing to say no to. You just become one with it.

Rick: You mean you as a person disappear?

Margaret: Yeah.

Rick: Kind of chilling, isn't it?

Margaret returned a week later. She immediately struck me as slightly but discernibly more animated as she strode into my office and sat on the floor cross-legged, leaning against my couch.

Margaret: (*with some satisfaction*) I claimed three bowls of soup since we met.

Rick: Claimed them?

Margaret: Ate ém. *Claimed them!*

Rick: That's a nice way of putting it—"claimed them." What's the meaning for you in that way of saying it? What's the difference between claiming them and eating them?

Margaret: Eating them doesn't have any entitlement.

Rick: So when you claimed them you not only ate them but felt you had a right to eat them?

Margaret: Yeah. Eating can become a rule or something you have to do. I wasn't forced into it. That's different!

Rick: I like that distinction a lot, the distinction between eating food and claiming it. Have you ever thought of that before or did it just come out of your mouth spontaneously?

Margaret: That just came out of my mouth. That's what it felt like. But it's not proper English.

Rick: It's not improper English. It's actually very proper if that captures your experience better than saying "I ate three bowls of soup."

Margaret: I claimed it.

Rick: Great!

Margaret had achieved a significant victory in her battle against anorexia. She had not only been able to eat, but also felt entitled to eat. She had not only opposed anorexia on the outside by eating, but had also undermined anorexia on the inside, which enabled her to experience eating as an entitlement.

Margaret: Part of it had to do with trying to name some of those soldiers [referring to the sandtray soldiers she used to represent anorexia].

Rick: Oh, really?

Margaret: Like, *You're to Blame* is one of them.

Rick: And what does You're to Blame say you are to blame for?

Margaret: For everything. For absolutely everything. For being weak, for not being strong. But its definitions of strong don't match mine.

During our last meeting I had asked Margaret to consider the effects of her allowing anorexia to equate strength with "not feeling." When anorexia's soldier You're to Blame accused her of being weak, Margaret contested anorexia's definition of strength. It was a relief and a pleasure to have her join me as cointerrogator of anorexia.

Rick: What do you think anorexia's definition of strength would be?

Margaret: My losing weight and losing my life.

Rick: Anorexia would call that being strong?

Margaret: Yes, but it doesn't present it that way.

Rick: How would it present it? That's you seeing through it, right? Is it okay to ask about that or would that be inviting anorexia's voice in here too much?

Because Margaret was separated from anorexia at that moment, I had some reservations about inviting its voice back into the room to make its case. I felt fairly certain that Margaret's anti-anorexia would not be endangered by this, but I wanted to play it safe and shelter her anti-anorexia if it was at risk. Margaret's current separation from anorexia made me confident that I could trust that whatever she decided would be on the side of anti-anorexia.

Margaret: I don't know. (*She pauses to consider, then chooses to proceed.*) It presents it more like I *am* stronger for listening to it.

Rick: Strength means listening to anorexia and obeying it. And what does that translate into? Strength means not eating ...

Margaret: (*decisively*) Willpower. Things like that, willpower, not eating.

I then returned to the anti-anorexic side of her experience, inviting her to elaborate upon her own definition of strength. This was identical to the process we engaged in during our last meeting when we worked to draw distinctions between anorexia-happiness and Margaret-happiness.

Rick: What's your definition of strength? What do you think it means to be a strong person?

Margaret: To be able to have my own voice, even when it's hard.

Rick: (*recording Margaret's words on paper to emphasize their significance*) "To be able to have my own voice." Okay. And what else?

Margaret: Even when it's hard. (*Margaret pauses to consider this question further.*) To be able to know what I know. That's strength.

I was moved by Margaret's definition of strength, as I knew how much the extreme abuse she experienced as a child had dispossessed her of her voice and of her knowing, and how bravely she had worked to reclaim them. Because her definition of strength struck me as powerfully anti-anorexic, I anticipated that anorexia would attempt to challenge and discredit it, so I tried to head it off.

Rick: Anorexia probably wouldn't put it this way, but would it imply that disavowing what you know would be a strength?

Margaret: Yeah.

Rick: (*looking for the trick*) How would anorexia sweeten it up for you, to make it sound like a positive?

Margaret: Like it did with the privacy thing. It just twists it.

Rick: You mean when it made my asking questions about what anorexia was allowing you to eat a violation of your privacy?

Margaret: Yeah.

Rick: So how would it twist things in such a way as to get you to think you were being strong by disavowing what you know?

Margaret: It says to me, "That's ridiculous ... not right ... wrong!" It would use majority opinions out there.

Rick: To disqualify ...

Margaret: (*finishing the thought*) ... my own knowledge, yeah.

Rick: Would it have anything to say about the respect that should be afforded to your own feelings?

Margaret: Yeah, but that was from another soldier. That comes into the soldier of *Rules*. That's where all my feelings come under.

Rick: Should we wait on that?

Margaret: No, that's fine.

Rick: (*summarizing*) Okay, You're to Blame blames you for everything, accuses you of being weak, and tells you that being strong means listening to and obeying it, which it calls "willpower." But you've held on to your own definition of strength, which includes having your own voice, even when it's hard, and knowing what you know. And naturally, You're to Blame tries to disqualify what you know. Well then, tell me about anorexia's soldier of Rules.

Margaret: The soldier of Rules and Rights. That's where feelings come in. He kind of controls a lot.

Rick: Does this soldier have a rule about feelings?

Margaret: He has rules about everything.

Rick: What would it claim about your feelings?

Margaret: That they are not legitimate, that they're out of proportion, they are not good. But it also uses them, too.

Rick: How does it use them?

Margaret: Well, like when I got here I forgot you said you might be a little late and immediately it was like, "You don't really want to see me." It plays it that way.

Rick: So are there certain feelings that it makes use of and other feelings that it has less use for? Or could it potentially use all feelings?

Margaret: It could potentially use all feelings. Except that it doesn't want me to have anger.

Rick: Not even at yourself?

Margaret: No. It would rather have me feel bad about myself rather than angry at myself. It would prefer me not to have any connection to my own anger.

Rick: Even anger directed at yourself is just potentially too ...

Margaret: (*jumping in*) ... threatening.

Rick: Threatening to anorexia.

Margaret: I mean it will allow it, but it would prefer I not do it.

Rick: Because it knows that it could be turned against itself too easily?

Margaret: Yeah. My anger might just allow me to see it. But I don't think it wants me to try to kill myself. It doesn't want me to die a quick death.

Rick: You mean that's why it opposes anger directed against yourself? I hope that you don't decide to die a quick death just to spite anorexia. (*laughing*)

Margaret: (*laughs*) No, I won't.

Rick: What other kinds of rules and rights ...

Margaret: The privacy thing that I told you about.

Rick: Was that a rule or a right?

Margaret: That was a right. It takes rights that I have like the right to privacy, the right to respect, any right that I feel I have and it twists it all around.

Rick: What's the nature of the twisting that it does? It takes rights you've already laid claim to and it . . .

Margaret: . . . seduces me with them. It makes me think it's backing me.

Rick: It makes you think it is backing you through these rights?

Margaret: Yeah. Supporting those rights. But it's really cutting me off from people, like it did with the privacy thing with you.

Rick: So it appropriates the talking about rights to actually deny you your rights while convincing you it's supporting them?

Margaret: That it's supporting them.

Rick: David [Epston] and I were talking about this very thing—how anorexia tries to infiltrate and appropriate anti-anorexia. He calls it "turning." You know how another country might try to turn a spy against the country he's working for and make him a double agent? It's like taking what is initially anti-anorexic and then turning it in an anorexic direction, so it starts working on anorexia's behalf.

Margaret: Yeah.

Having explored some of the tactics that anorexia used to oppose and co-opt Margaret's anti-anorexia, I was now curious about any strategies that Margaret might have discovered to foil anorexia's attempts. Often this anti-a/b knowledge operates reflexively without ever having been articulated. Richly describing this anti-a/b knowledge makes it possible for the person to: (1) fine-tune her anti-anorexic strategies, (2) share and celebrate her knowledge with League members and concerned and loving others, and (3) ground her anti-a/b in an alternative story about herself by speculating about what life experiences and relationships these knowledges may be connected to, and what they might say about the person's skills, abilities, purposes, values, and intentions.

Rick: Have you discovered some ways of frustrating anorexia's attempts to "turn" your anti-anorexia?

Margaret: Just questioning the thoughts that go on inside of me more. Questioning myself.

Rick: So the counter-tactic is "questioning the thoughts inside of me more."

Margaret: Yeah. And another thing that has helped me see it is to go along with the thoughts more to see where they take me. But I don't act on them. At some point I push back from them and check them out to see if they are really mine, if they really fit. It's like being on a boat on a river and letting it carry me a little ways. I have to always be looking ahead a bit to make sure it's not going to plunge over a waterfall. When I see something bad coming, I get the hell off.

Rick: Do you think this requires a lot of vigilance?

Margaret: A fuck of a lot! I'm sorry [for swearing]. I talked in the caucus about anorexia's voice coming back into my life again. It was a real internal battle but I managed to ask their permission to privilege their voices [over anorexia's voice] in order to sort of support my own. And that's been helpful. God was that a fight. The asking thing was hard.

Rick: What kind of response did you get back?

Margaret: Real positive. They were all honored. I'll show them to you.

Rick: I'd love to see them. What difference did that make? Did that create a sense that you had some anti-anorexic allies?

Margaret: Yeah, it sure did. And when I talked with them about the [homophobic] conversation, they experienced it very much the way I experience anorexia's voice. It was uncanny. Their way of trying to seduce us to listen to hateful, demeaning ideas about homosexuality was to call it "the voice of dialogue." It was real similar to the seduction anorexia does.

Rick: Are you referring here to how some people on the Internet list have taken what could be called verbal assault and called it "dialogue"?

Margaret: And made it "dialogue."

Rick: And you've been told it's for your own good?

Margaret: Right. "It's for your own good. And you should participate." The whole nine yards. "Be open and curious, inviting." (*growling with anger and frustration*) It makes me sick. And the whole time claiming that they care and this is good for us. But it doesn't feel good. They make lots of intellectual arguments to back it up. And many of us have been left hearing voices that tell us we're bad. It's left some people feeling guilty and some people feeling bad and powerless, like we all deserve this.

Rick: I'm glad you are beginning to see through this twisting. We are running short of time and I am wondering if there are some other rules that Rules and Rights have been laying down?

Margaret: Old ones about crying or the anger thing. (*speaking as anorexia*) "You can't cry. If you do you're a baby or weak. And you can't be angry."

Rick: And what would it say if you're angry?

Margaret: You're being violent, unreasonable, not nice. But it doesn't fight me if I happen to be feeling like shit about myself. That, it doesn't mind.

Rick: So you are allowed the experience of misery?

Margaret: Yeah. But it really prefers it to be only self-misery, nothing that connects me to others' misery.

Rick: Why wouldn't it want you to connect to other people's misery?

Margaret: Because that would connect me to other people, possibly in a way that would have me fighting anorexia.

Rick: Are you talking about noticing other people's anorexia-related misery?

Margaret: Not just that. Anything. I think it's more like the misery of anybody who's been oppressed. If I can feel outrage about the injustices that other people are experiencing, then perhaps I might begin to feel a bit more outrage on my own behalf.

I was intrigued by what Margaret was saying about how anorexia attempted to blind her not only to her own oppression but also to oppression and injustice in general. For Margaret, anorexia was allied with other discourses that render injustice invisible by blaming the person who has been victimized. But the fact that Margaret referred to these injustices suggested to me that she was keenly aware of injustices and the experience of people who are subject to them. I wanted to return to the subject of anorexia's soldiers at this point, but I made a mental note to inquire about the history of Margaret's capacity to perceive injustice when the appropriate moment presented itself.

Rick: Have there been any other soldiers that you've identified?

Margaret: I've been working on it.

Rick: What difference has it made to identify what these two soldiers get up to?

Margaret: Well, when I said I claimed the soup, identifying the soldiers contributed to that claiming. It's helped me feel more entitlement and it's enabled me to disagree with some of what those soldiers stand for, to step away from anorexia a bit. But it's still seducing. That's the other soldier.

Rick: What's the other soldier?

Margaret: The *Seduction* soldier.

Rick: I see.

Margaret: The I Love You one. But it's not love! And the Comparison soldier should be in there. I'm constantly comparing myself to others and even within myself.

Rick: What do you mean "within yourself"?

Margaret: Good feeling, bad feeling, good need, bad need. That kind of thing. Putting myself in little fucking boxes left and right. Comparing-boxes.

Rick: Like self-evaluation?

Margaret: Yeah, self-evaluation.

Rick: I'd love to hear more about this, but what I'd really like to ask you a bit more about right now is this: How has putting names to these soldiers and really noticing the operations of anorexia through these different soldiers helped you get more free from it?

Margaret: It helps me find my own voice.

Rick: How does it do that? Tell me the process that goes on in your own mind. Where are you standing in yourself when you are identifying these soldiers? Is there a place that you go to in your mind that makes these soldiers more visible to you? How have you become able to see them?

Margaret: It's almost like making anorexia into an entity, if that makes sense. Something concrete that I can see and hear. And then I can talk to it. Like it's not in me. Like a person outside of me. I get it out of me.

Rick: When you think about it as outside of you, how does it make it more clear to you?

Margaret: My own voice is clearer, for starters. And I can see it [anorexia]. I can see it for what it is.

Rick: One person said she could hear its voice better because her voice and its voice weren't so intertwined.

Margaret: Yeah. They aren't together. That's another one that's hard to keep up. Let down your guard for one second and it's right back in.

Rick: That's what she said, too. She said the minute she goes unconscious about it . . .

Margaret: (overlapping) . . . it's there. It's there all over again.

Rick: And then she kind of wakes up and catches it . . .

Margaret: And then you need to start again. (sarcastically) It's fun.

Rick: I know I'm asking you to be very detailed about it, but you know what they say—"the devil is in the details." Well, perhaps exorcising the devil is in the details as well. How do you push anorexia outside of you? Do you say something to yourself or do something in relation to your body?

Margaret: I get a glimpse of safety. It might not be very long.

Rick: And that glimpse of safety comes first before you push anorexia outside of you?

Margaret: Yeah. And at some level there's . . . I guess it would be like a dissociation kind of thing.

Rick: Say more. You'll get a glimpse of safety like . . . "I'm okay"?

Margaret: Yeah, like an "I'm okay" kind of safety.

Rick: And then what happens?

Margaret: I kind of grab on to it and feed it.

Rick: How do you do that? I know I'm asking hard questions but I'm thinking it might be good to be as conscious of your anti-anorexia as you are of anorexia.

Margaret: It's hard. Why is this harder?

Rick: I think it's stuff we usually don't notice or pay much attention to.

Margaret: I thought about my frog.

The frog Margaret referred to related to a camping trip her father took her on when she was a teenager. During this trip Margaret's father sexually abused her. This was not the first time he had abused her. In fact, by this point in her life, Margaret knew that time alone with her father would require her to summon all of her strength of spirit to get through what she knew would be a terrifying and humiliating ordeal. On this particular trip, Margaret's spirits ebbed. While walking by herself among the trees and rocks and streams, she felt despair descend over her like a black cloud. In desperation she looked up at the vast blue mountain sky and prayed for the arrival of a person who could take her away from all of the pain and fear.

Shortly after her desperate plea she stumbled upon a frog. She laughed at her misfortune: "I pray for a savior, and what do I get? A frog!" When she attempted to pick it up, she found the frog to be quite docile. It allowed her to hold it and even seemed to welcome it. An instant rapport grew between the two of them. As she cradled the frog, she found her spirit quieting and drawing strength from the frog and from what seemed like the frog's affection for her. She sensed something special about the frog but knew she could not bring the frog home with her because her father would harm it. But then it occurred to her that she could bring the spirit of the frog inside of her and carry this spirit with her. This arrangement seemed agreeable to the frog, and henceforth Margaret and her frog became inseparable.

When Margaret was required to participate in activities that were abhorrent and degrading, her inside frog would whisper to her in a voice only she could hear: "Do what he says, but play with me while you are doing it." This frog allowed Margaret's spirit to remain separate from and undiminished by these abuses. And by looking at herself through the eyes of her beloved frog, she knew that she was in no way to blame for what was being done to her body or for what her body was being compelled to do to others. Through access to this frog, she was able to continue to know that she was a good person.

Margaret: [The frog] sort of gave me . . . I was then able to step back and start naming them [anorexia's soldiers].

Rick: How did thinking about the frog facilitate that stepping back?

Margaret: Because I knew I was good.

Rick: You knew you were good through your relationship with your frog?

Margaret: Yeah. And when I have that knowing, anorexia's voice doesn't feel like it's mine. It's not there at that moment. Everything gets a little clearer.

Rick: Right. It takes a little bit of separation from anorexia's voice before you can step back and start naming it? You move into a position of skepticism in relation to it and begin questioning it?

Margaret: Yeah.

Rick: And so that platform that you're resting on that enables you to question it is a platform of goodness in some way, of feeling okay?

Margaret: Yeah. Right. And there's like that split moment where I have a thought or reaction that seems so out of character for me, so far from who I am. If I jump on it, I can stay separated from anorexia. It's like I'll have a reaction to whatever it was that distracted me, and then anorexia's voice will say something in response that is so drastically different to what I'm like. Then there's a moment of clarity like "ah ha."

Rick: So right away you can recognize the thought as alien. Anorexia's take is so at odds with . . .

Margaret: Yeah, and if you jump on that right away you can put it outside of yourself again. I don't want to agree with it and I say to anorexia, "No, you're wrong."

Rick: So rejecting it?

Margaret: Yeah.

In response to what might seem like annoying and picayune questions, Margaret had provided some of the details of the processes by which she was able to perceive and then separate from anorexia. She had identified some of the *micro-practices* of her anti-anorexia, the internal practices of thought and perception that often go unnoticed and unarticulated. I later shared Margaret's description of this anti-anorexic practice with other League members, many of whom also identified the significance of grounding themselves in some experience of themselves as "okay" or "good" as a platform from which to perceive and repudiate anorexia. As a result of these conversations, I now attend more carefully to the experiences that confirm people's goodness, and I work to strengthen their access to these experiences so that they figure more significantly in their identities.

In the following segment of the conversation, I made a rather glaring error. Rather than edit it out of the transcript, I decided to include it in order to illustrate just how easily anorexia can slip back into the therapy. It is important for therapists to approach anti-a/b work with a fair bit of humility and be prepared to make mistakes. Because a/b thrives on the expectation of perfection, if I really expected myself to be perfectly anti-a/b in my practice of therapy, I'd be playing right into a/b's hands. I also suspect that it might have been reassuring for Margaret to see me fumble without becoming critical of myself and instead use the mistake to learn something more about the way in which anorexia operates. Fortunately, Margaret gave me the opportunity to learn something by speaking out when she sensed that the therapy was turning in a pro-anorexia direction.

Rick: We're going to need to stop. I just wanted to ask you a question. You've told me there was a time long before we met when you were struggling with anorexia. You didn't really talk with anybody about anorexia, but you said you had some conversations that were very helpful. You said these conversations helped you reclaim yourself. Are you finding the conversations

we are having today as helpful? Are they in any way "reclaiming" conversations?

Margaret: I don't want to do this.

Rick: Okay.

Margaret: I don't want to compare it, please.

Rick: Okay, all right.

Margaret: If it's not helpful I'll tell you, okay?

Rick: Okay. Can you tell me why you don't want to compare? I'm not saying
I think we should compare them, I'm just curious about what the negative
effects of comparing them might be. Would comparing the two be colluding
with that soldier that has you evaluating and putting things in boxes?

Margaret: Yeah.

Rick: Saying this is good and this is bad?

Margaret: And anorexia will try to disqualify you. It's already made good attempts at that. I don't want to hear it. It sure is good at getting me to
disregard my own experience. For example, it takes you being postmodern,
which I experience as good, and turns it into "you're not a real therapist."
So I'm saying "wait a minute." That's the kind of thing it does in certain
relationships. With you, it's been a good thing that it has tried to do that.
I have a very different experience of you. It's one of those things we were
talking about where you go "wait a minute, that's really different from how
I really feel."

Rick: It's hard for it to talk you out of your experience with me?

Margaret: Yeah. It's not something where I just go, "Yeah, you're right."

Rick: That's another tactic of anorexia, discrediting therapists?

Margaret: Yeah. It's discrediting you whenever you're challenging it, asking
questions about it. It's just discrediting the positive part.

Rick: We've gone a bit over but I've got to stop now and eat something before
my next meeting. Anorexia's probably saying, "See, he's weak, he can't tune
out his hunger, he's a slave to his appetites."

Margaret: "That's because he's not a real therapist. A real therapist could do
it."

Rick: (smiling) "But he is thin, he does have that going for him."

Margaret: Yeah. (laughs) Anorexia's saying, "See, he's taking our position."
No, he's not, anorexia, he's making fun of you.

Part Four

BECOMING AN
ANTI-ANOREXIC/BULIMIC ALLY

Chapter 16

PARENTS AS
ANTI-ANOREXIC/BULIMIC ALLIES

A/b inflicts profound suffering on parents and, although this suffering is different in many respects from that experienced by the daughter, it can be just as excruciating. Few experiences are more agonizing than watching your daughter be deceived by something so terrible and deadly, witnessing her transformation into someone hardly recognizable, and being opposed and reviled with a newfound wrath, as if you were the very enemy, when you attempt to help.

Siblings, too, are greatly affected by the presence of a/b in their family. Although they share their parents' worry about their sister, they can also become angry and resentful about the amount of parental attention their sibling is absorbing and the anguish she is inexplicably inflicting upon other family members.*

Just as the daughter's life becomes engulfed by a/b, so too do parents' lives. It is all too easy to become consumed by fear and worry and gripped by feelings of worthlessness, inadequacy, and guilt. Many parents find themselves also becoming emotionally and physically depleted and preoccupied with the eating and weight of their daughter. However, although a/b may provide the daughter with a sense of success and control (no matter how temporary and illusory), it leaves parents feeling like failures and utterly out of control.

---

* This chapter addresses parents specifically, but much of the content can be applied or adapted to the relationship with partners, friends, and siblings.

When the stresses and the stakes are so high, not surprisingly, a couple's relationship often begins to fray and deteriorate. Thus, a/b often succeeds in denying parents the compassion and support of their partner at a time when they most need and desire it. Many parents we have spoken with emphasize the importance of each person's taking some time out to replenish his or her energy and regain a desire for life. If parents get caught up in constant worry, planning, and monitoring, they too have unwittingly been tricked by a/b into sacrificing their life and have been deprived of simple moments of joy and relaxation.

This was the case with Shelly, a mother who spent every waking minute with her daughter, providing around-the-clock surveillance to prevent her from throwing up the little she managed to eat, and taking her to the nutritionist, the doctor, and a therapist. After several inpatient treatments failed, Shelly became even more vigilant in her efforts to assist her daughter to eat. Both she *and* her daughter were trapped by anorexia, and it was wearing both of them out. It had her daughter hating herself, Shelly hating herself, and sometimes the two of them hating each other. They both felt helpless, angry, defeated, scared, blamed, and alone.

THE DILEMMA OF CONTROL VERSUS ACCOMMODATION

A/b can stymie and perplex even the most savvy and skilled of therapists, but the dilemmas therapists confront pale in comparison to those faced by parents looking after their stricken daughter. Foremost among these dilemmas is the question of how much power and authority parents should wield to prevent their daughter from engaging in a/b-required acts (e.g., not eating or drinking, excessive exercise, vomiting or laxative use) and how much to accommodate her seemingly ever-increasing compulsions, fears, and demands.

Initially, many parents respond by attempting to cajole, coax, and finally insist that their daughter refrain from self-injurious starvation, purging, or exercise. Eventually, however, their daughter's outright defiance or covert deceptions force them to admit the futility of this strategy and recognize the cost it exacts on their relationship with her. But relinquishing these attempts at limit-setting and control can leave parents feeling maddeningly helpless or, even worse, complicit with a/b. Either way, they can wind up feeling that they are not helping their daughter and perhaps are even injuring her. Under these circumstances, it is entirely understandable why so many parents defer to the advice of professionals and then just hold their breath and hope and pray for the best.

Entire books have been written to offer advice and guidance to parents of children beset by a/b, many offering potentially valuable information and suggestions for those trying to navigate these treacherous waters. Yet there is no "perfect" way to parent in this situation (or at all). And because a/b is so adept at turning its prisoners against those who wish to come to their aid, even general guidelines can make parents unwitting accomplices of a/b, undermining their relationship with their daughter and making her even more vulnerable to a/b.

For this reason, we largely avoid offering blanket prescriptions or specific advice about particular issues or dilemmas. Instead, our aim is to offer some options for thinking and speaking about a/b that can assist parents in establishing an anti-a/b alliance and collaboration with their daughter. This anti-a/b alliance can position the daughter in the role of consultant, allowing her to assist her parents in helping her reclaim her life from a/b. This makes it possible for parents to custom-fit their parenting practices to the particular strategies that a/b is using to dominate their daughter and to understand what their daughter is likely to experience as supportive of her efforts to free herself from a/b's deathgrip. Like the rest of this book, this section is based on knowledge we have gathered from insiders and their parents.

WHAT PARENTS AND OTHER ALLIES CAN DO TO HELP

Many of the practices described in this chapter depend on an external view of a/b (see Chapters 7 and 8). As discussed earlier, this entails viewing a/b as an external intruder that takes advantage of a daughter's fears and aspirations, rather than viewing it as a "disease" or as a feature of the person's "self," "character," or "makeup." An external view recognizes how the problem derives its power from specific discourses and values that are dominant in Western societies, especially those that relate to the cultural ideals of beauty, success, fitness, and strength. As we see it, a/b encourages people to achieve perfection in relation to these ideals. Women and girls attempting this engage in a/b practices that carry these ideals to an illogical and deadly extreme.

Recognizing a/b as an external force that, with the help of dominant cultural ideas, acts *upon* its victims rather than as an internal deficiency, abnormality, or disease that is somehow an inherent part *of* the person affords parents a much broader range of ways to deal with the problem. Following are some of the options and possibilities that are made possible when a/b is viewed as external. Keep in mind that some of these practices will only bear fruit after sustained attempts; others may have to be modified or abandoned altogether if they do not "fit" your particular situation.

Express Moral Outrage, Anger, and Frustration at A/B

Viewing a/b as separate from (external to) one's daughter allows parents to express their own moral outrage at a/b, as well as their frustration and fear, in a manner that makes it harder for a/b to exploit. Parents who do not distinguish between a/b and their daughter cannot help but become angry with, critical of, and disappointed in their daughter. Thus, they inadvertently fuel a/b in its efforts to make their daughter feel guilty, worthless, and hopeless. Two parents, Wendy and Winston, had this to say about the effect of thinking about anorexia as external in relation to their 16-year-old daughter Meg:

> Treating it as an external being, separate from Meg, has been really helpful. Anorexia does not seem to like being separated from its victim and given distinct form. However, doing so provides us with a much better target for our anger. It has given me something to (literally) yell at, threaten, and defy, in a way that never would have been possible if we thought of it as a part of Meg. It has also helped us express how much what anorexia is doing to Meg upsets us. Without this capacity to externalize it, we would end up targeting Meg with our upset, disappointment, and anger.

Help Your Daughter Distinguish Her Own Voice

Parents who live with their daughter day in and day out are in the best position to observe the myriad ways in which a/b is robbing her of prior joys, previously taken-for-granted liberties, and self-confidence. Speaking about a/b as external, either to or in the presence of your daughter, helps provide her with a platform from which she can begin to see, evaluate, and resist a/b's ideas, values, and practices. However, be prepared for your daughter to vigorously protest this way of speaking, especially if she still has an unquestioned belief in the premises and promises of a/b. She may adamantly say, "No, it is me who is doing this, not anorexia!" Or she may insist, "This is what I want! You are talking nonsense. You don't get it!" Her responses may be similar to those you might get if you tried to squelch your daughter's first romance on the grounds that her newly beloved was bad or unsuitable for her—prepare yourself for a good dose of bold hostility.

Your daughter's protests, however, provide you with an opportunity to further articulate the distinctions you perceive between your daughter and a/b. Every parent will find his or her own responses to these protests. Some examples we have heard include: "This is the way we see it and we suppose anorexia will have you see it differently"; "The Julie we know would never consent to being treated this way or voluntarily choose it"; "Could bulimia be promising you something really great to get you to go along with it, or threatening you with something terrible?"; "I think the person talking to me at this moment is the one who has been tricked into believing that her future happiness depends upon starving herself or following certain rules. But we believe there is another Julie lurking inside who knows better, and who may be concerned, confused, and fearful, and we are there for her one hundred percent."

The point is not to get your daughter to agree with your statements (this would be far too much to expect) but rather to maintain a conceptual space that differentiates between a/b—its confinements and torture—and your daughter's desire for freedom, happiness, and life. Maintaining this conceptual and linguistic distinction between a/b and the person allows your daughter to begin to separate from a/b.

Merrin, a young woman who overcame anorexia only to find it overtaking her younger sister 10 years later, had this to say about the importance of separating anorexia from the person:*

> It was 10 years ago that anorexia gripped me to the extent that it controlled me. I remember the day I finally stood up to anorexia and finally saw it for what it was. I stood staring at the pantry and looking up at the medicine shelf and I distinctly remember thinking that if I continued to starve myself, I would eventually die. So, I might as well take some pills and end it now, or I could choose life. Basically, I chose life. I don't mean in any way to sound dramatic, it's just that at that particular time it came to me in a flash. I could see anorexia for what it was. I don't know why or how that happened but it changed everything so dramatically. It's like suddenly I had regained my inner voice.
>
> The day after I made a choice to live and expel anorexia from my life (although at the time I didn't like to use the word *anorexia*), I got up and made myself breakfast. I'm sure, to my mum, it looked like a normal "getting ready for school" scene, but it was the most wonderful thing I had experienced for a year. I felt like a butterfly emerging from a chrysalis. I could participate in life again. I felt the strength building in me again. So, before I knew it, I was pouring out all my thoughts and feelings to Mum. I started voicing all my fears

---

* Merrin is the older daughter of the parents who tell their story in the next chapter.

and all the restrictions anorexia had been putting on me. I believe that part of what enabled me to reach that point was all the love from my friends and family.

I think my Mum and I must have talked for hours and hours those first few weeks. But the most incredible thing was that just by voicing my feelings, speaking out when anorexia was imploring me not to reveal it, I could feel anorexia shrinking and running from me. I think what you and the League have done is to articulate the process of separating the person from anorexia itself. It amazed me that (looking back), that's exactly what I saw that day I stood up to anorexia—anorexia is not me. It is astonishing what an effect the League and narrative therapy have had by raising a collective voice against anorexia while embracing the person with love and encouragement.

Help Your Daughter Evaluate the Effects of the Voice of A/B

Once a person is able to discern the voice of a/b, it then becomes possible for her to evaluate its effects on her life. By persevering (and we mean *persevering*) with questions about the effects of a/b, and by helping your daughter notice contradictions between what a/b has promised her and what is actually happening in her life, doubt can be sown about both the veracity and the benevolence of a/b and its spell can be broken (see Chapter 8).

Parents may be unfamiliar with querying rather than instructing. In circumstances such as these, where the desire is to reclaim one's daughter from a living death and prevent her demise, it can be incredibly difficult for parents to desist from pressing their point and instead ask about their daughter's thoughts. This is especially the case when a/b seems to have become a ventriloquist and their daughter its puppet. But the young women we know who now speak with great personal authority learned to do so by cutting their teeth in dialogues where the knowing rests with them. Anti-a/b parents can, with practice, become very skillful in the art of inquiry and interviewing.

Help Your Daughter Distinguish Her Own Hopes and Dreams

Once your daughter has become more aware of the actual effects of a/b on her life, in contrast to what it has promised, its plans for or intentions toward her can be inquired about. For example, you might ask some of the following questions: "Do you think refusing all of your friends' phone calls is furthering your hopes, dreams, or values or bulimia's plans for you?"; "Given what you have told us anorexia is doing to your life, what would you say anorexia's intentions toward you were?"; "Is it telling you the rewards are just around the corner or that you just haven't worked hard enough?"; "If a person promised to make you happy, how much suffering would you endure at his hands before you concluded that he was lying?"

Explore With Your Daughter the Tactics of A/B

One of the most important things that you can do is to learn about how the voice of a/b speaks to your daughter. Because a/b takes advantage of a person's own fears, hopes, aspirations, and life experiences, its rhetoric is always customized to appeal to the particular person. For this reason, off the shelf, one-size-fits-all guidelines for parents are often ineffective in countering a/b's persuasive arguments or lose their potency over time as a/b finds ways to twist or spin them.

For example, if a mother tells her daughter that she is ruining her life by not eating, that she is beautiful just the way she is, and gives her a hug, a/b may translate this as: "She is jealous of you and is trying to make you fat. Her hugging you is her way of trying to see if you have put on any weight." Or, a parent might say "You did good at lunch today" in an attempt to be positive and supportive, only to have anorexia twist it to mean "You gave in to her by eating. You are not even a good anorexic."

Viewing a/b as separate from but in relationship to your daughter allows for the possibility of jointly exposing, through co-research (see Chapter 7), the tactics and strategies of a/b and allows you to explore anti-a/b strategies and knowledges. By carefully tailoring your language (asking questions that eliminate evaluations, separating your daughter's own desires from those of a/b, encouraging attention to contradictions and highlighting actual experience and feelings) you can hinder a/b's ability to use your words as weapons against your daughter. In co-researching your daughter's values and hopes and the inevitable contradiction between her values and hopes and the actual effects a/b is having, your daughter will be empowered to make her own decisions based on the evidence. This is entirely different from trying to wrest your daughter away from a/b by reiterating the dangers to her health, arguing with her, or punishing her.

Disturbing as it might be, learning as much as possible about how a/b works, how it speaks to your daughter, when it is at its strongest, and so on will help you better understand what your daughter will experience as supportive and anti-a/b. Beyond this, you may even begin to be able to anticipate a/b's attempts to counter or co-opt your aid and thus head it off as much as possible. For example, avoiding comments about other people's weight or appearance may give a/b less opportunity to run riot. Remarks such as "Hasn't Judy got a nice figure?" are likely to encourage invidious comparisons between your daughter and Judy. Similarly, emphasizing the external achievements of others can also invite invidious comparisons, feelings of inadequacy, and a desire to excel. In addition, you may wish to speak to your daughter about the likelihood of a/b's twisting your attempts to support your daughter's anti-a/b—for example: "I'm guessing that when I say this, a/b will tell you what I really mean is . . . , but it will be lying to you. What I really mean is. . . . "

Finally, in availing yourself of opportunities to co-research a/b with your daughter, you actually help your child to more clearly identify the voice of a/b and to become more savvy with respect to its treachery. There is an ongoing need for this, for a/b operates very much like a chameleon, continuing to change its colors to avoid detection. However, the fact that such co-research has required a/b to transform itself can provide some hope that the tide is turning, as it is often the case that with each subsequent disguise a/b becomes more easily unmasked and more transparently fraudulent.

Co-research and Develop an Anti-A/B Parent-Child Relationship

Once your daughter has declared her intention to resist the ideas and practices associated with a/b (which is not to say that she can be expected to live up to this intention every moment), it becomes possible for her to make informed judgments regarding how she and others might participate together in an anti-a/b relationship. This allows you and your daughter to step into a relationship of teamwork rather than opposition. Once your daughter has become adept at recognizing the voice of a/b and the values that support that voice, she is in a position to identify the ways of relating that inadvertently side with a/b and those that assist her in breaking free of it. Such matters can only be broached during moments when your daughter is avowedly opposed to a/b.

Soliciting feedback from your daughter about what you, as a parent, are doing that is helpful or unhelpful is only useful if you are willing to openly examine the ways in which a/b may have infiltrated your own life or your parenting practices, and also willing to consider the possibility that your attempts to help are inadvertently strengthening a/b's grip on your daughter. This soul-searching has the potential to not only greatly assist your daughter (perhaps even save her life), but also can bring your own life more into harmony with your own values and enrich your relationships with family members. Believe it or not, parents have actually told us after their daughter's ordeal with a/b had come to a successful conclusion: "Anorexia was the best thing that ever happened to us." Such a sentiment would have been unimaginable while they were "in the thick of it."

We can understand why parents might be distrustful of their daughter's wishes and disinclined to honor them, given the deadly conclusions she has espoused when dominated by a/b. So, just as your daughter must continue to be vigilant in discerning her own voice from that of a/b, you must be equally vigilant in discerning whether it is your daughter speaking or a/b speaking through her.

Notice and Acknowledge Sparks of Resistance

Be on the lookout for moments when your daughter defies a/b in some small or seemingly insignificant way. These instances might include moments when your daughter takes some small bit of pleasure in her daily life or a renewed interest in activities that a/b has forbidden, puts her own desires first for a change, is more forgiving of herself for a mistake or "imperfection," and so on.

Unfortunately, these acts of resistance can easily go unnoticed because, initially, they are most likely to occur in domains of your daughter's life outside that of nutrition. Often parents' reasonable fears for their daughter's physical well-being lead them to focus on weight gain as the sole indication that she has turned against a/b in both thought and deed. In our experience, weight gain (except for weight gained to merely "get out of the hospital" or "not go to the hospital") seldom precedes the development of an anti-a/b vision and perspective. Often girls and women will tentatively try out anti-a/b acts in arenas of their lives other than the "big game" of body weight. These initiatives often include attempts to define their values and preferences, to accept and honor their own experience, or to stand up for themselves and their rights. We have regularly observed how a woman's resistance first leads to a reclaiming of her substance as a person and only then to a regaining of her bodily substance. When there are indications that your daughter is turning against a/b but weight loss is not immediately arrested or weight gain is not immediately achieved, you may need some reassurance (possibly from your daughter, her therapist, or other anti-a/b veterans) to allay your fears that "nothing is happening."

When parents notice acts of resistance to a/b, they are in a position to provide some acknowledgment of these acts and contribute to them being more richly described. These acknowledgments are not the same as "pointing out the positive," as that can be experienced as an evaluation—by referring to something as good, you imply that its opposite is bad. For example, if Sophie is commended ("That's good!") for having eaten more than usual, she may assume that, if she eats less than usual on another occasion, this is bad. With a/b's twist, she assumes that therefore *she* is bad. But if Sophie's parents ask her something like "Tell me, what are your thoughts about the fact that you have nourished yourself tonight instead of letting anorexia starve you?" she will be less inclined to feel evaluated by her parents. Likewise, a/b can turn this type of praise into a negative by convincing the daughter that she acted only to please her parents and therefore was just giving in to them or allowing herself to be controlled. The practice we are proposing has as little to do with evaluation as is humanly possible. Instead, it is intended to embolden your daughter's own movement toward her hopes and dreams.

Once you notice the sparks of resistance to a/b, you have a number of options. These include but are not limited to:

- Silently appreciating the act
- Mentioning that you noticed it
- Mentioning that you noticed it and asking your daughter if she noticed it too
- Asking your daughter if she considered her act, no matter how small, to have any anti-a/b significance and if so what she considers it to be
- Asking your daughter what moved her to take that particular step
- Speculating about the possible significance of such a step should your daughter be unable to accord it any ("Tanya, this is the first time in the last 7 years that we have witnessed you make yourself a cup of coffee without having to serve us first. If you can't make any sense of this, do you mind if we speculate? Is it possible that this is connected in any way to your standing up for yourself with your friends last week after you decided they were misusing you?")
- Asking what tortures or backlashings of guilt had to be endured for the sake of such "freedoms."

Much of what you learn through these queries may be distressing, but at least you will be informed of the anti-a/b courage it took for your daughter to do what free citizens take for granted, and admire her for it.

The options you choose will depend upon your sense of your daughter's readiness to entertain such acknowledgments and to engage with these questions. You can consult your daughter, preferably at moments when she is in an anti-a/b frame of mind, about what would support her anti-a/b fight. If she tells you to stop referring to such anti-a/b innovations, it would be wise to backtrack and try again later. However, if your daughter dismisses her actions as having little or no significance (e.g., "Any normal person can do that! What is so special about eating a muffin in public?"), you might choose to persist by asking her if a/b could be blinding her to what seems very significant to you.

Continue to Express Love, Even in the Face of Rejection

Parents can begin to feel overwhelmed, exhausted, and hopeless as their attempts to give their daughter love and support are repeatedly rebuffed. A/b often reinterprets a parent's love and support as something negative—for example, as an attempt to weaken her resolve or fatten her up. A/b may also tell your daughter she is unworthy of love and care and would be better off dead. These distortions or dismissals of parental love and concern can make it difficult for parents to persist in their expressions of love and to continue to believe in their daughter. Yet, by holding fast to whom you know your daughter to be and continuing to show love, affection, and faith in her, you can thwart a/b's attempts to portray her to herself in the most negative light. Instead, she may feel reassured that, at least in her parents' hearts, she is lovable and loved.

These efforts to ally with your daughter are much like talking to and stroking an unconscious patient. The hope is that something is getting through and that eventually—when your daughter is sufficiently separate from a/b—you might be able to reconnect with the daughter you know and love so well and witness her reclaiming her life. For some, such acts of love can best be sustained by a hatred of a/b, as odd as that may sound. Meg's father, Winston, called for "an unconditional love of Meg and an unconditional hatred for anorexia." Many young women have identified "love," "regard," and "belief in me" as some of the most potent anti-a/b practices.

However, you should be careful to express your hope for and faith in your daughter in a manner that does not take her efforts to retrieve her life for granted. For example, if you respond to your daughter's anti-a/b steps with something akin to "I knew you would come around" or "we always believed you would do it," a/b can turn such encouragement into pressure and burdensome expectations. If the hope you have for your daughter is heard as an expectation or presumption, your daughter may feel guilty or believe herself to be a hopeless failure at those times when she is unable to sustain or extend her anti-a/b initiatives.

We believe that these ways of thinking and speaking make it possible for parents to challenge the unique ways in which a/b acts on their child and to fine-tune and adapt their anti-a/b practice in order to respond to and foil a/b's attempts to neutralize their love for their daughter and the aid they wish to provide.

AN ANTI-BULIMIC CONVERSATION

We'd like to present a hypothetical example of an anti-bulimic conversation between a couple and their daughter. It would be highly unlikely for all the conversational threads included in this example to be present in an actual conversation; rather, they would probably develop over the course of many conversations. Furthermore, we do not intend for this example to be a "model" conversation—you will need to find your own unique ways of engaging with your daughter around these themes, patiently waiting for opportunities to codevelop, with your daughter, a common anti-a/b language.

Jessie's parents have learned, through conversations with their daughter, that bulimia is able to seize control of her when she begins to feel she is worthless or a failure. Jessie's parents ask, "When are you most likely to feel this way?" Jessie responds that this often happens during school and that she often compares herself to other girls in a variety of ways, including how her body looks, popularity with boys and other girls, and academic success. Attempting to look at the effects of bulimia, Jessie's mother asks, "How does bulimia take advantage of your feeling like a failure and worthless?" Jessie responds: "When I come home from school feeling really bad about myself, I start to eat. But this makes me feel even worse about myself because I think that I should have a lot more self-control. Bulimia tells me that with more self-control I might be able to lose some weight and become more attractive, and also maybe I'd do better at school. So now all my bad feelings are focused around just having eaten. So bulimia tells me that if I just throw up, I can get rid of all the bad feelings. Not just the feelings about having eaten, but all the other feelings from the day, too, because they got merged with the eating. It tells me I can have a clean slate. When I throw up, I do feel better for a little while because I was able to undo my failure. But I truly know, if not at that moment then later, that I am hurting myself when I do this, and then I feel bad about that failure, too, and I am back to feeling even more worthless. It's just a vicious cycle."

In delving deeper into the tactics and strategies that bulimia uses, the parents ask a few more questions: "What does bulimia tell you when you get a lower score on a paper than your friend?" "How does bulimia try to convince you that your body is not acceptable but hateful?" From her thoughtful answers, the parents learn that Jessie believes that if she is not the best, she is a failure. She upholds perfectionistic standards for herself, not just in academics but in just about every area of her life, including appearance and popularity. In so doing, she has absorbed the dominant Western ideals of thinness and achievement and hears these ideals supported every day in school by the comments both girls and boys make about the appearance of girls, and the value people everywhere else seem to place on appearance and performance. And even though she does speak her mind in many instances, she believes that the measure of how good and nice a person you are is based on the extent to which you are liked by others. If others don't like her, the only conclusion she can reach is that there must be something wrong with her.

Having figured out how bulimia is operating, the parents can now co-research with Jessie what they might do to extend their contribution to her efforts to leave bulimia behind. One aspect of this co-research might be to investigate the ways in which the parents might be un-wittingly subscribing to proposals very similar to those that bulimia thrives on. Because it is sometimes difficult for children to be critical of their parents, especially for daughters who are invested in being "nice" and prone to feeling guilty, the parents may need to initiate this part of the co-research with some enthusiasm and reassure their daughter (if they can do so sincerely) that they are eager on their own behalf to take apart their values—values they now suspect a/b may be using to guide their daughter to despair and death.

If you have already co-researched the particular ways in which a/b speaks to your daughter and the ideas and assumptions that allow a/b to gain a foothold or maintain a chokehold, you are often in a good position to ask more specific questions. For example, Jessie's parents might say, "We have been considering how perfection plays too large a part in our lives. We have decided that we both have been too hard on ourselves and have made a family decision to let up on ourselves and others. We were wondering if you have any thoughts about our trying to become more carefree." Or they might say, "Your dad and I have been looking into how we have uncritically accepted the idea that women are more beautiful if they are thin. We suspect that this has limited our ability to appreciate a range of body types, and we have put too high a value on appearance and not enough value on what is inside a person. We were wondering if you have any thoughts about our critique of the culture we live in? We have decided to take some action against this and here are some of the things we are considering doing."

COUNTERING PARENTAL GUILT WITH COMPASSION

If you feel guilty upon learning that you have been unwittingly contributing to the problem, we suggest that you be prepared to offer yourself the same compassion you show your daughter. A/b thrives on guilt. If you respond to feedback from your daughter with guilt and a sense of inadequacy, you may not only be falling into the trap of measuring yourself against perfectionistic standards, but also inadvertently making your daughter feel bad for having hurt your feelings, which may lead her to avoid being honest with you in the future. Furthermore, she may conclude that if you blame yourself for harboring a/b beliefs, then she, too, must be to blame for her "disorder." Hopefully you will recognize that your daughter is not to blame for trying to live up to omnipresent ideas and ideals and will conclude the same about yourselves. As Susan, a 23-year-old, emphasized, "It is important that we all look at ourselves with curiosity instead of blame—we are all given these messages. We believe it is important for you to be open to looking at your family with curiosity rather than self-blame, which ultimately might lead to avoidance when things are difficult to face."

Parenting Practices Insiders Have Found Helpful

Ali asked a group of insiders at her place of work (a residential program for women struggling with a/b) to identify the things their parents did that they found supportive of their attempts to reclaim their lives from a/b. Although different people (including your daughter) will find different things helpful, we present a few responses from the group here to give parents some sense of the range of practices that have been found to be anti-a/b.

- Asking me what a/b wants me to do in this situation and what the ultimate consequences of doing that will be.
- Opening themselves as fully as possible to me, listening, and being present.
- Just saying, "I can see how hard this is for you," or just listening, rather than trying to strategize a plan and implement it as if it were a problem that could be solved like any other.

- Asking me what I want for my life or reminding me of what I've said at other times.
- Gently encouraging me when I'm not eating without getting confrontational or pushy.
- Helping point out when anorexia sucks me in and deprives me of having fun with friends.
- Asking how they can help.
- Noticing things I try at.
- Avoiding making comments about how my body looks.
- Not talking about diets, plans to diet, how full someone is from "overeating," or needing to exercise.
- Pointing out things I do well so I can remember that I do not see myself as positively as others see me.
- Reminding me there is no "perfect."
- Having faith in me and believing that I'll be okay while appreciating the challenge in front of me.
- Honesty, tenderness, and patience.
- Understanding the power of anorexia in my life and the ways I am trying to resist it, even if I haven't "won."

The ways of thinking and speaking about a/b presented in this chapter may assist you to establish a collaborative relationship with your daughter so that she can serve as an advisor to you and assist you in custom designing an anti-a/b parent-child alliance. The following chapter shows how two parents put such strategies to work in helping their daughter free herself from anorexia.

Chapter 17

LIGHTING A TORCH IN THE GREAT DARKNESS OF ANOREXIA

ANN AND RICHARD'S STORY

H ere, Richard and Ann describe in their own words the story of their daughter's battle with anorexia and their own evolution as anti-anorexic parents. At some point (described below), Richard and Ann consulted with David and met with him regularly over a period of about a year. Diana, their daughter, refused to join them and her parents could not enforce her attendance. This meant that Richard and Ann had to become more than just their daughter's anti-anorexic allies but her "therapists" as well. Dire necessity became the mother of their many inventions.

The fact that Richard and Ann succeeded in engaging with Diana therapeutically and transforming the culture of their family to one that was very inhospitable to anorexia supports our conviction about how significant parents can be as anti-anorexic allies. As you will see, learning how to be anti-anorexic allies to their daughter required them to struggle with themselves, each other, and their daughter. This struggle ultimately resulted in a radical revision of their ways of relating both to themselves and each other. Their account illustrates the many ups and downs that lie along the path to freedom.

We are grateful to Ann and Richard for speaking directly to the parent readership of this book. We believe that other parents will strongly resonate with some of their trials, tribulations and joyous victories and gain some measure of courage and hope that can inspire them to unite with their daughters against anorexia.

Ann

Our recognition of the silent intruder dawned slowly. When Diana first showed signs of having a problem, it seemed it was a physical one: Sore stomachs, headaches, and generally feeling unwell. I felt very protective of her at this time and kept her home from school a lot. When the tests showed no physical disorder we were referred to a child psychologist at the hospital. We never made it to that appointment. One night Diana secretly swallowed a number of pills and medicines.

She seemed in a very strange state the next day and, not knowing what had happened, I took her to the doctor. He thought she was suffering from anxiety and was hyperventilating. Later that day Diana admitted to a friend that she had taken the medicines. I called an ambulance which took us to the Children's Hospital.

The happiness, the liveliness, the energy of youth had deserted her. She couldn't smile, she couldn't laugh, she felt empty and alone. Diana became a day patient at the hospital and was given medication for severe depression. She was 14 years old.

Richard

One day in August Ann called me at the office: Diana had tried to commit suicide. Shocked and nervous, I got to the hospital as they waited to see a doctor. Diana was sitting beside her mother, curled in a fetal ball, grim, hard-faced, skin tightening after months of being "off her food," gaunt and unhappy. It was strange and disturbing. How do you feel about your child trying to kill herself? Was it really serious, I wondered?

I was assailed by a wild mixture of feelings: Shock and horror, anger at her silliness, an uncertain guilt and confusion. I was embarrassed, sitting there and having to answer questions about our private thoughts and feelings and listen to Diana fielding questions I couldn't help her with. In many ways she was in this on her own and I had no say. It was a strange situation for me. I wasn't used to the children having their own opinions and feelings in any important sense and I certainly wasn't used to letting them cope as adults without us helping them. Fortunately she turned out to be fine, which left us free to ask the question: Why did she do it?

Ann

I felt so confused. Why could I not help her smile and be happy again? How had I contributed to this dreadful situation? At the same time I felt strangely numb and distant. I still had a 2-year-old and a 7-year-old at home and life compelled me to get on with domestic things. Diana seemed to have lost her appetite, which, we were told, was a symptom of depression.

Richard

She was admitted to the hospital's child and family unit, which deals with emotional and mental problems in youth. They questioned us in family conferences as Diana's weight continued to decline. After some weeks they pronounced two related conditions: depression and anorexia. Just to hear them made us depressed. They thought the loss of appetite might be caused by depression. They wanted to give her shock treatment (electroconvulsive therapy, ECT) to remove, perhaps, the depression. They explained carefully how the modern version of ECT was humane and sensitive, that they used anesthetic, and what they expected from the procedure. If it worked, the depression would be gone and it wasn't anorexia. If it was anorexia, ECT would have no effect. We were horrified.

Ann

We were so desperate by this time that Richard I agreed for this to be done. However, I was deeply troubled. It seemed like such a severe measure and if Diana was suffering from anorexia the shock treatment wouldn't work. Before this was carried out, I went in desperation to a respected friend and mentor, who made a very practical suggestion. Let Diana go away from her normal environment and especially away from the hospital, which was full of troubled young people, spend some time with her beloved aunt and uncle and see if the depression lasted.

During the 2 weeks she was away, Diana's spirits lifted again. Working with her aunt picking orchids in their shade houses, playing cards, cooking, and soaking up the peaceful countryside warmed and nourished her spirit. However, her eating did not improve and she was steadily losing weight.

When she returned to the hospital, the professor heading the treatment team spoke to me angrily on the phone about Diana's weight loss. He demanded to know why I let it happen. I was hurt and felt unfairly blamed. After all, we had shown that anorexia was the culprit and now we could get her some real help.

Richard

Now they suggested we attend clinics at the eating disorders unit (EDU) at the hospital to treat the anorexia and see how that went. The first meeting was a family conference which all our five children managed to attend, bless them. We were asked if we felt responsible for Diana's predicament and Michael, a few years older than Diana, answered that he didn't feel responsible. He was told very forcefully: "We'll make you feel responsible." They meant we'd feel guilty. That was an early example of what we came to perceive as an extremely unsympathetic therapy.

Ann

The very first meeting set alarm bells ringing for me. The whole family was there: our children, aged 22, 18, 14, 7, and 2, with my husband and myself. We listened with all the urgency that might be expected of parents whose daughter's life is threatened, to be told at the end of the session that we had not given enough attention to our youngest child, who had been running around energetically like any 2-year-old. I found the psychiatrist's manner disturbing, confrontational, and full of blame.

I asked if we could continue the counseling sessions with only Richard and myself. This was partly a protective move on my part—I did not yet trust these people to care for my children. I felt right from the outset that there was something amiss. A major problem was that they didn't speak to Diana. I felt very protective as a mother going there. I felt a lack of sensitivity, of heart or spirit or something—they could easily lead us into feeling we had done something really wrong. It's still hard to talk about it.

Richard

Ann and I started going once or twice a week. Diana would come, too, but only to be weighed. We would come to see the weighing as being itself a practice that supported anorexia, but at that time it seemed the right thing to do. It was what the doctors said should be done, and we had great faith in the doctors. So we went to the meetings—they were going to show us how to deal with anorexia, and they said they didn't have to talk to Diana. It became clear that we had to deal with it because we were the cause of it. Diana consistently denied she had anorexia, she wouldn't use the word and got angry at the very mention of it.

The examination of emotions was new ground for us, although much stranger for me than for Ann. I seemed to have spent most of my life denying I had any feelings, avoiding even using the word *feelings*. I tried very hard to be reasonable and describe everything in concrete terms. I thought that emotions could not be described in "concrete" terms. Ann, like most women, hadn't done this. The psychiatric team showed us how our responses are governed by emotions that are often very old, even left over from childhood, not examined or resolved, hanging around in the heart long after conscious reason would have let them go.

From example after painful example from our own lives and from conversations and responses right there in the meeting, this principle was shown to us. They had great knowledge of these things, and revelations were frequent. I eventually saw this as helpful. However, by focusing their questions on all the negative things, they were leading us to tell our life stories in a way that was degrading, painful, and debilitating.

I think part of their intention was to help us understand emotions, so we might deal more sensitively with anorexia. But with their negative approach it was hard to be open and free in that understanding, because we ended up blaming ourselves for everything. It was clear early on that anorexia fed off hidden, unstated, or covered-over feelings, so it was vital to know what was happening emotionally, either in oneself or someone else—not only discern it, but speak about it. So you had to have the insight and the vocabulary to discern and express emotions. Anorexia used such a complicated, twisted logic that if you were just a little unsure of your ground, you got swept away by the storm and lost your ability to help.

And what a storm it was. It was around this time that the violence began. Diana was screaming obscenities, throwing things, hitting, scratching, punching, kicking, and mutilating herself. I was the most frequent target, and I still carry the scars (I view them proudly now as medallions of honor), but Ann suffered, too. And writhing and hurt in the center of the storm, Diana was suffering more than all of us. It was horrible to experience this from such a gentle, sweet-natured young lady. Diana was well known for her agreeable and helpful nature. We were to learn more about how anorexia had perverted this for its own purposes and filled her with anger. But at the time it was a horror we could not understand.

We slowly began to see that anorexia used things you knew, things you'd done, or others had done, that you were attached to. For example, it would re-accuse us of offenses from the distant past. It seemed to raise prison walls around each of us. The walls appeared to be for our own protection but they made it difficult to communicate. Anorexia was very personal. It knew how to push our buttons. It could make us defensive, ashamed, angry, or self-righteous very easily.

Diana continued to deny that she was unwell. Anorexia made her speak of death as a good thing, her increasing thinness as beautiful, our ordinary shapes as grossly fat. She said she hated us. People hate me, she said, I'm no good. It doesn't matter if I die. I want to die.

Ann

We were told that if Diana continued losing weight at the rate she was, she could be dead in a few weeks. They recommended that we force feed her. In desperation once again, we agreed, and, in doing so, we deepened the nightmare.

It is difficult to describe the horror we felt when we did this, holding down our gentle, loving, beautiful daughter as she kicked, punched, bit, and swore at us as we forced food into her mouth. We ended up puréeing her meal, jamming her mouth open with a door stop and pouring it in. We acted with the resolve of paramedics saving a drunken victim fighting the treatment, but the horror of what we had to do shook the very roots of our beliefs and ideals of how to care for our children. We never did it again.

Richard

The psychiatrist asked if we were prepared to do whatever was necessary to save our daughter. We said yes and asked, "Do you mean force-feeding her?" He said we needed to do "Whatever is necessary." So we took this to mean we must force the food into her and he did nothing to correct us. At that time we saw no alternative. This was all about food, right? Or even if it wasn't, it was only the lack of food that was imperiling her. What else but food could save her?

That night we made her understand we were prepared to do this, and even forced some food into her. It was unpleasant and ugly but at stake, we thought, was our beloved daughter's very survival. We didn't really know what we were doing but we wanted to make a stand for her welfare. To show someone—or something—that we meant business, we were determined and we had strength. So we bullied Diana to show how much we cared for her. We bullied her to prove we would not bow down, we would not accept defeat. Diana gave in but only partly. Anorexia encouraged Diana to see food as so negative that she could not justify eating it for herself and therefore negotiated (through Diana) that Ann must physically put the food into Diana's mouth.

Diana did agree to eat but she refused to feed herself any longer. So the nightmare deepened some more.

Ann

This day was the beginning of 9 months of counseling and "refeeding." Every day I sat with Diana on one side of me and Christopher (age 2) on the other, feeding them their food. They both refused food, threw food about, argued about food. It was truly exhausting and took such a lot of time and patience.

Richard

For the next 9 months Diana put no food into her mouth. She (that is, anorexia) tightly controlled the quantity and the sort of food but she did not participate in the feeding except to submit to it. Even in public. What courage from the both of them, can you imagine it? In a coffee bar or in the hospital cafeteria after visiting her grandma, a 15-year-old girl being fed by her mother. What anorexia makes you do!

Around mealtimes tempers became brittle and oversensitive. We tried not to say anything that might upset Diana. With the slightest excuse, Diana would flee to her room and refuse any food. Ann would spend hours with her, try to calm her down and eventually she might return to the dining room and eat a meager meal. At other times she wouldn't eat a thing. Sometimes, when she'd calmed down, Ann might take a favorite food, perhaps a pot of yogurt, to the bedroom and coax her to eat some. When she was upset she would never accept it from me. But sometimes at the table if Ann was called to the phone, I could carry on with feeding her. It gave me a secret sense of pride when I was allowed to do this, although I never mentioned it.

Anorexia caused Diana to become very well-informed about food. She knew precisely the calories in all manner of foods, the calories required for ordinary living or strenuous activity or bare maintenance, with the result that not quite enough food was consumed. Her weight continued to decline. Anorexia's promises motivated Diana's intense self-deprivation.

Ann

It is painful to remember the counseling we received through this period, and it was so confusing. We went there for help and on most days we left feeling deeply depressed, confused, and blamed as parents. One memory that sticks in my mind was Richard being told that if he did not go home and feed our daughter more food, he might as well resign as a parent. I was terribly upset to hear this. It completely negated the contribution he'd always made and was still making to the welfare of our family.

My world was beginning to fall apart. Diana was still alive and was attending school again, but only through enormous efforts on my part to feed her, listen to her protests and fears, sometimes for hours at a time, hold her or sit by her bed as she cried in pain and frustration.

After about 2 months of counseling at the EDU, my mother was suddenly taken to hospital desperately ill, first in intensive care for 3 weeks and then on intravenous feeding that would keep her in hospital for 16 months. All of my time was spent caring for others and the stress of the counseling drove my husband and me to the brink of separation.

There was an incident that captured the dilemma I faced trying to care for everybody. Diana and I were sitting alone waiting to visit my mother in the intensive care department and I carried the remainder of Diana's lunch. She hadn't had time to finish it before leaving the house. An argument developed between us about a sandwich. She wouldn't eat it. I said she should. The argument intensified until Diana ran away. Now the dilemma arose: Should I follow her or wait to see my mother, who might die at any time? My mother's sister arrived at that moment, and there I sat crying. She was so angry at Diana and could not understand what seemed like complete selfishness. I went and found Diana. I don't remember if she had the sandwich, but we hugged and cried and wondered how we had reached this sorry state of affairs.

Richard

I found it difficult to concentrate on my work. I attended the office grudgingly, much of the time wondering what was happening at home. The fear of Diana dying from anorexia was vivid, alive, and present most of the time. It seemed we didn't have too many mistakes to make before it would be too late to save her. The fear interrupted every task I engaged in, slowed everything down, made me inefficient and unreliable. I arrived late and often left early. Each counseling session meant about 2 hours out of the office, once or twice a week. I took many days' sick leave. But I did my best to keep my boss informed, and he made extraordinary efforts to support me.

However, at my annual performance review my boss was unhappy that the manual had not been finished and many promised deadlines had gone by. He made it perfectly clear my performance had been unacceptable. He knew the problems I was facing, but he had problems of his own. I knew I must increase my efforts. Over the next couple of weeks, I became increasingly afraid I would lose my job, which would make a horrible situation intolerable.

I wasn't sleeping well. One Sunday night, unable to sleep, I went into the office about 2:00 in the morning. It felt like a new beginning, so from then on, I started arriving at the office at 6:00 in the morning. I noticed at that hour I was fresh and worked well, and there were no interruptions. I kept this up for many months, and it saved my job. I would return home at 2:30 or 3:00 in the afternoon and there was usually time to talk to Ann before the children arrived home from school. The best part of this arrangement was the chance to discuss what was happening, how we felt, how we might act in concert, whether against anorexia or simply handling one of the children. One of the worst things anorexia had us do was argue when one of us had decided, alone, to take a particular action, and we could prevent this by discussing things first.

Ann

Diana and I retained a great closeness during this time, but Richard took the brunt of most of Diana's anger and frustration—he suffered extreme physical violence at times. It was impossible to comprehend what was happening. For example, we would often arrive at a counseling meeting to be told Diana had lost a bit of weight. Sometimes this would be dismissed with "Don't be concerned. Anorexia is not about food or weight." But another time the psychiatrist would attack us for letting our daughter lose weight: "Don't you realize you are killing her?" Sometimes he would reach a point in the session where we were really upset, confused, and angry, and then he would suddenly stop the session and send us away. Diana later told me that when she saw us upset she felt so bad and responsible for all this anger and misery.

During these difficult times our friends and family began to be alienated by the seeming impossibility of the problem. None of them had any idea what to do to help when they saw the enormous pain we were going through after each counseling session. Many of them later told us that they felt the counseling was doing more harm than good, but what can you do when you feel you have no alternative?

We tried having people visit, and sometimes we went out, but it was extremely difficult when, wherever we were, I had to feed Diana her food with all the accompanying arguments. Under the spell of anorexia, Diana was not always troubled by this, but I saw the looks on people's faces as they tried hard not to react. Anorexia was subtly silencing everyone, making this our new reality. We were all so afraid of upsetting Diana and the consequences that might bring.

The thing that most surprised me was the ability of the human spirit in the most difficult situation to keep rising to meet the challenge. There were times when I felt extremely low, even fleeting moments when death would have seemed a friend. But a walk on the beach or a smile from a stranger, a kind word, a new morning, some beautiful music, or the laughter of a child would bring me back from that dark place to carry on.

I had reached the end of my tether with the EDU counseling when an anti-anorexic angel told me of a therapist called David Epston. After speaking with the mother of one of David's former clients who had suffered with anorexia, I decided to contact him.

I was struck by the very first conversation I had with him on the telephone. David made it clear that my inner knowledge was important and he was willing to help. He clearly believed my opinion was worth something, he spoke to me as a person who could be trusted, and he treated me with extreme respect. Our first conversation filled me with hope.

I mentioned to the EDU psychiatrist my desire to change counselors and he gave me an ultimatum. I had a week to decide whether to make a change and he warned me that Diana would deteriorate rapidly if I did such a thing. My husband was uncertain. Some of the counseling had really opened his eyes and heart and he was reluctant to let it go. Indeed, I too had learned some valuable lessons, though it had come at a great cost in pain and humiliation. I had little difficulty in leaving and choosing this new path. I never saw or talked to the EDU people again. Richard lovingly joined me in this decision.

Richard

Ann had been told about this private counselor and was very keen to try him out. I felt suspicious. I wondered what he knew. I was aware Ann had had a much more difficult time with the psychiatrist than I (and my experience had been painful enough), so I suspected her decision was more about leaving the old than joining something new. But she was desperately unhappy and we both knew something had to change, so I went along with it, asking the EDU people if I could continue with them on my own, if I wished. They hesitated at this, but then agreed, so I felt I had a safety net.

I spoke to David by telephone and tried to get some idea of his experience, his capacity to take care of us. The conversation did not go well.

I may have been a bit too aggressive and he perhaps misunderstood my intentions. I remember him later saying our first conversation hadn't gone well, and could we start again? That impressed me deeply.

I went alone once to the EDU, the week after our final joint session, and felt unwelcomed. I started describing a crisis during the week with Diana, and he cut me off, saying we should talk only about Ann and me. I never went back. Later, this decision to leave them created great difficulty in getting Diana admitted to the hospital.

Ann

Our first session with David was very different from what we were used to. He asked questions that were perceptive but unthreatening. He listened to our story with interest and compassion. Although Diana did not speak much, she told us later that for the first time she felt a glimmer of hope that somebody understood something of what she was going through.

David showed us that anorexia had crept in at a sensitive time in Diana's young life. We had a new, unplanned baby at a time when we were losing our house and our business due to financial trouble. The baby had an immune deficiency and was sick a lot of the time. Our older son had come back home to live with his pregnant girlfriend who was vomiting all day with morning sickness. We were living in a strange, rented house. Diana was quiet and very supportive at a time when she could have done with a lot more fun and support for herself.

She had begun as early as 10 or 11 years old to worry about her image, both physically and as a person, wondering why she did not have more friends, and so on. She had borne the brunt of some cruel teasing at school about her weight and began to find it difficult to eat in front of the other children at lunchtime. Being a quiet, sensitive person, she continued to try and be friends and do what she thought would make others like her. She did not talk to us about this much and when she did, we had not learned to really listen. As her insecurity grew our situation worsened and we were terribly preoccupied. The stage was set for anorexia to strengthen its hold on her, promising that if Diana would only follow a few simple rules things would get better.

Anorexia usually prohibited Diana from attending the sessions with David. We were faced with a unique situation. Because Diana was not there, it was up to us to learn the language of anti-anorexia, and learn fast. David was involved with an organization called the Anti-Anorexia Anti-Bulimia League, which supports sufferers and their caregivers. Members around the world wrote stories of their experiences. These stories were moving and full of insight. They broadened our understanding and let us know we were not alone.

In our conversations there was a respect for myself and for Richard in the very way David spoke to us about "anti-anorexia." He talked about speaking anti-anorexically with each other and with Diana. So now anorexia became something you could actually fight back against. Instead of Diana being a problem we could see that Diana had this problem and we were trying to fight it and to find out more about it. So there was anorexia almost with its own persona. You could say: "This has come in and intercepted Diana and overtaken her. This is *not* Diana. She is separate from it." That was very important. Very important!

Externalizing anorexia, recognizing it as separate from Diana, gave us the liberty to vent our anger and frustration at the real culprit. Diana hated it at first when we started saying things like: "We hate it when anorexia treats you like this and makes you so unhappy"; "It is so sad when anorexia stops you from enjoying your food"; "Anorexia is trying to stop you from doing the things you really want to do." But it was such a relief to get angry at anorexia and not at Diana.

It was really hard work at first. Diana did not even want to hear the word anorexia, and she sure didn't want us separating her from it. The new language seemed forced and unnatural. We said it but we did not feel it. I wasn't comfortable when I first tried to speak anti-anorexically. I was uncertain because it sounded so awkward. When I began speaking like this, Diana seemed to think: "Mum and Dad have really gone 'round the bend and they're losing it." But we persisted, and eventually I saw breakthroughs in Diana.

David sent faxes to Diana when anorexia would not allow her to attend the sessions. They were short, she read them and did not comment. It took a lot of faith and perseverance. Sometimes David would ring to ask how we were getting on or offer us a new idea. Sometimes sessions would last for hours as we soaked up as much anti-anorexic fuel as we could, in the form of stories or practice conversations. There were times when my mind longed to return to the familiar, the well-worn ideas, the old habits. My comfort zone was being stretched to the limit.

Richard

As soon as I saw David the first time, I knew he was different. The way he made way for us and set us comfortably down, his friendly, chatty, disarming conversation all established him in my mind as a man who would care for us. In time, I would occasionally disagree with him, but I never disliked him. And, contrary to my experience of the psychiatrist, I would never, ever, distrust him.

But he asked odd questions. He asked Diana to imagine being free, in the future, of anorexia ("the big A" she called it, to avoid using the word) and to speculate now on how, then, she could help other young women to become free. What a question that was! I could see her future free of anorexia. I forget now what her illuminating answer was, but I cannot forget that question.

David was so understanding of every difficulty. He would never put blame on you for feeling bad or doing something wrong. He would always have an interpretation that was free of criticism. He seemed to explain everything you did and felt and thought in your own terms, from your own point of view, and so you started to have faith in yourself, and stop criticizing and blaming yourself. This was essential anti-anorexia—for one of the ways anorexia affected us was in how we spoke to ourselves: in critical, blaming, demeaning ways.

Though by all accounts highly qualified, experienced, and sought after, he deliberately and overtly abandoned any "position" or "authority" you might expect him to have. He never talked to us in the manner of other professionals, giving to us from his store of knowledge. Rather, he called himself a "co-consultant" with us on the problem of anorexia, and he acted just like that, too.

We were amazed. We were honored. Then, after we got used to it, we would share insights and suggestions freely with each other. He continually drew on examples from other people's experiences to illustrate his points or to support our experiences and confirm them for us. Consistently, he stressed that nobody but we ourselves would know what to do in our own situation.

Until our meetings with David, in our minds, Diana had been a problem. And somehow or other we were engaged in fighting Diana. Certainly Diana was engaged in fighting us. The evidence was all there. But when I understood that anorexia was the problem, that anorexia made her fight us, my approach to her was transformed. I must say that when David started talking about anti-anorexia, anti-anorexic language and practices and so on, I was offended. It felt as if I were being recruited into a strange new political movement. But when I started to get what anti-anorexia was all about, the offense gave way to understanding.

Although we called it "anti-anorexia," I came to see it as "unity," where anorexia is disunity, division, discord, hatred, and violence. The anti-anorexic language of narrative therapy gave us the precise tools to bring about or to reflect this unity, and there was a complete turnaround. We were given dignity and respect and we were able to start respecting ourselves and Diana again. Elsewhere, the professionals left us feeling "grilled" and blamed, and Diana feeling vilified and scorned. But now we were being understood and acknowledged for standing on our own feet. That was very strengthening. We had felt weak and helpless for a long time and the sense of having strength again was truly liberating.

I think I found it harder than Ann did, initially, to get a grip on how anorexia operated. A good thing the EDU did was to let me approach somewhat the feminine perspective on feelings, that they exist and that I had them. I still felt lost to some extent, but with the warmth and understanding of David's approach it started to make sense. You cannot comprehend anorexia and how it does what it does without understanding something about feelings, but my approach was analytical and logical. I tried to discount my feelings and I suppose I tried to discount other people's feelings too. And that was so anorexic, it wasn't funny. Understanding emotions contributed greatly to my understanding of anorexia.

As a man, I found this was new. As soon as we started talking about anorexia, I recognized in myself a deep lack of understanding about emotions, and I decided early on to confront this. So, since the crisis had begun, I had spent time reflecting on what we were learning. Every chance I got, I would simply sit down and quietly reflect on the topic of *feelings*. At the office, every hour or two I would go outside for a cigarette. As I sat down and lit up, the single word *feelings* would resound in my mind, and I would simply watch what the mind brought in about that. It would change from day to day, from week to week, but it was always relevant, and very instructive. I went from being suspicious of feelings to understanding that they cause action. By very definition, emotion means "that which moves." Every word and action has an emotion behind it, impelling it into being. And far from being suspect, emotions are trustworthy. I began to trust the feelings I had, to name them and voice them. I noticed that understanding the emotion let me understand the action. So I went from being rather out of touch to being closest of all to the real action.

One time Diana told me angrily: "You have a real problem with anger!" I immediately felt angry right back at her, just because she spoke to me angrily. But somehow I managed to listen to what she was saying and to let go of my own angry response. That gave me a brief space to think clearly. In that minuscule space we looked at each other. I saw her face, angry but firm, and I remembered that she was my beloved daughter but that anorexia was in there somewhere distorting things—and

I tried to slow down and figure out which one was speaking. Then I saw that this was *not* anorexia speaking and understood why she had said it—because I *would* get enraged at anorexia's taunting and needling of me, and I did have a problem with anger because I didn't know how to deal with it. So I acknowledged that she spoke the truth.

Before, I thought any anger from my children was always deliberate, unjustified, threatened my position as a father, and must be put down strongly or punished. I realized that was just the way I had been brought up. But studying emotions has shown me that they arise quite independently of our conscious will and are difficult to control. The only thing we each can control is our response to them and even then it takes effort and time to learn. So the children weren't threatening any "position" I held, they were simply expressing themselves and all I had to do was try to understand them. In an instant I let go of the anger that rose in me and I relied simply on: "Right." And in the way I looked at her and by my tone of voice she knew I genuinely agreed with her. From then on I tried even harder in all situations not to angrily manifest the anger I felt. Letting go of the anger was very hard to do, but letting it go made me an even better father, as the children themselves told me later.

When we first came to practice the things David was teaching we were adopting an emotion or attitude that was not really there so it felt false. Diana saw through it—we all saw through it. But we persevered and eventually when we said something as simple as "How do you feel about that?" it was believable, because it was not a false or insincere question. And because it was a real question, we got a real answer.

Ann

In order to fight anorexia, Richard and I had to transform our relationship. What happened in the past was that, if we had a discussion about something, we would have reached an impasse and stopped. I would have said: "Well, that's what I believe," and he would have said: "This is what I believe." So we would have parted at that point, saying: "This is as far as it's going to go." And we would have stormed off, leaving resentments to build up.

We can now get past those limits. So even if we get to a point where we feel really upset and are thinking "I'm right—I know what I'm talking about and you don't know what you're talking about," we just keep going. We are willing to persist with difficult things. We are hitting brick walls but we refuse to give in. I used to drop things because they were upsetting. Now we keep going until we find a place where understanding is starting to dawn: "Oh, I see. That's why he feels like that," and "That's why I feel like this." And it's okay for him and me to disagree on something and both of our opinions can be right.

Richard

Compared to our old relationship, our renewed relationship is full of love. We've come to respect each other's differences rather than trying to press the other person into seeing everything the same way and being terribly offended and mad when that doesn't happen. Our enjoyment of each other has risen a thousand-fold. It has affected our relationships with the children in the same manner. The same principles apply to them and our attempts to resolve differences with them. I used to be very autocratic: He's 3 years old, he'll do as he's told. End of story. Now we are able to work with them to resolve differences or examine feelings in ways I had never imagined. The children respond to this and you can see them gaining confidence.

Ann

It was breaking my heart to see what anorexia was doing to Diana, but I thought I should be stoic and brave. I didn't know how to have my feelings and help Diana at the same time. I suppose at that time I would have seemed withdrawn and remote from everybody, especially Diana. I kept my distance, trying to be brave and soldier on, not letting myself feel all the feelings I was having. I suppose I would have appeared to outsiders as a bit cold.

David told us stories about how some parents found ways of expressing their feelings that actually led to a sense of solidarity with their daughters against anorexia. I remember in particular the story he told me about a daughter who was screaming and the parents joined in and screamed with her. Some of those stories made me realize that part of Diana's anguish was directed against anorexia. At those times when, in my heart, I could really feel this, I could go from crying and crying to becoming *angry* that anorexia was doing this to her. And because I was now clear that it was anorexia that I was angry at and not Diana, I let myself give voice to my outrage: "*Look what it's doing to you, it won't let you eat or feed yourself, it makes you lie there on the bed curled up, you can't speak to anybody, it makes you lash out at everyone!*"

I allowed myself to really feel what anorexia was doing to her, and I could be really angry about it. It was a while before I could explain to my mother, whose house we were living in while she was in hospital, why she has so few plates left. I was standing at the kitchen sink and things got so difficult I said to Diana: "I can't stand what anorexia is doing to you," and I picked up a plate and threw it into the sink. Then I took another and did it again. And again. Smashing and crashing into the sink. I had never done anything like that before. Diana was shocked: "My God, what's Mum doing? Here is my mother so angry that she's breaking plates." But I wasn't angry at Diana. I was just really angry at anorexia and it was so different. I couldn't have been angry at Diana.

Richard

I came to feel that we all "have" anorexia to some extent. So I think of the person "with" anorexia as just "having" more of it than the rest of us. If the person with the most anorexia says "How are you?" and you say "Fine!" and that's not true, that's because the bit of anorexia that's in you is wanting you to be perfect, to smooth the waters, to have everything okay. But the other person knows what the truth is, too, so you should try to look through your own anorexia to tell the truth, which might be "I'm pissed off" or it might be "I'm feeling joyful."

Ann

I wouldn't like to count the number of hours I sat with Diana and talked or just sat. She would cry and all I could do was hold her hand. Sometimes she would start to talk. Some of these conversations were very rich anti-anorexic conversations. But this came only after months of trying to talk with Diana in an anti-anorexic manner while she declined to join in these conversations. She started to get better about 6 months after we began seeing David.

Richard

Developing the ability to tell the difference between exactly what was Diana and what was anorexia was a key skill. Looking back now, it was absolutely vital. You made the slightest mistake and anorexia was in and Diana felt betrayed. It was awful. But if you could clearly identify who was who, Diana calmed down. You understood her, she felt she was being understood and heard, and anorexia, simply by being *identified*, had much less power.

Because this discrimination is such a silent, invisible action, I got the feeling sometimes that I hadn't done anything. But of course I had done something—the mere attempt is doing something. The difference between the anorexia and Diana was so tiny and unremarkable but the results of seeing the difference were clear, obvious, and distinct. The one leads to misunderstanding, misery, and deepening alienation, while the other fosters understanding, compassion, and unity.

Another part of our anti-anorexic practice was learning how to praise Diana. To our conventional thinking, there was absolutely nothing at all to praise in what Diana was doing! We didn't exactly need instruction in praising, but rather in finding things to praise—they were such small things, normal-thinking people don't notice them. After David explained it to us, we would watch for these small things that we could praise Diana for. We would almost pounce on them! It had to be something that was praiseworthy—you couldn't make it up. You had to tell the truth and you couldn't fake it. These statements of praise, admiration, and support changed the atmosphere tangibly. You could almost measure the lift in the air when we found something to praise and said so simply and honestly. And yet these moments of freedom could be easily forgotten. Anorexia's daily drudgery and carping criticism would weigh like a gray burden upon yesterday's moments of freedom. We worked at it constantly and had to be most vigilant in remembering to praise her.

Praise is brightness and anorexia is darkness, there are no two ways about it. Praise nourishes self-respect and confidence and supports a person, whereas anorexia is eternally deprecating. When we started acknowledging Diana's small victories and moments of resistance, it was like lighting a torch in the great darkness of anorexia.

Ann

Cracks began to show in the armor that anorexia had built around our beautiful daughter. She would start to say something and then break down and cry. We would speak about how anorexia was causing this to happen. And she would often just cry. This was like a gentle reminder of her real nature and that we were working together against a common enemy.

Richard

There would be moments of that gentle crying where there was relief and sadness that wasn't the bitter, strong crying of desperation, anger, and frustration. By the gentle surrender in her, anorexia seemed to have been defeated for a moment.

Ann

One significant victory was when Diana was offered a job at the super-market. It was something she really wanted to do. The job represented new freedoms and she did not want anorexia to take this opportunity away from her. I recall her saying: "I would really love to try to fight back against anorexia because *it* is going to stop me getting the job. Or keeping it as well." I remember thinking, "Wow! She is actually saying there is an enemy." That was the first time I really heard her admit to the existence of anorexia in her life, and that it was an enemy which was trying to stop her from doing what she really wanted to do.

This was an incredible moment. The demon was finally visible. Un-fortunately, seeing the demon can make life harder at first. When its existence is threatened, it fights back with a vengeance. She would make efforts and it would torture her with guilt. I was still feeding her. She later told me that she planned many times to cook herself a meal and eat it. She pored over recipe books, she prepared food, but the relentless nagging of anorexia stripped her of the courage to eat it.

Finally, with her health fading, she cried out for help: "Why won't someone help me? If I'm so sick why don't they put me in hospital?" She finally saw that her life was in danger and she did not want to die. I think Diana had made the decision to turn against anorexia even before she went to the hospital. But she got so sick she didn't have the energy any more to fight. She really needed some medical support at that stage.

She was eventually admitted to the children's hospital in the first stage of kidney failure. She looked like a concentration camp victim but anorexia forbade her to eat. Diana's powers were severely depleted from lack of food and exhaustion from trying to fight. There were two important effects of this: First, Diana didn't understand much of what was said to her; second, the unknowing attitudes of the medical staff let them hear only anorexia. For example, she was asked: "Will you allow us to feed you through a gastric tube?" Anorexia heard only "will you allow" and "feed" and of course replied "No." They became openly angry. Diana may have agreed to the proposal if it was stated as: "Anorexia has put your life in danger. We'll slip this tube by it for a while without telling it." That is supposition, but there may be possibilities here to be explored by others.

The only way the doctors could cope with this was to have her de-tained under the Mental Health Act. We were desperate and agreed. This meant that, legally, Diana was being forced into the hospital to accept treatment against her will. We had, to all intents and purposes, passed over all responsibility and authority to the hospital doctors.

They told me I should have a rest, not visit too often, allow them to take over for a while. It was tempting, but except for one special nurse, they did not have the anti-anorexic language. I tried to visit every day and kept up an anti-anorexic dialogue, as Diana was fed through a nasal tube and then gradually encouraged to eat small amounts again. They worked on a reward system. Eat a certain amount and you get to have a shower. Eat more and you get to walk to the television room, and so on. Diana hated it.

Richard

I visited Diana most afternoons after work. If Ann was still there, I'd take her home. Diana and I would talk about all sorts of things, and I found myself returning again and again to the themes of self-determination, self-will, choice, and freedom. Later she reported everyone was on about the same thing. She meant everyone connected with David. None of us were criticizing her, no matter what she did.

Earlier, when we'd started to practice this, we went through ten kinds of hell trying to trust her judgment about the food. It was the hardest thing we'd done. We wanted her to eat enough to live, yet wanted to avoid forcing her, wanted to support, encourage, praise, love her enough so her decisions would become free of this demon inside her. That would be the real freedom, not the mere eating of food.

I remember a conversation in the hospital just before she started to turn and get better again. Anorexia was controlling what she did, what she thought, and what she abstained from doing. I said: "What you want is perfectly valid. It is entirely respectable—so what is it?" That seemed to go to the heart of it. I was deep in anti-anorexia (unity). There was nothing false, nothing being practiced. I was no longer even concerned about success or failure. I think about that now, and I marvel. Success meant she lived, failure meant she died. And I wasn't concerned either way, I just loved her.

I had reconciled myself to the possibility of her dying, but I wouldn't use force any more, because to compel her was to become anorexia itself. My resistance now took the form of an unwavering belief in her and an unshakable opposition to the ignorance assailing her. For all of us, this campaign was a battle for self-discovery. I found myself and, in doing so, I connected with Diana in a real and vibrant way. There was just honest love of Diana and antipathy and complete opposition to anorexia. There was constant discrimination between my daughter and anorexia, and I was always true to myself and true to Diana, just talking to her, never losing faith and never getting angry with her.

Ann

David gave us a piece of writing from a young woman who had reached Diana's stage in the battle and Diana clicked with it immediately. Lorraine was telling Diana's story. Although she was still terribly tormented she was beginning to see some of the more subtle moves of anorexia. Freedom was looking more and more attractive.

One evening Diana rang me at home. "Mum, I want to do something anti-anorexic, what shall I do?" Now, I recognized the trap I could fall into. Anorexia concentrates on giving orders. If I were to say what I thought she should do, I was being no different from anorexia. So I asked her: "That's great, what would you like to do?" She said, "Well, there's some banana cake in the dining room, I might eat a few crumbs." And she did.

Richard

She told us much later that she had suddenly needed to do a spontaneous act that wasn't forced on her. She said she had been talking to her aunt on the phone at the nurses' station and returned to her room. She was sitting there for a while and she just wanted to do something anti-anorexic. She had been increasingly aware that day of having no control over her life. She had to shower at a certain time, eat when they had time to feed her, she even had to tell someone when she wanted to use the toilet, and now she just wanted to do something that only she had decided to do.

Ann

The next day I visited her in the hospital. The transformation was nothing short of miraculous. We went for a walk and she asked for money to buy potato chips. We walked along laughing and joking as she ate them. Only we could know the true joy of this moment. It was as if a spell had been broken.

Until Diana went into the hospital she was being spoonfed by us. Anorexia made her feel quite comfortable about the spoonfeeding. She wasn't even humiliated. I saw that anorexia was totally blinding her to what was going on. She just couldn't see that spoonfeeding wasn't a normal way to carry on. Diana and I decided together that we never wanted to do that again, no matter what. We had to find another way. After Diana left the hospital, she fed herself from that point forward.

Diana came home to rebuild her life. She laughed, she cried, she made plans, she ate food she enjoyed, she walked in the sun, restyled her hair, renewed her friendships. Anorexia did not leave completely. It still whispered in her ear, but she had seen how much it had stolen from her, and she had a life to get on with.

Sometimes Diana thought we were trying to trick her or just playing games with her. But in actual fact, we were genuinely helping her find her voice which anorexia had taken away. Anorexia had been speaking through her so much that we had to help her rediscover her voice.

One morning soon after Diana came home from the hospital, Emma, our daughter, said: "In a way, anorexia was the best thing that could have happened to our family!" "Yes," I said, "but why do you say that?" She said: "Well, all these things that we all have been feeling and thinking wouldn't have come out, would they?" I replied, "Yeah, it was a pretty awful way for it to happen but at least everyone has learned to say how they feel and talk about things, so this won't have to happen to anybody else." She said: "Yeah, that's right!" She was only 8 years old then.

As parents we gained strength and renewal from Diana's courage and we are forever grateful to David and all the members of the Anti-Anorexia/Anti-Bulimia League who helped to pull back the shadows and fill the deadly silence with their support and knowledge.

Chapter 18

TOWARD SPIRIT-NOURISHING APPROACHES

A life-threatening "eating disorder" can engender tremendous fear among not only a woman's family and friends, but also professionals entrusted with her medical care. When these professionals perceive that the person, for the most part, is embracing her murderer (if not her very murder), they understandably feel justified in taking whatever measures they deem necessary to save her life. Unfortunately, these measures often amount to what Victoria (see Chapters 11, 12, & 13), referred to as a "transferred dictatorship," with the treatment team, instead of a/b, now in control of the person's body and life.

As discussed earlier, this type of treatment approach mirrors the tactics of a/b itself, often ultimately reinforcing a/b and making the woman more vulnerable to its attack upon discharge from the hospital. Victoria argued for an approach to treatment that avoids becoming another form of tyranny and instead supports and inspires the person to fight against a/b on her own behalf:

> At present, an anorexic patient is often stereotyped as being deceitful, angry, resistant to help, and incapable of making decisions regarding her own body. This last claim may contain a grain of truth in that anorexia has severely compromised her ability to think for herself. But the fact is that this is an individual who, if supported anti-anorexically, can make the decision to fight back. I am one example of this. If a patient can be inspired to fight against anorexia through recognizing the terrible atrocities it commits on her mind, body, and spirit, then

it is much more likely that this rebellion against anorexia's demands can be sustained after discharge.

Margaret (see Chapters 10, 11, 13, & 15) described her experience of the transferred dictatorship she encountered as a teenager in a psychiatric hospital. She contrasted this "anorexia-fattening" approach to treatment, based on obedience to the authority of treatment professionals, with her current anti-anorexic means of resisting anorexia, founded on the reclaiming of her own authority.

> In my first round with anorexia when I was put in the hospital and force-fed, I learned ways of fighting anorexia that actually fattened anorexia and starved me more. I think that may be why I feel like anorexia was never really engaged in battle until now, but was dormant and waiting to pounce on me when it had the chance. I found this writing of mine in an old journal. I wrote this while in the hospital after being punished for not eating. The voice of anorexia completely takes my voice and had me thinking about my life as no more than a game that I had to win.
>
>> Dear Journal,
>> I'm scared. I hate the time-out room. I hate me. I don't know how to be good here. I'm winning, though. They can put me in this room till hell freezes over. I won't eat. They don't understand. I can't eat in a half an hour, it makes me sick. I hate these stupid fucking doctors and I hate it here. They can force me to weigh_lbs before they let me out but they can't force me to keep it on. I won't be ugly, I won't be a loser, and I won't be fat. Fuck them. I'm smarter than these idiots any day. Eat your dinner or you go to the torture room. Fuck your tortures, no one is going to stop me. I'm winning this game.
>
> Looking back, one of the things that kept me "alive" but without a life I really wanted was the therapist spending all this time on finding "safe" foods: Foods that anorexia liked that were low-fat and nonfat. There were never desserts. At the time I was going through this, the therapist set a goal weight of_lbs and then I would be free. It was pro-anorexic fighting because it wasn't from a place of self-love or care of my body that houses my spirit, but out of terror of being punished for not obeying. The only difference became who I was obeying—doctors or anorexia.
> None of the ways I was taught to fight anorexia ever allowed me to claim the food I was eating because eating was just a rule that I had to follow. All of this kept me alive, which is good, but there wasn't any

claiming of myself in any of this—of what's important to me, what I want, and what I enjoy. It was more about how I looked and getting my weight to a certain number. For me that's pro-anorexic. I felt like I was a problem because I had some form of "eating disorder" and needed to be cured and fixed. This time around, at moments of clarity, I don't feel like I'm the problem. I feel like I'm in a war but if I win I get *me* out of it, not just a different-appearing body.

Residential or inpatient treatment for "eating disorders" is often necessarily focused on addressing nutritional emergencies or trying to stabilize and improve the patient's physical health. Many of these practices also aim to get the patient's weight into a "normal" range. Although this is true in outpatient treatments as well, the methods used in inpatient programs usually rely to a greater extent upon coercion and the imposition of authority.* Sometimes a young woman may encounter staff who interact with her in ways that rekindle and nourish her spirit and inspire her to claim the initiative to fight against a/b. Unfortunately, it seems that practices aimed at restoring people's physical well-being all too often take a toll on their spirit.

Margaret described a more recent treatment experience that included both a relationship with a social worker who was nurturing of her spirit and a relationship with a well-meaning and caring psychiatrist who used his power and authority in ways that nearly crushed Margaret's spirit. She poignantly described the effects that each of these two forms of practice had upon her relationship to anorexia:

> It all started when I had to have surgery for a medical condition unrelated to anorexia. My surgeon, with the best of intentions, thought it would be a good idea to put me in a short-term convalescent hospital. Because of my past experiences of abuse, some of the treatment protocols were absolutely terrifying. I was tied in my bed for safety precautions. If I didn't have a bowel movement by 6 P.M., I was given an enema and a stool softener. At 10 P.M. I was given a sleeping pill and the lights were turned out. The feeling of falling asleep against my will was terrifying. I felt like I had no dignity, no privacy, and no rights whatsoever. I felt like a body and a body that didn't matter and that was supposed to be like every other body. I had to be weighed every morning with all the other patients and that gave the all-out go ahead

---

* Some speculations about why this is the case include: (1) patients in hospital or residential settings are usually more acutely malnourished; (2) these settings allow for more surveillance and control over patients' actions; (3) hospital-based eating disorder units are usually overseen by psychiatrists trained in the traditional hierarchical model of doctor-patient relationship and see the patient as sick and therefore unable to be incited to resist a/b.

for the voice of anorexia. It felt like my weight was the only thing left I could control. Anorexia seized on that idea.

Like all patients, I had a social worker and I lucked out with Judith. She came to talk with me because, as she put it, it had been noted in my chart that I had lost a fair bit of weight and that I had a history of being "anorexic." She was the only person during the entire stay who bothered to ask *me* what I had found helpful in the past, or if there was anything that I might find helpful now. When she first asked me that, I started to cry. She was the first person there that I felt tried to connect to me as a person.

I told Judith it would be a lot easier if I could eat in my own room and explained my loss of appetite in the cafeteria (most people were on pureed diets due to swallowing difficulties and were tied to their wheelchairs). I told her about my Internet caucus group that stands with me when I'm struggling with anorexia. I also told her about feeling horrible about the enema and being tied up at night. She heard me and she came up with the idea that my occupational rehab therapy could be getting me onto a computer with Internet access so I could talk to the other caucus members. She completely understood why I would prefer to eat in my room, and she arranged for me to have a laxative as an alternative to the enema, though I was still required to be tied up at night. We talked about what might make that easier for me to endure and I shared with her about my stuffed animal (a frog) and my having it with me while I slept. Things were beginning to look up.

Then my surgeon, who also noticed my weight loss, decided to call in a psychiatrist. That's when things went from hopeful to hellish. The first thing the psychiatrist informed me of is that I wasn't to talk to my therapist. I asked why not and he told me it would undermine my therapeutic relationship with him [the psychiatrist]. I didn't understand why he and my therapist and I couldn't work together for what's helpful to me. Instead of my feeling safer and more trusting with him, [the psychiatrist] I couldn't talk to him at all and wouldn't.

Next, he found out that the social worker had let me eat in my room and that I had been talking to my Internet caucus group. He was furious with Judith when he found out. He called her out into the hall and came and got me from the computer room and then proceeded to scream at her as I was being escorted back to my room. He told her that she was "splitting" the team. He said, "Don't you know that anorexics can't be trusted alone while they eat? She's probably throwing her food up and flushing it." I felt like garbage and sick inside. I honestly wasn't throwing up and had actually started to eat a bit.

When we got to my room, he saw my stuffed frog on my bed. He picked it up without my permission as if it was his right. He then declared that my having a stuffed animal was a sign of "regressive behavior." Judith was starting to tear up and I wanted to scream, "It's my frog…it makes me know I'm safe…my frog helps me know I'm okay."* I was so angry that I swiped the water pitcher off the bedside table and water spilled everywhere. I was crying and hurting and afraid and angry. The psychiatrist had me restrained and sedated for my outburst of "regressive" behavior, but it felt good to fight back. It felt like the only way I had of standing up for me. Unfortunately, everything I did was proof to him of what he claimed. After that, anorexia had me throwing my food up and then not eating at all.

I started exercising for as long as I could, as anorexia told me that if I spent as much time as I could on machines in the gym, I would be too drained to feel, and I wouldn't get angry and punished anymore. I lost more weight. I stole ankle weights from the gym and hid them under my jeans so no one would know. But the nurses, when they examined me, heard an irregular heartbeat, and my electrolytes tested abnormal.

I had already told Judith that I wasn't real keen on a NG [naso-gastric] tube but that if it meant saving my life I would agree to it. However, without any warning, four people, led by the psychiatrist, stormed into my room. The psychiatrist forced a NG tube down my nose and throat saying, "Anorexics are often noncompliant with life-saving procedures."

I didn't want to be punished by having what's mine—the people I am in relationship with, the ideas that help me—confiscated. When I talk to my therapist, we talk about the voice of anorexia not "the anorexic," and I have a voice that's mine. I can find it and, while it's a struggle sometimes, it's there in me. Later, when I spoke of the voice of anorexia, the psychiatrist asked me if I was hearing voices. I said "no" and then he tried again to talk about me being anorexic and again I talked about the voice of anorexia. He said I was in denial about being anorexic. If I had adopted his ideas of me, I would have just given up in relationship to anorexia and accepted its descriptions of me as wrong and bad and fat.

Margaret's poignant story illustrates the hazards of therapy that is single-mindedly focused on a person's physical well-being. Margaret remained visible to Judith, the social worker, but invisible to the psychiatrist. We believe that the differences in their approaches had more

---

* See Chapter 15 for an explanation of the significance of frogs for Margaret

to do with the differences in the discourses that inform their respective disciplines (and perhaps their gender socialization) than they did with purely "personal" differences between the two professionals. The psychiatrist invested a great deal of concern in his "treatment" of Margaret; his intentions were undoubtedly positive, but the effects of his treatment approach (constrained as they were by ideas about "anorexics" and by a traditional, hierarchical approach to treatment) were not.

When the will of the treatment team is imposed upon the person, violations of spirit are bound to occur. At times these impositions may be necessary to save a life. However, unless these violations are addressed, the person's life may be saved for the time being but a/b will be strengthened, increasing the likelihood of "revolving door" hospitalizations. Chloe (see Chapters 11, 12, & 13) had this to say about the possibility of combining life-saving and spirit-nourishing treatment approaches:

> Imposition is anathema to anti-anorexia because it flies in the face of all that anti-anorexia values. Imposition from "outside" simply mimics anorexia's imposition upon the person. Anorexia invades a person with no regard for their values, and tricks them into believing that it [anorexia] is "right" and they are "wrong." It makes them lose all faith in their own judgments and knowledge of who they are as a person. The hospital treatment programs also step in as "the savior" and the "right way." In effect, while they save lives, they diminish the spirit within the person just like anorexia does, in contrast with anti-anorexia which nourishes the spirit and celebrates its discovery and growth.
>
> A year ago to this day, I was being airlifted to the hospital against my will and placed in a position that was indeed very spirit-breaking rather than enhancing. Yet, if my will had been honored in this instance, I would probably be dead. All my past "life-saving" experiences have, in many ways, been spirit-breaking experiences. I would dearly like to discover a way where the two—live-saving and spirit-nourishing—could coexist when anorexia is at its strongest. I think it would come down to respecting the person yet being unabashed in defiance of anorexia.

RECONCILING LIFE-SAVING AND SPIRIT-NOURISHING PRACTICES

Chloe raises an extremely important question—one we feel needs to be carefully considered by the larger community of "treaters" and "caregivers." When a/b is at its strongest, desperate measures such as hospitalization and tube-feeding are often necessary to save someone's life. And it is often (though by no means always) the case that these measures are necessarily imposed upon the person, who may be too captured by a/b to recognize or care about her own peril.

Mitigating Spirit-Breaking

It is vital to consider how one might minimize the experience of spirit-breaking when dire circumstances require life-saving impositions. When the possibility of hospitalization (and the impositions often associated with that) is on the horizon, the therapist and insider can develop an anti-a/b perspective whereby she takes a/b to the hospital rather than viewing her hospitalization as her incarceration.

Prior to hospitalization, most women, if consulted about their wishes should tube-feeding be deemed necessary, will consent to this procedure. These women may more willingly consent to them or even insist upon such measures if they are given trustworthy assurances that care will be taken to minimize any sense of violation. Perhaps the most reassuring practice would be to consult these women about how the insertion of an NG tube, should it become necessary, be best carried out. For example, a woman might choose to prepare a document addressed to her medical team that provides her consent ahead of time. This type of document might read like the following:

Dear Doctor and Medical Team,

You may find this hard to believe, given what anorexia is having me tell you right now, but I have prepared this document so that you will never lose sight of my anti-anorexia no matter how hard it is for you to see it right now. If you are reading this letter, then no doubt anorexia has taken over both my mind and body to the point where I am at its mercy. The trouble with that is that it has no mercy. That is why I am asking you now to save my life so that I can live to fight another day.

Anorexia is probably telling me that I am not worth the hospitalization and it is unnecessary because, according to it, I've never felt better or looked better. Anorexia, through me, will probably raise any number of protests against the life-saving measures you are taking or intend to take. I ask that you ignore anorexia but take me into account. That may be very hard for you to do right now, so let me just tell you who I am and what I wish my life to stand for.

My values and aspirations couldn't be more different than anorexia's plans for my life and death. It is of great importance to me to live my life in a way that, when I leave this world behind, I will have savored its beauty and many pleasures, and I will have helped make it a better place. For me to make a positive difference in this world, however small, I need to live a lot longer than 16 years. I need further study and much wider experience of life. I need the love of others as much as I would hope to give love to others. I would like you to take whatever measures necessary to see to it that I survive, although I ask you to do so thinking of me the way I do rather than the way anorexia might have you think about me.

I ask that you read this to me even if I appear to hate what you are reading and try to destroy it. I am hoping that this will help counter what I imagine will be anorexia's attempt to paint you as my enemy and to view this procedure as punishment for being a treatment failure. Thank you very much.

Any variety of letters in a similar vein—whether addressed to the medical staff, to a/b, or to the woman herself—could serve similar purposes.

Engaging in Reparative Practices

When a woman's situation becomes dire enough that life-saving measures must be imposed, reparative practices can lessen the sense of violation. These reparative practices can come in the form of acknowledgments of or apologies for the violation or offers to redress the violation in some way. Chloe commented on the importance of such practices:

> David, you asked me, "How differently would you have felt if, as soon as your life was secured, those who 'broke' your spirit came to you and apologized and asked how they might assist you in its repair?" This question really touched me. If someone had said this to me at the time, I think it would have changed the whole experience of being tube fed.

She then proposed another reparative practice: consulting with the woman about how the team might go about their life-saving efforts without further damaging her spirit. Her proposal attempts to outline a treatment practice that is both respectful and unabashed in defiance of a/b.

> I also think that reparations could have taken place through discussions with me about how they could best keep my spirit intact while maintaining their life-saving efforts. I can see that these people are doing their job and, even when anorexia's at its strongest, I can still

respect that they have to go about their life-saving measures. Just by treating people with a bit more respect and dignity, I think that treaters would get a lot more understanding and cooperation from their patients.

David and Chloe worked out an example of something that a treater might have said in anticipation of a life-saving measure that had the potential to be experienced as an assault on the spirit. Chloe believed that had the following been said to her prior to these measures, they would have gone a long way to mitigate any injury to her spirit.

> Chloe, I suppose anorexia has convinced you that you want to die and, given the way it has been tormenting and torturing you for twenty-five hours a day over the past so many years, if I were in your shoes I would certainly be thinking the same. But I hold to the fact that you are not anorexia, for your parents have told me how as an 8 year old, you . . . and how as a 7 year old, you. . . . I refuse to listen to anorexia when it tries to have me think you are a "sick little girl" who is "out of her mind." In fact, I believe anorexia is 'in your mind' and if I had my way, I would do everything in my power, short of neurosurgery, to remove it. It is your mind, your spirit and your body that I intend to save and I will do so by any means I have at my disposal. I do not wish to attend your funeral but some day I want to attend your graduation. Chloe, I do not expect you to agree with me. All I am asking is that you will look into my heart and see if I have malice or hatred for you. If you see hatred or malice in my eyes, please know that I am staring at anorexia and thinking how immoral it is for trying to talk you out of your life.

Externalizing A/B

Viewing a/b as an external influence rather than an internal disorder opens up the possibilities for collaboration between "treaters" and "patients." It can also help subvert the polarizing effects of perceived impositions. Chloe described such a collaboration in terms of *surveillance* versus *support*:

> I was wondering if "surveillance" could somehow be turned into "support." That is, rather than being engaged in surveillance practices, could the shift be made to support practices. For example, at meal times, rather than the nurses feeling like they have to surveil the patients and watch out for any "manipulative" or "sneaky" behaviors, could they make their position one of anti-anorexic support? That is, could they develop a different sort of relationship with the

patients so that, rather than it feeling like "us against them" (nurses against patients), which is the way it so often feels like from the patients' perspective, could it become "us against anorexia"? Could they be unequivocal in declaring to the patient that they are not there to watch over the person but rather to watch over anorexia because they know that it often gives the person a particularly hard time around mealtimes and they want to be there to make sure it doesn't get up to any nasty tricks? While the patients might still feel unhappy about being watched and feel like they aren't trusted, perhaps it would be an important step for the clear distinction to be made between who the nurses are watching out for (anorexia) and who they are in support of (the person).

A proposal similar to Chloe's had earlier been implemented by Ann Epston and the staff of a hospital unit to which Judith, aged 23, had been admitted. The staff had produced a "wellness plan" for Judith. Written in the typical way, it listed restrictions placed upon Judith for "her own good." Ann, Judith's therapist, recognized that the manner of speaking in this plan implied Judith's "oneness" with anorexia and could create the "us against them" relationship that Chloe referred to in the previous extract. Ann worked with the staff to create an anti-anorexic version of the plan that made it clear that the staff were going to ally with Judith by placing restrictions upon anorexia's attempts to dominate her. Nurses roles were revised by referring to their task as one of shielding her from anorexia rather than surveilling her. The original and revised plans are juxtaposed:

Plan to Ensure Judith's Wellness	An Anti-Anorexic Draft of Judith's Rest Plan
1. Bed curfew: Judith has to be in bed (under the covers) totally ready for sleep at 10:30 P.M. Therefore, she needs to get ready in plenty of time.	1. Bedtime: Anorexia must stop procrastinating and claiming that sleep isn't necessary. Anorexia must let Judith get right into bed and be completely ready for sleep by 10:30 P.M. Judith deserves a good night's sleep to rest and heal.
2. Judith will not set her alarm for 6:00 A.M. These rules are to ensure that Judith receives adequate rest.	2. Anorexia must stop demanding that Judith set her alarm for 6:00 A.M. Judith deserves to sleep in naturally as much as possible.

3. All Judith's visitors will have to abide by the visiting times of the ward. This includes Marla and Peter [her parents]. This, too, is to ensure that Judith receives rest.

4. Judith is to stop playing ballgames or other "active" games. This is to enable the goodness of her food to heal her body rather than be used up in activity.

5. Judith can go outside or leave the ward once a day for 30 minutes only. She has to stay in the wheelchair during this time. No exceptions. This is to allow enough time for Judith's body to heal. It is also to enable the nurses to monitor Judith's progress. (When attending occupational therapy Judith has to go directly there and come straight back.)

6. Judith has to stay on her bed for 30 minutes to 1 hour at a time. She can play quiet games during this time only if her bottom is on the bed. This is to ensure Judith has enough rest for her body to heal (even more important now that she does not have a cast on).

7. If showering twice a day, Judith is to wash her hair once only. During her showers, she is also only to spend a maximum time of 15 minutes. This is because excessive hair washing expends excess energy and is damaging to the hair itself.

3. Staff want Judith to share the same visiting hours as all other patients, and want her to get as much rest as possible both during and outside visiting hours.

4. Anorexia has to stop using games as a pretext for subjecting Judith to torturecise. Judith deserves to play for fun and to rest and heal.

5. Judith is entitled to leave the ward for half an hour each day for pure pleasure, such as visiting the rose gardens and enjoying trees and nature. Anorexia must not make Judith get out of her wheelchair; she needs and deserves the rest it provides. Anorexia may not divert Judith on her way to or from occupational therapy.

6. Anorexia must allow Judith time to rest on her bed for 30 minutes to an hour at a time. Anorexia has got to let Judith sit so she can play diverting games. Judith deserves mental stimulation, but she must not be required to pay a physical price for this right.

7. Anorexia must not turn pleasure showers into torturecise. Anorexia has no right to demand hairwashing more than once a day. Judith is fully entitled to warm, relaxed showers for up to 15 minutes.

8. The seminar room is to be used for quiet seated games only. If games that involve activity continue to be played here, the seminar room will become out-of-bounds.

8. Anorexia must not turn the seminar room into a torture-room. Judith is entitled to use this room for restful and thoughtful purposes, including quiet seated games. See item 4 above.

The anti-anorexic draft concluded with this statement. At all times staff will reaffirm and warmly encourage Judith as she learns to accept and acknowledge her right to rest and heal. Staff will be vigilant in detecting anorexia's attempts to undermine this healing process and will sternly reject any of anorexia's lies, excuses, and procrastinations.

ADDITIONAL EXAMPLES OF SPIRIT-NOURISHING IN TREATMENT

As discussed earlier, treatment providers often end up focusing their conversations and interactions exclusively on measurements and numbers and on food and weight, and consequently they lose sight of both a/b (in the broadest sense) and the person. This, along with inpatient programs structured around compulsory eating and the processing of the fears that arise in relation to weight gain, severely limits opportunities for "bigger," more significant conversations which nourish the spirit rather than focus on the body.

Ironically, many spirit-nourishing encounters between "treaters" and "patients" occur outside of what is regarded as the "treatment." They may come through a passing comment, a casual conversation during down time, or an interaction with someone who is not regarded as part of the clinical staff, such as a cleaning person. Because spirit-nourishing encounters are often incidental to the treatment program or occur in spite of it, they may often overlooked and unrecognized. Consequently, we suggest that hospital staff question their residents about what they experience to be spirit-nourishing and use this information to develop and extend their spirit-nourishing practices.

Chloe described some of the spirit-nourishing encounters she had while in hospital-based eating disorders treatment programs.

Treating Me as a Person

I have met many spirit nourishers over the years and they will remain engraved in my memory forever. One nurse in particular comes to mind. I met her when I was at one of my lowest points and she was able to reach me at a time when others found it impossible. I guess she was one of the few nurses who genuinely (and I think the genuine part is really important) treated me as a person (as opposed to an anorexic) first and foremost.

Because there wasn't much of "me" left at the time, as I was so consumed by anorexia and depression, Dad told me how she sought him out one day and asked him if he could tell her about who I was when anorexia wasn't dominating my life. At the time, I didn't like this too much because I thought they were talking behind my back about what a problem I was, but now I can appreciate what she was trying to do. This enabled her to have the background and understanding to talk to Chloe rather than anorexia. At the time, my mind was filled with anorexia's shoutings, but she was able to give me a break [from it] for fleeting moments when she engaged me in talking about books (I'm a keen reader). We discovered we had read many of the same books and both shared a love of Charles Dickens' works.

She also engaged me with nature—she would just sit with me when I was distressed and keep on bringing my attention back to the view outside my window and get me to look at and appreciate the shadows on the trees, the birds, etc. Usually such distraction techniques have not only been unsuccessful but have actually inflamed anorexia and frustrated me; the last thing I want is simple attempts at distraction when World War III is raging in my head. I'm not quite sure why it worked with Daphne but I know she did it in a really skillful way.

It usually takes me a while to get to trust people but, with Daphne, I felt a sense of connection almost immediately. Although she wasn't "experienced" in dealing with anorexia, she was one of the first nurses who ever took the time to really understand. For the first time I felt I'd come across someone who could truly help. She just sat with me for ages, talking me through things when anorexia got really bad. Rather than just get impatient or dismissive, she stuck with me until she'd seen me through.

Believing in Me

Another example of one simple action that nourished my spirit occurred 10 years ago during my first hospital admission. I was being tube-fed at the time and I'd been tampering with the feeding pump to slow it down when the nurses weren't around. Eventually I was discovered and the shame I felt was unbelievable. To make sure I didn't "manipulate" the system any more, the doctors counted out the exact number of cans of nutritional supplement that should be gone through in 24 hours. If, at the end of the day, there were cans left over, they'd know that I'd been slowing down the pump. After being found out, I was determined not to do it again and was humiliated by the fact that no one trusted me anymore, and angry at myself for breaking their trust.

One evening there were two cans of supplement left over. I was horrified as I hadn't touched the feeding pump and knew that no one would believe me. The nurse that was on [duty] that night was someone who'd known me for a while and was a really soft-spoken, caring person. Upon discovering the two extra cans, she came to me and asked me if I knew why there were cans left over. I spoke of my innocence in the matter and assured her that I hadn't done anything untoward. I spoke of my fears of what the doctors would think when they found out. She looked at me in the eyes and said, "I believe you." I then said, "But what about the doctors?" And without another word she quietly slipped the two cans into her handbag on her way out the door. She risked trusting that I was not just a lying, manipulative anorexic and instead believed in me to the extent that she put herself on the line by taking the cans home with her. In that one gesture, she nourished my spirit and strengthened me against anorexia.

Reconnecting Me with What's Important

Another spirit nourisher was a woman who worked as a cleaner in one of the hospitals I was in. She came to know me over the years and whenever she came to clean my room she did a lot more talking than she did cleaning! She would stand and talk with me for ages, sharing stories with me. She would tell me about her childhood growing up on a farm (I had lived on a farm my entire life so her reminiscences reconnected me with home); about her current pets and their exploits; and also about her husband, children, and grandchildren. She would bring me photos from her holidays and also of her animals and family, and she would tell me the stories that went with them. We never talked about anorexia or how I was doing (in terms of progress) or anything "illness" or "hospital" related. In essence, through sharing her stories and her quiet, caring ways, she created a space for me where I could reconnect with what was important to me in life (e.g., animals, nature, family) which was so often buried in the hospital surroundings. By reconnecting with these things, I was reminded of my values and was inspired to fight against anorexia to reclaim them.

ACCOUNTABILITY PRACTICES

If a therapy is to become spirit-nourishing rather than spirit-violating, it is crucial that therapists solicit the input of the people who are consulting them. This means asking them about their experience of "the work" and, in particular, about what they are finding helpful or problematic about the conversations. To some, this line of questioning may seem like a low priority when a person's life is at stake. But we believe that this kind of co-critique is of vital importance during life-threatening situations because these are the times when life-saving interventions with potentially devastating consequences are most likely to occur.

The questions we ask people in order to solicit their experience of our conversations extend our co-research of a/b and anti-a/b into the therapeutic relationship itself. The overall "research" question becomes "What constitutes an anti-a/b therapy?" This question is approached by engaging with people in an evaluation and critique of the micro-practices of the therapy.

However, we cannot assume that everyone we meet will feel free to share with us their experience of our work, especially if they have found aspects of the work unhelpful, off-putting, or even destructive. In some cases people may feel that being critical of us could jeopardize our goodwill toward, commitment to, or caring of them. Others may believe that "complaining" or "being negative" would be petty, ungenerous, or impolite. A/b may also make it difficult for people to connect with and affirm their own experience and to say or do anything that might be construed as challenging authority. These are but a few of the reasons why people might find it hard to enter into a critique of our work.

If we are going to engage in more than just a pro forma or pseudo critique, it will be essential to discuss with people the things that might prevent them from fully engaging with us in such a critique, and to find ways of overcoming or mitigating these constraints.

Accountability practices must be suited to the therapist's own style and setting. On-the-spot consultations from anti-a/b veterans and "outsider witness groups" (White, 1995, 1997) can be excellent and convenient means of establishing accountability for therapists working in residential settings. Outpatient or private practice practitioners may need to ask questions of their clients, while trying to make it as safe as possible for them to be forthcoming in their responses.

We often begin by asking general questions about what people have found helpful and unhelpful, but we quickly move on to more specific questions that invite more detailed responses. Over time, we seek to gain a better understanding of where and how our practices might inadvertently support a/b as we believe that such support is unavoidable. The particular set of questions we tend to ask people at any given moment is informed by what we have already learned about our own individual propensities and blind spots as therapists, as well as by the vicissitudes of the relationship with the client and her relationship to a/b. Because we are interested in the person's response rather than in a/b's response, we ask accountability questions only during moments when the person is relatively free from a/b's domination.*

We have found that people are often reassured about our genuine desire to know their experience if we take the first step in the critique. This might look something like: "In looking back on that conversation we had about__, I'm not sure if I was really listening or grasping what you were saying. Did you feel heard or understood on that particular occasion?" Responses to these questions are typically followed up with other questions about the effects, both positive and negative, of a particular comment or question (or the lack of one) and what implications this might have for how we understand what it means to be working anti-anorexically/bulimically.

The following is a sample of such questions. Therapists will undoubtedly generate other questions that relate more directly to their own work. Although it is equally important to ask about what the person is finding helpful in their therapy, we have included only questions that pertain to potentially unhelpful practices, as this side of co-research can be more challenging for both insiders and therapists.

- How are you finding these conversations so far?
- Do you feel, at times, that I haven't listened well enough to what you were saying?
- Were there times when I didn't appreciate how hard something was for you?
- Do I get ahead of you at times? Do I sometimes make incorrect assumptions about your degree of disloyalty to or disaffection from a/b? How does this affect you?
- Are there times when I fail to keep up with your anti-a/b and overestimate the extent to which a/b has a hold on you? What effect does this have on your anti-a/b?
- Are there times when you felt my faith in you waver? Did this cause you to lose faith in yourself? Were there times when my faith in you was absolutely essential to your anti-a/b?

* Because A/B's domination is rarely total, we believe these moments may occur even in the midst of hospitalizations.

- Were there times when I asked questions or made statements that left you wondering where I was coming from? Do you sometimes feel that I am taking a position without acknowledging it or without explaining why? Do you feel imposed upon at these times?
- Do you think there have been times when I have failed to grasp the significance of your anti-a/b acts? Were there things you would have wanted me to acknowledge or ask questions about that I didn't?
- Do you ever feel that I am making too much of positive developments or am thinking something is a positive development when you think it isn't?
- Do you ever feel that I get angry with you or blame you instead of a/b?
- Are there times when I am too much on the frontlines of the anti-a/b battle instead of inciting or supporting your own anti-a/b resistance?
- Are there times when our work has focused too much on nourishing your body and not enough on nourishing your spirit? Are their times when I haven't paid enough attention to helping you resist a/b by looking after your physical health?
- Are their times when you felt I expected too much from you?
- How do you think my being a man has influenced our relationship and conversations? How might they be different if I were a woman? How do think my being an outsider (or an insider, if that is the case) has been a handicap or an asset in our work together?
- Has my introducing you to other anti-a/b veterans by reading from the archive inadvertently fostered a sense of competition and not measuring up? If so, how might this be avoided or minimized in the future?
- Is there anything you would like to comment on that I didn't think to ask about?
- Has a/b infiltrated our therapy (or tampered with it) in ways that I was obviously unaware of?

It is inconceivable to us that a consistently spirit-nourishing relationship could be created without regularly soliciting the insiders experience of the "help" being offered them through questions such as those listed above. Questions such as these can be adapted by parents, partners, friends and other caregivers in order to increase the likelihood that those relationships are experienced by the insiders as spiritually nourishing and anti-anorexic/bulimic.

Chapter 19

CONCLUSION

U nlike authors of most books that aim to assist their readers, we are hoping that what follows reads more like a commencement than a conclusion. This is because the practice of anti-a/b has hardly begun: We do not regard the knowledges and practices presented in this book as the blossoming or fruition of anti-a/b, but rather, as the sowing of anti-anorexic/bulimic seeds, and the nurturing of seeds already sown. We trust that you will take the baton as we pass it to you, and move these ideas and practices forward in the course of authoring your own anti-anorexic/bulimic lifestyles, relationships, families, and therapies. We hope that this book will assist in launching a thousand, if not hundreds of thousands of new anti-a/b lives. It is time for us—its compilers, archivists, and coproducers—to hand it over and entrust it to those who will carry anti-a/b in directions we cannot anticipate. This book and the accompanying Web site* are intended merely as starting points and havens to return to when need be.

We decided to close this book with two letters: one written by a father to his daughter in 2001, and the other written in 2002, by that same daughter to another young woman who was close to perishing. We can think of no better distillation of the spirit and practice of anti-a/b.

Dear Chloe,
David's initial question was: "How did we not surrender to despair?"
Obviously I can't answer for your mum, but for me I think the most

---

* See Archives of Resistance at http://www.narrativeapproaches.com

important anti-surrender preventative was that we were like a tag wrestling team. That is, when one of us was weakening to the siren calls of despair, the other could step into the ring and take up the struggle with anorexia. Not that we rested or took a vacation while the other was "in." Rather, when one of us was down, the other was sufficiently up to step in.

When you were in the hospital, luckily we were not captured by the pathologizing descriptions of you which could have led us to despair; we always knew and remembered you were more than that. It's quite amazing that the thinner you got the thinner the official descriptions of you got. This is a really sinister ploy of anorexia; just when you needed a fuller description to sustain your sense of self, you were being described, captured, and belittled by the apparatus of unyielding psychiatric descriptions. Although I was aware that you were being disparaged, I rarely publicly contradicted their idea of you as "anorexic" because I would have been pathologized as being in "denial."

I also think there is an important difference between "powerless" and "hopeless." Very early on, I accepted and ultimately embraced our inability to do anything that would "solve the problem." In the early days we thought we could do something that would free you from the grip of anorexia. Letting go of this was a powerful learning experience because it was the first time in my life that I had not been able to "do something"! At other times in my life I felt in charge, even if I wasn't always effective. With anorexia, I had to surrender my sense of personal efficacy, but this was not a debilitating defeat; it was more a graceful surrender in the Buddhist sense.

Hope is something quite different. Hope is not contingent on outcome. That is, hope is relational—it sits between us. It is sustained and nourished by memories, conversations past and present, and faith in who you are in some deep, enduring sense. We never surrendered to despair because our hope sat between us, sustained by all those small, everyday exchanges and little acts of resistance on your part: They act as harbingers of hope for us. What I'm trying to say is that we did not sustain hope on our own, independent of your struggle, but it was not dependent on your successes. It sat outside of this—in our knowledges of who you were, what you stood for, and your incredible strength. Of course these knowledges had to be remembered and rekindled in conversations. This must have pissed anorexia off. I've never really thought of it from anorexia's point of view but it must have been severely taxed by our ability to keep on turning up on your team.

David asked us what we know about you that sustains our hope. I don't want to just list what we know. Rather, I want to remember the numerous occasions we had to contest the thin descriptions through which you were being confined, by declaring your honesty, ethicality, and our unshakable trust in your goodness. We knew that anorexia would never get you doing things that went against your sense of fairness and justice. Anorexia totally failed here; it never got you to give in to anything that compromised your ethical precepts. I'm still amazed at that and wondering what enabled you to do that.

What sustained me through the darkest times is my belief that the only constant is change. This does not mean that I believed that things would therefore get better, merely get different. This enabled me to resist getting demoralized by the present, because everything, including our pains and sorrows, is impermanent.

Safeguarding your hopes and dreams was the one small source of joy for us during the lean times—to be able to occasionally return them to you, or at least show you that they were still in our care. I can recall coming home from hospital visits feeling quite positive when we had conversations about your hopes and dreams that you had left in our care. Remember when you would ask us why we don't give up on you, or why we thought you got stuck with anorexia? Well, I can now see that these were your attempts to rediscover that the hopes and dreams we were temporarily safeguarding were still intact and awaiting your reclaiming.

David asked if we knew our safeguarding was inspiriting of you; all I knew was that these conversations were inspiriting of me. I came away thinking that I had been helpful. It's only now that I see that all I was doing was showing you that we were holding onto your dreams and hopes with loving kindness. I didn't realize that I was merely returning to you what was on loan with us.

I guess I anticipated David's next question about the joy we felt in inspiriting Chloe; it was a powerfully moving joy, reminding us of the need to stay connected with you in your struggles with anorexia. This connectedness is vital when you're in a medical system that callously says, "Just deposit your daughter here, she's got the problem." Just writing the words down offends and appalls me: As if "the problem" could be contained inside your skin. That seems insane to me. Leaving you there, in such a system, was, for us, the other side of joy.

Yes, anorexia often attempted to have us rewrite history by looking for stories that accorded with its accounts of you. Fortunately we were somehow or other able to resist this. Cherished memories were important but I think we were not so much engaged with the past as with the present. Because we looked beyond anorexia's description of you, we were always able to see your many anti-anorexic actions no matter how deep the hole anorexia had pushed you into. Our great sadness was that these were inevitably ignored by the hospital staff.

Even though these small but heroic counter-anorexia actions (and they were numerous) were visible to our loving eyes, we usually did not say anything to you because we thought anorexia would beat up on you if it knew of your secret opposition. I think it smugly thought it had your measure but we could tell you were waging a secret war, mobilizing all your allies to defeat its plans for you. For us, it was never a question of if you would go free, but rather a question of when, and we trusted you enough to know when.

I hope this does not seem contrived, saccharine, or sanguine. These words are being spoken with the breath of the heart and often bring with them ten thousand pains and sorrows but these are insufficient to derail our hope. It's actually not our hope, it's Hope, it's the air we breathe.

I hope you are able to feel the joys and sorrows that writing this has reawakened for me and to realize the gift that anorexia has mistakenly given us. I bet it never realized that it would be so instrumental in getting us all to learn so much about ourselves and life. It strikes me as a paradox that it thought it was just delivering untold grief, and it has, but it has also delivered you as you are now, and we as we are, and us. Personally I could not ask for more.

Loving kindness,
Dad

Dear Thalia,

It's just me, Chloe, back again to let you know that I'm still thinking of you. Before proceeding any further, I'd like to say something to anorexia, because I don't want it to try and twist my words in order to use them against you. Anorexia is very good at doing this to me and it sounds like it is very good at doing this to you as well. I know that it won't stop anorexia but I will write this all the same, in the name of truth and justice and in repudiation of anorexia's demands and lies.

Anorexia!
This letter is not to you but to Thalia. I don't care for you at all but I care about Thalia very much and this letter is for her alone. You have already stolen so much from Thalia and I don't intend to let you steal this letter away from her without putting up a fight. I know you will probably try to steal it from Thalia by telling her that she is stupid if she doesn't "perfectly" understand everything I write or isn't feeling up to reading my letter. Do you know what

I think of that, anorexia? I think you are despicable for making Thalia believe that she should be "perfect" and always be able to understand everything straight away despite the fact that you (anorexia) aren't allowing her to nourish her brain to be able to think freely and clearly. How dare you make such unreasonable demands of Thalia? Anorexia, I despise you and what you do to young women like Thalia. And so, anorexia, however hard you may try to infiltrate my words and twist this letter for your own evil purposes, you can never succeed in stealing it completely because you can't take away the fact that it was written with anti-anorexic spirit in total and utter defiance of you and with caring and solidarity towards Thalia. You might claim that she doesn't deserve this letter or that I am writing to her because I feel sorry for her or feel like I have to write to her. But I am writing Thalia because I *want* to and because I despise you (anorexia) for trying to take Thalia's hopes, dreams, and values away from her.

Sorry about that long conversation with anorexia, Thalia, but I wanted to make sure it knew where I stood.

Thalia, I understand that anorexia is very close to snatching your life away and that many people are so fearful for your life that they are prepared to take desperate measures such as putting you back in the hospital for tube-feeding. I can only imagine how much fear this must fill you with and how much you must wish that everyone would just leave you alone. I don't know how to take away the anguish you must currently be feeling. I was in a very similar position a year and a half ago and I was placed in the hospital against my will for tube-feeding. So, Thalia, I think I have some idea of what you must be going through right now and just want to say that I'm thinking of you and sending you all of my anti-anorexic strength and hope.

This afternoon, I went on a walk up into the park that is near our house and, while I was out there, I thought of you. The last time I walked there it was just before I was committed to the psych ward and anorexia was making me walk even though I had no energy. My face was awash with the rain that was pouring down and mingling with the tears streaming down my face. As I was walking there again today, I remembered so clearly what it felt like that day—to feel so very desperate and sad, to have such intense hatred for myself and wish myself dead. When I compared this to how I felt today as I walked amongst the very same park, I thought of you and was struck by an intense sadness about the fact anorexia is making you feel the same desperation and sadness that I felt back then, and that it is also trying to convince you that you don't deserve to live or are better off dead.

Thalia, as I walked through the bush today, I didn't have tears pouring down my face, nor was I thinking of how I'd be better off dead. Instead I noticed the tiny wildflowers growing amongst the grass, the butterflies flying free in the breeze, the birds twittering to each other in the trees and felt the sun warm upon my back. It was then that it struck me how evil anorexia is for trying so hard to rob you of your life and convincing you that you deserve to die.

Your therapist, Mary, told me about your questions about me—"How did she get better? I must be just a crazy person because I just can't do it, I give up." I can't believe how familiar those questions sound to me because so many times I have asked myself the very same questions in relation to other people. And do you know what I've discovered? Anorexia wants us to believe that we are just "crazy" and "weak" because then we will feel like we're hopeless and just give up. And that way, it can keep ordering us around and imprisoning us. As corny and cliched as this may sound, if there is anything I have learned over the past 10 years is that there is hope! No matter how much it may not feel like it at the time, things change.

I can almost laugh, finding myself in the position of writing these words to you because, not so long ago, I had given up all hope. I never, ever believed that I would find myself gaining as much freedom as I have from anorexia today and I sincerely hope (and believe) that the day will come when you too will be able to look back and find yourself in the same position that I am today. It might be a long time coming and I have no illusions that it will be a long and rocky road but it is possible and, above all else, the journey is worth it.

Don't get me wrong, I still struggle with anorexia every day. It often tells me that life is not worth living and that I don't deserve happiness. It still tells me that I don't have the courage needed to beat it. And if truth be told, often I still believe what it says. However, I have discovered that I have people who care for me who don't agree with what anorexia has to say about me and I know that you do too—like your family, and Mary (and me if I count!). They see something in you that anorexia is blinding you to at the moment. Perhaps anti-anorexia is about going against anorexia even when you might believe what it says. For me, anti-anorexia was about realizing that I had people who loved me and who wanted me to regain the freedom and happiness anorexia had stolen from my life.

It was then that I decided that, even if I didn't believe I deserved to live, I was going to try to live anyway and create a life for myself that fit with my values, such as family, friends, helping others, and nature, rather than lived according to anorexia's values. What keeps me going everyday when anorexia tells me that I must go back to starving myself is the fact that this is my life and I want to live it according to my values; that although I may feel worthless, I might just be of worth to somebody. If I can make a small difference in just one person's life, then to me, life, however hard, is worth living.

Until recently, anorexia had me give up in despair, thinking I'd never be able to make any difference in the world. Now when it tells me that I'm hopeless or worthless and that I'll never be able to help anyone, I say to it: "That may well be true, anorexia, but I'm not going to give up on my dreams without trying. And the worst thing that can happen is that I won't achieve what I set out to but it's worth trying just on the off chance that you (anorexia) might be lying to me." It has taken me a long time to be able to do this and I never thought in a million years that I would be able to stand up to anorexia in such a way but here I am—*doing it!*

Before I made a decision to reclaim my life, Thalia, I felt I was living only because people wouldn't let me die. I'd get angry with my parents and the hospital staff for not just leaving me alone and letting me die. I felt like it was unfair that they could decide whether I could starve myself or not and wished that they would all go away. When I first decided to live, I ate not because I necessarily wanted to live but because I realized that my life was important to other people. This is the amazing part though . . . after a long time of living my life just because people wouldn't let me starve myself to death, I am slowly but surely coming to find that I'm living my life because I want to create a life of meaning and value for myself. I am finding that, more and more, I have moments like today, when I am out in nature and can appreciate its beauty. I never thought that this day would come but it has. And I guess what I wanted to share with you, Thalia, is that the impossible is possible—that sometimes you don't have to feel like you are fighting against anorexia to start off with. Sometimes it's just a matter of living life because you "have to" because people value and care about you and after a while, you find that you want to take back your life and regain your lost freedom.

I sincerely hope that this day will come for you too, Thalia. It is a terribly long and often painful process and anorexia will try to trip you up every step of the way but the journey is well worth it. If only to be able to once again experience the beauty of nature and be able to take pleasure in the simple joy of the birds in the trees and the sun on your face.

With all my hope,
Chloe

BIBLIOGRAPHY

WORKS CITED IN TEXT

Bell, R. (1985). *Holy anorexia.* Chicago: University of Chicago Press.

Binswanger, L. (1944). Der Fall Ellen West. *Schweizer Archiv für Neurologie und Psychiatrie, 53,* 256–277.

Burns, M. (in press). Eating like an ox: Femininity and dualistic constructions of bulimia and anorexia. *Feminism and Psychology.*

Carey, M., & Russell, S. (2002). Externalizing—commonly asked question. *International Journal of Narrative Therapy and Community Work, 2,* 76–84.

Epston, D. (1999). Co-research: The making of an alternative knowledge. In *Narrative therapy and community work: A conference collection* (pp. 137–157). Adelaide, Australia: Dulwich Centre Publications. An extended version can be found at http://www.narrative approaches.com/antianorexia%20folder/AAcoresearch.htm

Epston, D., Morris, F., & Maisel, R. (1998). A narrative approach to so-called anorexia/bulimia. In D. Epston, *'Catching up' with David Epston: A collection of narrative practice-based papers published between 1991–1996* (pp. 149–174). Adelaide, Australia: Dulwich Centre Publications. Previously published in K. Weingarten (ed.), *Cultural resistance: Challenging beliefs about men, women and therapy* (pp. 69–96). Binghamton, NY: Haworth.

Freedman, J., & Combs, G. (1996). *Narrative therapy: The social construction of preferred realities.* New York: Norton.

Freeman, J., Epston, D., & Lobovits, D. (1997). *Playful approaches to serious problems: Narrative therapy with children and their families.* New York: Norton.

Gillyatt, P., & Reynolds, T. (1999). Sharp rise in eating disorders in Fiji follows arrival of TV. Retrieved November 8, 2003, from http://www.hms.harvard.edu/news/releases/599bodyimage.html

Gremillion, H. (2001). A canary in the mine: An anthropological perspective. In *Working with stories of women's lives* (pp. 135–150). Adelaide, Australia: Dulwich Centre Publications.

Horton, M., & Friere, P. (1990). *We make the road by walking: Conversations on education and social change.* Philadelphia: Temple University Press.

Morgan, A. (2000). *What is narrative therapy?: An easy-to-read introduction.* Adelaide, Australia: Dulwich Centre Publications.

Payne, M. (2000). *Narrative therapy: An introduction for counsellors.* London: Sage.

Russell, S., & Carey, M. (2002). Re-membering: Responding to commonly asked questions. *International Journal of Narrative Therapy and Community Work, 3,* 23–31.

Scott, J. (1990). *Domination and the arts of resistance: Hidden transcripts.* New Haven, CT: Yale University Press.

Simmons, S. (2002, January 13). Eating disorders on rise for South African blacks. *Los Angeles Times.* Retrieved March 21, 2002, from http://www.latimes.com

Stearns, P. (1997). *Fat history: Bodies and beauty in the modern west.* New York: New York University Press.

Thompson, B. W. (1994). *A hunger so wide and deep: A multiracial view of women's eating problems.* Minneapolis: University of Minnesota Press.

White, M. (1995). *Re-authoring lives: Interviews and essays.* Adelaide, Australia: Dulwich Centre Publications.

White, M. (1997). *Narratives of therapists' lives.* Adelaide, Australia: Dulwich Centre Publications.

White, M. (2001). Narrative practice and the unpacking of identity conclusions. *Gecko: A Journal of Deconstruction and Narrative Ideas in Therapeutic Practice, 1,* 28–55.

White, M. (2002). Addressing personal failure. *The International Journal of Narrative Therapy and Community Work, 3,* 33–76.

White, M., & Epston, D. (1990). *Narrative means to therapeutic ends.* New York: Norton.

RELEVENT WORKS ON NARRATIVE THERAPY

Abels, P., & Abels, S. (2001). *Understanding narrative therapy: A guidebook for the social worker.* New York: Springer.

Beels, C. (2001). *A different story: The rise of narrative in psychotherapy.* Phoenix, AZ: Zeig/Tucker.

Bird, J. (2000). *The heart's narrative: Therapy and navigating life's contradictions.* Auckland, New Zealand: Edge Press.

Durrant, M., & White, C. (eds.) (1990). *Ideas for therapy with sexual abuse.* Adelaide, Australia: Dulwich Centre Publications.

Carey, M., & Russell, S. (2002). Externalizing- commonly asked questions. *International Journal of Narrative Therapy and Community Work, 2,* 76–84.

Epston, D. (1989). *Collected papers.* Adelaide, Australia: Dulwich Centre Publications.

Epston, D. (1998). *'Catching up' with David Epston: A collection of narrative practice-based papers published between 1991–1996.* Adelaide, Australia: Dulwich Centre Publications.

Epston, D. (1999). Co-research: The making of an alternative knowledge. In *Narrative therapy and community work: A conference collection* (pp. 137–157). Adelaide, Australia: Dulwich Centre Publications. An extended version of this article can be found at http://www.narrative approaches.com/antianorexia%20folder/AAcoresearch.htm

Epston, D., Lobovits, D., & Freeman, J. (1997). Annals of the 'new Dave': Status: abled, disabled or weirdly abled? *Gecko: A Journal of Deconstruction and Narrative Ideas in Therapeutic Practice, 3,* 59–85.

Epston, D., & White, M. (1992). *Experience, contradiction, narrative and imagination.* Adelaide, Australia: Dulwich Centre Publications.

Friedman, S. (ed.) (1993). *The new language of change: Constructive collaboration in psychotherapy*. New York: Guilford Press.

Friedman, S. (Ed.) (1995). *The reflecting team in action: Collaborative practice in family therapy*. New York: Guilford Press.

Freedman, J., & Combs, G. (1996). *Narrative therapy: The social construction of preferred realities*. New York: Norton.

Freeman, J., Epston, D., & Lobovits, D. (1997). *Playful approaches to serious problems: Narrative therapy with children and their families*. New York: Norton.

Gilligan, S., & Price, R. (1993). *Therapeutic conversations*. New York: Norton.

Griffith, J., & Griffith, M. (1994). *The body speaks: Therapeutic dialogues for mind-body problems*. New York: Guilford Press.

Hoyt, M. (ed.) (1994). *Constructive therapies* (Vol. 1). New York: Guilford Press.

Hoyt, M. (ed.) (1996). *Constructive therapies* (Vol. 2). New York: Guilford Press.

Hoyt, M. (ed.) (1998). *Handbook of constructive therapies*. San Francisco: Jossey-Bass.

Jenkins, A. (1990). *Invitations to responsibility: The therapeutic engagement of men who are violent and abusive*. Adelaide, Australia: Dulwich Centre Publications.

Lane, K., Epston, D., & Winter, S. (1988). Mad fax Sunday: Are some virtual communities more real than virtual? *Gecko: A Journal of Deconstruction and Narrative Ideas in Therapeutic Practice, 1*, 45–61.

Lobovits, D., Maisel, R., & Freeman, J. (1995). Public practices: An ethic of circulation. In S. Friedman (ed.)., *The reflecting team in action: Collaborative practice in family therapy* (pp. 223–256). New York: Guilford Press.

McLean, C., Carey, M., & White, C. (eds.) (1996). *Men's ways of being: New directions in theory and psychology*. Boulder, CO: Westview.

Mcnamee, S., & Gergen, K. (eds.) (1992). *Therapy as social construction*. London: Sage.

Madigan, S., & Law, I. (eds.) (1998). *Praxis: Situating discourse, feminism and politics in narrative therapies*. Vancouver, BC: Yaletown Family Therapy.

Madsen, W. (1999). *Collaborative therapy with multi-stressed families: From old problems to new futures*. New York: Guilford Press.

Monk, G., Winslade, J., Crocket, K., & Epston, D. (eds.) (1997). *Narrative therapy in practice: The archaeology of hope*. San Francisco: Jossey-Bass.

Morgan, A. (2000). *What is narrative therapy?: An easy-to-read introduction*. Adelaide, Australia: Dulwich Centre Publications.

Neimeyer, R., & Raskin, J. (eds.) (2000). *Constructions of disorder: Meaning-making frameworks for psychotherapy*. Washington, D.C.: American Psychological Association.

Neimeyer, R., & Mahoney, M. (eds.) (1995). *Constructivism in psychotherapy*. Washington, DC: American Psychological Association.

Nylund, D. (2000). *Treating Huckleberry Finn: A new narrative approach to working with kids diagnosed add/adhd*. New York: Guilford Press.

Parker, I. (ed.) (1999). *Deconstructing psychotherapy*. London: Sage.

Payne, M. (2000). *Narrative therapy: An introduction for counsellors*. London: Sage.

Parry, R., & Doan, R. (1994). *Story re-visions: Narrative therapy in the postmodern world*. New York: Guilford Press.

Russell, S., & Carey, M. (2002). Re-membering: Responding to commonly asked questions. *International Journal of Narrathive Therapy and Community Work, 3*, 23–31.

Smith, C., & Nylund, D. (1997). *Narrative therapies with children and adolescents*. New York: Guilford Press.

White, C., & Denborough, D. (eds.) (1998). *Introducing narrative therapy: A collection of practice-based writings*. Adelaide, Australia: Dulwich Centre Publications.

White, C., & Denborough, D. (eds.) (1999). *Extending narrative therapy: A collection of practice-based papers*. Adelaide, Australia: Dulwich Centre Publications.

White, M. (1983). Anorexia nervosa: A transgenerational system perspective. *Family Process, 22* (3), 255–273.

White, M. (1989). Anorexia noervose: A cybernetic perspective. In M. White, *Selected papers* (pp. 65–76). Adelaide, Australia: Dulwich Centre Publications. Previously published in J. Elka-Harkaway (ed.) (1986), *Eating disorders*. Rockville, MD: Aspen Publishers.

White, M. (1991/1992). Deconstruction and therapy. *Dulwich Centre Newsletter, 3,* 21–40. Reprinted in D. Epston & M. White, *Experience, contradiction, narrative, and imagination: Selected papers of David Epston and Michael White, 1989–1991.* Adelaide, Australia: Dulwich Centre Publications.

White, M. (1995). *Re-authoring lives: Interviews and essays.* Adelaide, Australia: Dulwich Centre Publications.

White, M. (1997). *Narratives of therapists' lives.* Adelaide, Australia: Dulwich Centre Publications.

White, M. (2000). *Reflections on narrative practice.* Adelaide, Australia: Dulwich Centre Publications.

White, M. (2001a). Folk psychology and narrative practice. *Dulwich Centre Journal, 2001* (2), 1–37.

White, M. (2001b). Narrative practice and the unpacking of identity conclusions. *Gecko: A Journal of Deconstruction and Narrative Ideas in Therapeutic Practice, 1,* 28–55.

White, M. (2002). Addressing personal failure. *International Journal of Narrative Therapy and Community Work, 2002* (3), 33–76.

White, M. (2003). Narrative practice and community assignments. *International Journal of Narrative Therapy and Community Work, 2003* (2), 17–55.

White, M., & Epston, D. (1990). *Narrative means to therapeutic ends.* New York: Norton.

Winslade, J., & Monk, G. (1999). *Narrative counseling in schools: Powerful and brief.* Thousand Oaks, Ca.: Corwin/Sage.

Winslade, J., & Monk, G. (2000). *Narrative mediation: A new approach to conflict resolution.* San Francisco: Jossey-Bass.

Zimmerman, J., & Dickerson, V. (1996). *If problems talked: Narrative therapy in action.* New York: Guilford Press.

RELEVENT WORKS ON ANTI-ANOREXIA

Epston, D., Morris, F., & Maisel, R. (1998). A narrative approach to so-called anorexia/bulimia. In D. Epston, *'Catching up' with David Epston: A collection of narrative practice-based papers published between 1991–1996* (pp. 149–174). Adelaide, Australia: Dulwich Centre Publications. Previously published in K. Weingarten (ed.) (1995). *Cultural Resistance: Challenging beliefs about men, women and therapy* (pp. 69–96). Binghamton, NY: Haworth Press.

Grieves, L. (1997). Beginning to start: The Vancouver anti-anorexia, anti-bulimia league. *Gecko: A Journal of Deconstruction and Narrative Ideas in Therapeutic Practice, 2,* 78–88.

Kraner, M., & Ingram, K. (1997). Busting out-breaking free: A group program for young women. *Gecko: A Journal of Deconstruction and Narrative Ideas in Therapeutic Practice, 3,* 31–54.

Madigan, S., & Goldner, E. (1998). A narrative approach to anorexia: Discourse, reflexivity and questions. In M. Hoyt (ed.)., *Constructive therapies* (Vol. 2, pp. 380–400). San Francisco: Jossey-Bass.

Mådigan, S., & Epston, D. (1998). From 'spy-chiatric gaze' to communities of concern: From professional monologue to dialogue. In D. Epston, *'Catching up' with David Epston: A collection of narrative practice-based papers published between 1991–1996* (pp. 127–148). Adelaide, Australia: Dulwich Centre Publications. Previously published in S. Friedman (ed.)., *The reflecting team in action: Collaborative practice in family therapy* (pp. 257–276). New York: Guilford Press.

Zimmerman, J., & Dickerson, V. (1994). Tales of the body thief: Externalizing and deconstructing eating problems. In M. Hoyt (ed.)., *Constructive therapies* (Vol. 1, pp. 295–318). New York: Guilford Press.

RELEVENT WORKS ON ANOREXIA, FEMINISM, AND FOUCAULT

Bordo, S. (1993). *Unbearable weight: Feminism, western culture and the body*. Berkeley: University of California Press.

Butler, J. (1993). *Bodies that matter: On the discursive limits of 'sex'*. New York: Routlege.

Conboy, K., Medina, N., & Stanbury, S. (eds.) (1997). *Writing on the body: Female embodiment and feminist theory*. New York: Columbia University Press.

Crawford, R. (1985). A cultural account of 'health', self-control, release, and the social body. In J. Mckinlay (ed.), *Issues in the political economy of health care* (pp. 60–103). New York: Tavistock Publications.

Diamond, I., & Quinby, I. (eds.) (1988). *Feminism and Foucault*. Boston: Northeastern University Press.

Eckerman, L. (1997). Foucault, embodiment and gendered subjectivities: The case of voluntary self-starvation. In A. Petersen, & R. Bunton (eds.), *Foucault, health and medicine*. London: Routledge.

Faith, K. (1994). Resistance: Lessons from Foucault and feminism. In H. Radktke, & H. Stam, *Power/gender: Social relations in theory and practice*. Thousand Oaks, CA.: Sage.

Fraser, N. (1989). Foucault's body language: A posthumanist political rhetoric? In N. Fraser, *Unruly practices: Power, discourse and gender in contemporary social theory* (pp. 55–66). Minneapolis: University of Minnesota Press.

Gallagher, C., & Laqueur, T. (eds.) (1987). *The making of the modern body: Sexuality and society in the 19th century*. Berkeley: University of California Press.

Gremillion, H. (1992). Psychiatry as social ordering: Anorexia nervosa, a paradigm. *Social Science and Medicine, 35* (1), 57–71.

Gremillion, H. (2001). A canary in the mine: An anthropological perspective. In *Working with stories of women's lives* (pp. 135–150). Adelaide, Australia: Dulwich Centre Publications.

Gremillion, H. (2002). In fitness and in health—crafting bodies in the treatment of anorexia nervosa. *Signs: A Journal of Women in Culture and Society, 27* (2), 381–414.

Gremillion, H. (2003). *Feeding anorexia: Power and gender in a treatment center*. Durham: University of North Carolina Press.

Grosz, E. (1994). *Volatile bodies: Toward a corporeal feminism*. Bloomington: Indiana University Press.

Hepworth, J. (1999). *The social construction of Anorexia Nervosa*. London: Sage

Hekman, S. (ed.) (1996). *Feminist interpretations of Michel Foucault: Re-reading the canon*. University Park: Penn State University Press.

Heywood, L. (1996). *Dedication to hunger: The anorexic aesthetic in modern culture*. Berkeley: University of California Press.

Jaggar, A., & Bordo, S. (Eds.) (1989). *Gender/body/knowledge: Feminist reconstructions of being and knowing*. New Brunswick, NJ: Rutgers University Press.

Laqueur, T. (1990). *Making sex: The body and gender from the Greeks to Freud*. Cambridge, MA: Harvard University Press.

Lawrence, M. (1979). Anorexia Nervosa: The control paradox. *Women's Studies International Quarterly, 2*, 93–101.

Littlewood, R., & Lipsedge, M. (1987). The butterfly and the serpent. *Culture, Medicine and Psychiatry, 11* (3), 289–335.

McNay, L. (1991). The foucaultian body and the exclusion of experience. *Hypatia 6* (3), 125–139.

McNay, L. (1992). *Foucault and feminism: Power, gender and the self.* Boston: North-eastern University Press.

Malson, H. (1998). *The thin woman: Feminism, post-structuralism and the social psychology of anorexia nervosa.* London: Routledge.

Malson, H., & Ussher, J. (1996). Body poly-texts: Discourses of the anorexic body. *Journal of Community and Applied Social Psychology, 6,* 267–280.

Malson, H., & Ussher, J. (1996). Bloody women: A discourse analysis of amenorrhea as a symptom of Anorexia Nervosa. *Feminism and Psychology, 6* (4), 505–521.

Nichter, M., & Nichter, M. (1991). Hype and weight. *Medical Anthropology, 13,* 249–284.

Ramazanoglu, C. (1993). *Up against Foucault: Explorations of some tensions between Foucault and feminism.* New York: Routledge.

Sawicki, J. (1991). *Disciplining Foucault: Feminism, power, and the body.* New York: Routledge.

Steiner-Adair, C. (1986). The body politic: Normal female development and the development of eating disorders. *Journal of American Academy of Psychoanalysis, 14* (1), 94–114.

Steiner-Adair, C. (1991). When the body speaks: Girls, eating disorders and psychotherapy. In C. Gilligan, A. Rogers, & D. Tolman (Eds.), *Women, girls and psychotherapy: Reframing resistance* (pp. 94–114). Binghamton, NY: Haworth Press.

Szekely, E. (1988). *Never too thin.* Toronto, ON: The Women's Press.

Thompson, B. (1994). *A hunger so wide and so deep: A multiracial view of women's eating problems.* Minneapolis: University of Minnesota Press.

Weedon, C. (1987). *Feminist practice and post-structuralist theory.* Oxford, U.K.: Basil Blackwell.

INDEX